# Finding God in Unexpected Places

Wisdom for Everyone from the Jewish Tradition

**Rabbi Jack Riemer**

**Read The Spirit Books**
an imprint of
David Crumm Media, LLC
Canton, Michigan

For more information and further discussion, visit
**FrontEdgePublishing.com**


ISBN: 978-1-942011-87-3
Version 1.0

Cover art and design by
Brad Schreiber
www.bydesigngraphicarts.com

Published By
Read The Spirit Books
an imprint of
Front Edge Publishing, LLC
42015 Ford Rd., Suite 234
Canton, Michigan, USA

To the Fiedlers
with all
good wishes
Jack Rieser

Lovingly dedicated by Beatriz and Harold Jacobsohn

In memory of
Rosita (Z'L) and Carlos (Z'L) Kugler
Whose interest in preserving our traditions never faltered

# Contents

"Painter Paint—and Then Hush" ........ viii

Goodbye, Dubai ........ 1

ROSH HASHANA

A Short and Simple Story ........ 11

For the Sin We Have Committed Against You on the Computer ........ 15

Zindig Nisht ........ 27

Smile! You are on Candid Camera ........ 35

What Should You Do When Your Time Is Almost Up? ........ 50

Adam Greenberg at the Bat ........ 60

YOM KIPPUR

Dancing with Alzheimer's ........ 70

Four Phrases to Live By ........ 88

The Man Who Created the Jewish State ........ 98

SUKKOT

Siz a Rachmones off der Goy (It Is a Pity on the Gentile) .... 105

When Should You Listen to Your Wife and When Should You Not Listen to Your Wife? ........ 113

The Last Eight Lines … ........ 119

Announcing the Formation of a New Organization ........ 125

An English Critic and a Yiddish Poet Raise the Same Question ........ 133

Can We Grow Old and Still Stay Young? ........ 141

HANUKKAH

Did a Miracle Really Take Place in Los Angeles This Year? If So, What Was It? ........ 148

TU BISHVAT

How Come Jews Are Always Late? ........ 155

PURIM
Search Committee Report to the Congregation .................. 161
The Enormous Cultural, Political and Economic
Influence of the Latke on the Modern World ..................... 166
How a Major Halachic Crisis Has Been Averted ................ 182

PESACH
Reflections on the Four Children ........................................ 186
What Should You Pack When You Go on a Trip? ............... 194
Four Lessons from One Dollar Bill: A Story for Children
(and for Adults, Too) ........................................................... 201

YOM HASHOAH
"But I Do It Anyway ..." ....................................................... 213
How Can They Weep and Rejoice at the Same Time? ......... 219

YOM HA'ATZMAUT
What Makes Israel So Special? ........................................... 227

SHAVOUT
The Real Reason Why We Eat Dairy on Shavuot ................ 235
How Do You Say Goodbye? ................................................. 247

TISHA B'AV
What Should We Do When This Neighborhood Changes? . 254
The Marie Antoinette of the Talmud .................................. 261

PERSONAL REFLECTIONS
What Should I Do with the Rest of My Life? ...................... 270
Gone with the Wind ............................................................. 287
The Lessons You Have Taught Me ...................................... 300
How Should You Live in Old Age? ...................................... 306
Reflections on a Birthday .................................................... 318
What Does It Mean to Be a Rabbi? ..................................... 329
How Should We Live In a World
That We Cannot Control? ................................................... 341

Jewish Holidays ...................................................................... 362
Glossary .................................................................................. 369

# "Painter Paint— and Then Hush"

I no longer remember where I found this quote. It may have been in Goethe or in Heine or in some lesser soul, but whoever wrote it, it is good advice, not only for painters, but for playwrights and for poets and for preachers, too. For if a picture or a poem or a sermon is beautiful, you do not have to explain why, and if it is not, then all the explaining in the world will not make it so.

And yet I feel the need to introduce this bouquet of writings with a few words.

First, I need to say thank you to my parents, who first taught me that the Torah was the meaning and the measure of our days. And then to my teachers, who taught me that our task is not just to translate the Torah from Hebrew to English, but that our task is to translate the Torah from words upon a page into a guide for our lives.

Second, I need to say thank you to Sue, who has lived with these pages and who has made them better with her keen eye, her sharp pen and her wise heart.

Third, I need to say a word of blessing to Yosef, Vitina and Adena, and to Nathan, Lisa and Naomi with hope that they will find within these pages wisdom that will help guide them on the path of life.

Fourth, I need to say a word of blessing to Robert and Judy, Steve and Sterling, and Richard, Grace and Peter, for the ways in which they have enriched our lives. And I need to say a special word of thanks to Steve, who has cared for my computer and for me, and who has kept us both from having a breakdown, with his great skill and his remarkable patience.

Fifth, I need to say a word of thanks to the many sources of the stories and the ideas that are found in this collection, some of whom I can identify by name, and some of whom whose names I have forgotten. Know, dear reader, that no one but the *Ribono shel olam* ever creates anything *yesh mey-ayin*—out of nothing. Every writer, every poet, and surely every storyteller absorbs wisdom from books, from conversations, and from encounters with others, and then uses this wisdom in whatever he creates. Sometimes he remembers where he got these insights and so he is able to thank those that have taught him, and sometimes these insights become so much a part of him that he forgets where he first learned them. And so, let me thank, not only those whose names I still remember, but those whose names I have forgotten. May those whom I am no longer able to acknowledge by name forgive me, and may they find a measure of pleasure in knowing that their words have affected me, and that, through me, they have reached beyond me to those whom I have taught.

Sixth, let me thank those who have listened patiently to these words over the years. Without you and without your responses, these words would never have come into being, or they would have floated away and disappeared as soon as they were uttered. I am grateful—more than I can say—to those of you who have told me that these stories have made a difference in your lives, and I hope that I can repay your goodness to me by listening to you when you speak, and by sharing in your moments of joy.

And I hope that it is not too vain for me to say that I hope that these words have not yet finished their journey, and that there may be some new people out there who will read them and who will find them helpful. For this is the greatest reward that any teacher can ever hope for.

And last but by no means least, let me thank Harold and Beatriz Jacobsohn for the generosity that has made this book possible. May God bless them for their goodness.

And now let me hush and let these words speak for themselves.

—Rabbi Jack Riemer

1

# Goodbye, Dubai

## Parshat Mattot

I have two announcements to make this morning. And let me tell you, in advance, that I do not want to hear any applause when I tell you either one.

The first announcement is that I woke up Monday morning and decided that I am going to resign from this congregation, I am going to leave my family and I am going to move to Dubai.

The second announcement is that I woke up Tuesday morning and decided that I am not going to resign from this congregation, I am not going to leave my family and I am ***not*** going to move to Dubai.

The reason that I want to talk to you about these two decisions today is because all of us, at some time in our lives, are faced with the same question that faced me this week: How do you make a decision when you are caught between two conflicting values or desires? How do you choose between something that seems to feel right for you, and something that you feel is your obligation to the people with whom you live? How do you choose between enjoying your rights and fulfilling your responsibilities?

At first, I had no hesitation about leaving this congregation. After all, you only pay me a pittance. I don't know if everyone here knows this, but my salary from this congregation is only in the low seven-figures. And you may not know this, but I am a person who has enormous wealth from my investments, so there is really no financial reason for me to stay here.

The second reason why I decided to resign and move to Dubai is because I read an article about life in Dubai this week that was very, very impressive. The article said that Dubai is the number one city in the world to live in today. Dubai has dozens of brand-new, sumptuous shopping malls where you can shop for hours and where you can buy the latest fashions that come from Paris and every other fashion center of the world. Dubai has dozens of brand-new skyscrapers that reach up toward the sky, and some of these buildings are taller than any other building that exists—in Europe, in Asia or even in America. Furthermore, Dubai has a great many 12-lane highways that take you wherever you want to go with no traffic jams, while on both sides of these highways there are rows of lovely palm trees that are beautiful to behold. Not only that, but Dubai has almost-free gas, almost-free food and many other products are subsidized by the government. In short, Dubai is a man-made paradise.

And so I said to myself on Monday: Why should I not move there? If I do, I will be happy. And is being happy not what means the most in life?

And then, on Tuesday, I reconsidered. On Tuesday, I said to myself: What will happen to this congregation if I leave and move to Dubai? Where will they be able to find another rabbi to take my place? Where will they find a rabbi who is as talented and as modest as I am, and who is willing to work for a measly pittance, as I am? And if they cannot find a rabbi like me, then how can I abandon them, and leave them Torah-less?

How can I do that? It is just not right.

And then I thought about my family. What will happen to them if I leave and move to Dubai? Where will my wife find another husband who is as devoted, as loving, as generous and as kind as I am? If I go to Dubai, who will take care of her and minister to her every need with the same love and skill and thoughtfulness and devotion that I do? How will she survive the unbearable loneliness that she will feel every day if I move to Dubai?

And so, I was troubled by that age-old question: How can I reconcile the conflict that I feel inside, between my rights and my responsibilities?

For on the one hand, I surely have the right to move to Dubai if I want to, and on the other hand, I surely have a responsibility not to move to Dubai if, by doing so, I will do harm to my family and to my congregation. What should I do—and what should you do—if we are torn between our rights on the one hand, our responsibilities on the other, and we have no third hand to help us to decide?

I don't know about you, but whenever I face a question that I cannot resolve, I turn to the Torah for guidance. And sure enough, right in the middle of this week's Torah reading, I found a story about the two and one-half tribes of ancient Israel who faced the very same question that I am struggling with: How do you reconcile your rights with your responsibilities? And so I studied what the Torah says that they did, in the hope that their experience would provide some wisdom and some guidance for me (and perhaps for you, as well).

This is the story as it is found in today's Torah reading—just a little bit reworked and simplified by me:

> *The tribe of Reuven and the tribe of Gad had a tremendous amount of cattle, and they saw that*

*the land of Yazer and the land of Gilad were especially suitable for cattle. And so they came to Moses, and to Elazar, the high priest, and to the chiefs of the tribes, and they said four things. They said, "Ataroth, Dibon, Yazer, Nimrah, Heshbon, Elealeh, Sebam, Nevo and Beon: which are the territories that the Lord has conquered for the people of Israel—are very good cattle country? And then they said, "Your servants have many cattle." And then they said, "Could this land be given to us as a possession?" And finally, they said, "Please do not make us move across the Jordan."*

Did you notice that the leader of the two tribes, whoever he was, speaks four times in a row, and then—and ***only then***—does Moses say anything at all? Isn't that strange?

Let me slow the camera for a moment, and let us try to imagine the scene the way it probably unfolded:

*The heads of the tribes of Reuven and Gad come forward, and they ask for a meeting with Moses. The appointment secretary of Moses says to them, "Can you please tell me what this meeting is about?" And they say, "It is a personal matter. We would rather not say." And so the secretary gives them an appointment for 4:30 the next afternoon, and she puts the meeting on her boss's schedule. The next day, precisely at 4:30, the heads of the tribes of Reuven and Gad show up for the meeting, feeling very nervous and very self-conscious.*

*The heads of the two tribes look at each other, and one says to the other, "Would you please speak for both of us? You are smarter than I am." And the other one says, in response, "Would* **you** *please speak for both of us?" You are smarter than I am." And finally—after they go through this game of* *"after you," and "no—after you" for a while—they finally decide which one will speak for the two of them, and the discussion begins.*

*The one who was chosen hems and haws. He wipes his brow. He clears his throat and he musters up his courage, and then finally, he says to Moses, "Ahem. You know … you know … you know … you know that this land that we are sitting on right now is really very good for cattle." And then he stops, and waits to see what Moses will say in response.*

*And what does Moses say?*

*He says nothing.*

*Nothing at all.*

*There is just a long silence, during which these words hang in the air.*

*And so the spokesman for the tribes of Reuven and Gad has to speak again. This time, he says, "You know … eh, you know … hmm, you know, eh, you have probably noticed … hmm, that our two tribes have a lot of cattle …."*

*And what does Moses say in response?*

*He says nothing.*

*Nothing to all.*

*And again, silence hangs in the air. Each side waits for the other side to speak.*

We wonder: Will the spokesman for the tribes of Reuven and Gad have the courage to say what they want to out loud, or will Moses help them through this difficult moment by granting them the request that they are too shy to make? We wait, and we wonder: Will the spokesman for the tribes of Reuven and Gad break the silence—or will Moses?

> *Finally, the spokesman for the tribes of Reuven and Gad musters up his courage and says, "Would you please give this land to us?"*
>
> *And what does Moses say?*
>
> *Moses says nothing.*
>
> *Nothing at all.*
>
> *And so, finally, the leader of the tribes of Reuven and Gad has no choice but to say the words that he has been reluctant to say until now. He says, "Al tavireynu et hayarden" ("Please don't make us cross over the Jordan").*

Now they've said it. Now they have said that what they want is to stay in Transjordan while their kinsmen go into the Promised Land without them. They have finally said that they want to desert the Jewish people, and that they want to opt out of the struggle to conquer the Promised Land!

When they say this, Moses goes ballistic.

> *Moses lashes out at them in anger, and he says to them, "Do you mean that your brothers should go off to war* ***while you stay here?*** *Do you realize that if you do this, you will weaken the morale of the people and that you will discourage them from going forward into the land that God has promised them? How* ***dare*** *you make such a request?"*

And what do you think is going to happen next?

Now, before we go any further, let me point out one tiny detail in the story. It is a detail that I would not have noticed in a million years, but my colleague, Rabbi Vered Harris, caught it. She says that if you look very, very carefully, you will notice that after Moses makes this angry tirade, there is an end to this paragraph. And then there is a space. And then the story begins again, with their reply.

What is the purpose of this space? Why is there a pause between the speech of Moses, in which he accuses the two tribes of treason and of breaking faith with God, and their reply? Why is there a gap between the speech in which Moses compares the tribes' behavior with that of the 10 scouts—who, a generation before, had demoralized the people with their bad report about the land of Israel—who cost the people of Israel 40 years of wandering in the wilderness as a result—and their answer to this accusation? Why is there a space between the tirade by Moses and the response of the two tribes?

Rabbi Harris suggests that, during the silence that is symbolized by this break in the story, the two tribes huddled and considered what they should say next. They talked about how they could resolve the conflict between their rights and their responsibilities. They asked themselves: How can we find a balance between our desires—as cattle owners, for whom Transjordan would be good—and our obligations—as members of the people of Israel, for whom going with our brothers is the right thing to do?

They could have lashed back if they had wanted to, the way we are tempted to do when someone speaks to us in anger. They could have become defensive, which is what most of us would do if someone accused us of treason or compared us to the 10 spies who demoralized the House of Israel years before. Instead, they huddled together until they came up with a compromise plan, and then they came back and offered this compromise plan to Moses, to the high priest and to the rest of the people, as an alternative to their original proposal:

> *In response, they say, "How about we do this: We take a timeout here, during which we will build sheepfolds for our flocks and towns for our children, and then we will go with the rest of the Israelites and join them in their fight to conquer*

*the Promised Land? And not only that, but what if we agree to go out to battle in advance of the rest of the other soldiers? What if we agree to be the advance guard in this struggle, and then—and only then, after we have helped our brothers win their land—will we come back to this place? Isn't that a fair compromise?"*

*And then they wait for Moses to respond.*

*And what does Moses say?*

*He says, "It's a deal."*

*And then Moses makes just one small correction in the deal that they have proposed. He says, "You've got your priorities wrong! You should build towns for your children* ***first****, and* ***then*** *build sheepfolds for your flock. For your goal in life should not be just to care for your sheep and to become wealthy cattle ranchers. Your children should come first, and you should express that by the order in which you build. But with the exception of this one detail, I accept your compromise. If you will go across the Jordan with your brothers, and if you will fight at their side until they win their land, and if you will even go in the vanguard of the army; if you understand that this is not some ordinary land, but that it is 'the land that the Lord has given,' then—all right, you may come back and live here after the war."*

What is the purpose of this pause in the story—between the tirade of Moses and the second offer by the tribes of Gad and Reuven?

It was a timeout in which the two tribes could get together and think about what counteroffer they could make that would be both fair to their rights and consistent with their responsibilities.

And that, I would suggest, is the lesson that all of us should learn from their example today. Whenever we are caught in a conflict between our rights and our responsibilities; whenever we are caught between doing what is good for us and doing what is good for our families and our society; whenever we are caught between our desire for personal fulfillment and our obligations in this world, we should call a timeout and see if we can come up with a compromise that will be fair to both sides. For if you only do what is good for you, you are a sadist, and if you only do what is good for others, you are a masochist.

And therefore, this is what I have decided I am going to do:

I have decided that I am ***not*** going to resign from this congregation and leave you Torah-less. I can't do that, because you mean too much to me. For how would you get along without me?

And I have decided that I am ***not*** going to leave my wife here with no one to take care of her, and with no one to guide her. I am not going to do that, for how would she manage without me?

And therefore, I have decided that I am going to say: ***Goodbye, Dubai!***

But I ***am*** going to make a compromise between my needs and my responsibilities, and this is what the compromise will be: I am going to take a day off—not once a week, that would be too much—but I am going to take a day off once in a while, in order to nurture my own soul and satisfy my own needs.

And on that day I am going to read and study so that I can broaden my own horizons, and so that I can acquire fresh insights that I can share with you.

I am going to get a hold of some brochures that describe the wonders of Dubai, and I am going to put them up on the walls of my study both at home and here in the synagogue. I am going to post them all around—not to remind me and not to remind you of how much I am giving up for you, for I am not the kind of person who would do that. I am not the kind of person who would remind you every day of how much I sacrifice on your behalf. No. I am going to post these brochures all around in order to remind myself, and in order to remind you, of the need that we all have to balance the driving forces within us and to seek compromises between them. For now I realize that if I moved to Dubai and left you behind, and if I left my wife, whom I love, behind, I would not really be happy there for very long—no matter how many skyscrapers and no matter how many shopping malls and no matter how many superhighways they may have there.

For a life that is only devoted to oneself and to one's own rights, and that has no room in it for others and for the responsibilities to them, is really not a human life at all. And a world in which people are concerned only about their own fulfillment—in which people are never willing to make any compromises for the sake of those whom they belong to, and who belong to them—that is not a world in which people can live truly human lives.

And to this, if you agree—if you are pleased and relieved by my decision to stay here and not move to Dubai, and if you realize the power and the value and the need for compromise in our lives, and if you understand the need to somehow strive to strike a balance between the conflicting drives within us whenever we can, and if you will promise me that you will try, as I will, to look for compromises that will make peace between the various drives within us and between us—will you please join me, and to this, will you please say: Amen.

*Author's note: I wish to acknowledge the help of my good friend, Mrs. Susan Das, who suggested to me the title of this sermon: "Goodbye, Dubai." For this, and for many other blessings that she brings to our home, I am truly grateful.*

2

# A Short and Simple Story

## Erev Rosh Hashana

*Gut shabbos*, *gut yontif* and a *shana tova* to you all.

I am not going to give a formal sermon tonight, because we all want to go home and celebrate Rosh Hashana with our families and at our tables. Instead, let me just tell you a simple story.

You should know that all of my stories are true ... some even happened.

Did this one happen? Probably, although I can't prove it. Either way, it is a lovely story, and one that I think we can learn from—so let me tell it to you tonight.

There was a great rabbi in eastern Europe named Rabbi Yitzchak Elchanan Spektor. The rabbinical school of Yeshiva University, in New York, is named for him. The story is told that once he was asked to adjudicate a case—a very complicated case—that involved tens of thousands of rubles.

The rabbi did not want to take responsibility for deciding such a complicated case by himself, and so he chose a *beth din* to hear the case with him. And since this was such a complicated case, and since it involved so much money, he chose a *beth din* of very distinguished scholars who came from different cities.

When the *beth din* members had arrived, unpacked and rested, the rabbi summoned them to sit together so that they could hear the arguments of both sides and examine the Talmudic sources that related to the case. Just as they were about to begin their proceedings, somebody came to the door. The man at the door said, "Rabbi, I hate to interrupt you, but I was sure that you would want to hear the good news. Chaim has been released from jail. It turns out that the accusations against him were false, and so the accusers have been jailed and Chaim was released this morning."

Rabbi Spektor's face lit up with joy. He hugged the man who had brought him the news, and he said, "*Really?* Thank you—thank you so much for bringing me this good news. I am so grateful." He questioned the man about all of the details, and he offered him some refreshments before he showed the man out.

The court sat down again to begin the proceedings, when somebody else came to the door. The man at the door said, "Rebbe, I hate to interrupt you, but I was sure that you would want to hear the good news. Chaim has been released from jail. It turns out that the accusations against him were false, and so the accusers have been jailed and Chaim was released this morning."

The rabbi's face lit up with joy. He hugged the man who had brought him this news, and he said, "*Really?* Thank you—thank you so much for bringing me this news. I am so grateful." And he questioned the man about all of the details, and then offered him some refreshments before he showed the man out.

The court sat down again to begin the proceedings when, a few minutes later, there was another knock on the door, and a man came in. He said, "Rabbi, I hate to interrupt you, but I was sure that you would want to hear the good news. Chaim has been released from jail. It turns out that the accusations against him were false, and so the accusers have been jailed and Chaim was released this morning."

Rabbi Spektor's face lit up with joy. "*Really?* Thank you—thank you so much for bringing me the news. I am so grateful." And he questioned the man about all the details, offered him some refreshments, and then showed the man out.

By this time, the members of the *beth din* were becoming confused. They said to him: "Rabbi, would you please tell us what is going on here? Why have you treated every single person who came in here to bring you the news as if he was the first one? And why have you pretended to be so surprised, so happy and so grateful every time one of them came in here—even though you already knew the whole story? What's going on?"

Rabbi Spektor explained, "Each one of these people who has come in here today came here only in order to make me happy by bringing me this news. Can you imagine how disappointed they would have felt—how crushed they would have been—if I had said, 'Oh, I know already. I heard all about it,' I would have ruined their day.

"If I had given them the brush-off and told them that I already knew, they would never have wanted to do a *mitsvah* like this again. This way, by treating each one as if he was the first one—and by thanking each man for the good deed that he had done—I encouraged them to feel good about themselves and to feel that it is good to do a *mitsvah*.

"And if, technically, I lied ... *nu*. I hope that the *Ribono shel olam* will forgive me for lying if by doing so, I made another Jew happy and made him feel that it is good to do a *mitsvah*."

End of story.

As I told you, tonight's story was not fancy; it was not philosophical. It was just a plain, simple story. But it is a story that I like anyway, and I hope that you do, too, because it teaches us how careful and how sensitive a person should be to the feelings of other human beings. It teaches us how careful that we should be in making the people around us feel good about themselves. It teaches us that the purpose of studying the Torah is to become a *mentsch*.

So, that's my story for tonight. It is short and simple. Yet I think it is a story worth carrying into the new year with us, is it not?

Let me make two wishes for you tonight. If both of them come true, you will be blessed indeed.

My first wish for you is that, in this new year that now begins, may more than one person do an act of kindness for you.

And my second wish for you is that if that happens, may you say to the second person—just as you do to the first one—"Thank you, how good of you that was, and I am so grateful." Even if you don't need the second favor, and even if the first person has already done it for you, say this anyway. For if you remember to do that, how proud and how happy you will make the people who do good for you feel. And if you remember to do that, how proud and how happy you will feel, too.

These are my two wishes for you for the new year. And may they both come true.

*Lishana tova tikateyvu.*

3

# For the Sin We Have Committed Against You on the Computer

## Rosh Hashana

This is the season of the year in which we are supposed to examine the way we live—in every single corner of our lives. It is the season in which we are supposed to think about how we behave: in our stores and in our offices, in our cars and in our clubs, in our kitchens and in our dining rooms, in our libraries and in our living rooms, and in all the other places where we spend so many hours of our lives.

Therefore, what I want to do today is take a long, hard look at how we behave in that room in our homes in which many of us—myself included—spend more hours than we do in any other room.

Can you guess which room it is? The room we spend more hours in than any other?

I don't know about you, but for me, the room in which I spend more hours than any other room in the house is this: the room in which I keep my computer.

Is that true for you, too?

The computer now occupies a tremendous amount of time in our lives.

I spend more time on the computer than I do in the kitchen, the dining room or the library—or in any other part of my home. Do you do that, too?

I don't know about you, but I send more letters a day by email than I do by what is now called "snail mail." Do you do that, too?

And therefore, I believe that it is in order that at least once each year, we look at the way we behave on the computer. Are there any sins that we commit while we are online that we need to atone for?

I must tell you that I never realized how central the computer has become in our lives until last summer. I was flying from Florida to California, and I happened to glance at the magazine that they put into the pouch in the seat in front of me. And this is what I found:

There was an ad in this magazine for a hotel in Texas. The ad stated that the hotel has a 2,300-acre lake, which is ideal for fishing—and then it said that they have ***wired*** this lake, so that ***while you are fishing***, you can have internet access—***in the middle of the lake***! The ad stated that the system is operated from an underground bunker in the center of the lake that provides ***the entire area of the lake*** with wireless, high-speed, broadband connections and "wide area 802.11"—whatever that means.

And then the ad stated—and this is a direct quote, I haven't made up a single word—"While you are fishing, you can now host a national sales meeting, or check your email, or surf the internet, or download voice data or video files or hold live video conferences—from wherever you are on the lake."

Think of that! Fishing used to be a place of ***serenity*** and ***tranquility***. You went fishing in order to get away from the office and relax. Now you can download, send and receive email, and even hold video conferences—***while fishing***!

Isn't that crazy? Why would anyone want to be in contact with his office while fishing?

Evidently, this hotel is for people who are addicted to the computer. People who feel tense and anxious and ill at ease if they are away from the computer for any length of time.

I laughed at that ad, and I felt very superior to such people. I said to myself, Boy, am I glad that I am not like them. And then I turned the page, and I found another ad.

Listen to this one:

"The days of the simple, electronic notebook are long gone." (I didn't know that they had arrived, but evidently, they are now gone.) "Now you can buy the ***newest*** PC … which is truly different from all the other personal computers on the market."

This PC has, according to the ad, the sharpest high-resolution color screen available. And it has many multimedia features. It has such-and-such number of megabytes and memory. (I don't remember exactly how much memory it has, but I am sure that it has more memory than I do.)

And then the ad went on to say, "You can listen to your favorite music, or you can download an audio book with stereo-quality sound, or you can play video games on the 16-inch color screen or take photographs with your built-in audio camera."

So far, I had not been impressed. There are lots of computers that can do all of the things listed. What was so special about this one?

The ad stated that it had Wi-Fi technology built into it, which enables the user to go wherever he wants to go. I don't know what Wi-Fi is. I have something called WIFE, which enables me to go wherever I want to go. So what made this PC so special?

The ad stated that the computer enables a user to create, edit, sort and print Word, Excel and PowerPoint files. So? A lot of computers can do that. Is that such a big deal that the computer is worth $4,999?

And now comes the *chidush* of this computer. The ad said that this computer, unlike most others, came with a soundless, illuminated keyboard, so that users can ***work in bed at night without disturbing their spouse.***

Now, I ask you: Why on earth would you want a personal computer with an illuminated keyboard so that you can work at night without disturbing your spouse? Maybe you should ***sleep*** in bed at night, instead of being on the computer. Or maybe you ***should*** disturb your spouse at night, instead of typing away in the middle of the night!

When I read these two ads, I said to myself, My God, these people must be addicted. And it felt so good to know that I was not like them.

And then I got to California, checked into my apartment and went down to the office where they kept the computers for tenants' use—and I found, much to my shock and dismay, that the office that had the computers that guests are permitted to use was only open from 9 a.m. to 5 p.m.

This meant that for ***two-thirds of the day***—from 5 p.m. to 9a.m.—for ***16 long hours of the day***—I would be completely cut off from the computer. My first reaction when I realized that was ***My God, what am I going to do***?

And that is when I realized that I, too, am addicted to the computer—just as much as the people in the ad that I read on the plane, who need a lake that is wired with Wi-Fi when they go fishing. I am apparently just as addicted to the computer as those people who buy computers that are illuminated so that they can work in bed without disturbing their spouses.

I have a friend named Mindy Agler, who is the wife of Rabbi Richard Agler, the rabbi formerly at Congregation B'nai Israel. Mindy is a therapist, and she works with people who are addicted to drugs, alcohol and cigarettes. So I asked her, "Is there a support group for people who are addicted to the computer?"

She said, "Sure there is."

So I said to her, "Really? That's wonderful! Where is it, and how can I join?"

And she said to me, "You can find it online."

Now, before you make fun of me, let me say that I suspect that I am not the only one who is in denial about being addicted to the computer. I suspect that there are probably some other people sitting here right now who suffer from the same compulsion that I do.

So let me give you a simple test, to see whether you are addicted or not:

1. How many years has it been since you last played Solitaire—using real cards?
2. Do you need to dial at least 15 numbers of your code, plus the phone number, before you can reach any one of the three members of your family who live out of town?
3. Have you ever entered your password, out of habit, when you wanted to start your microwave?
4. Do you find yourself using email in order to connect with your co-worker—even though he or she works at the desk right next to you?
5. Do you keep in touch with friends and relatives who do not have email?
6. Did you get this list from eight different friends—many of whom you never hear from anymore except when

you receive their forwarded jokes and lists (like this one)?

7. Do you ever stop to check your messages when you are on the way back to your bed, coming from the bathroom, at night? (Or do you at least ***think*** about doing it, and have to resist the temptation?)
8. Do you disrespectfully refer to regular mail as "snail mail," even though you know that it is delivered by people and not by snails?
9. Have you reached the stage at which, when you disconnect your computer, you feel like you are pulling the plug on a loved one?
10. When you read this list, did you smile and nod your head in recognition?

How many of these questions did you say "yes" to?

1? 2? 3? 4? More?

Be honest!

There is no doubt that the computer has taken over our lives.

There was a time when, if I needed to know the answer to a question in Jewish law, I would turn to the "*Shulchan Aruch,*" or look up the question in the Talmud or in the Code of Maimonides. Now I ask Reb Google, and he gives me the answer in milliseconds! This man, Reb Google, is undoubtedly the biggest *talmid chacham* I have ever met.

And therefore, in all seriousness, I want to make a suggestion to you for how to overcome this addiction. Therapists will tell you that you can't go cold turkey—that you can't go from smoking six packs a day to quitting completely—and that instead you have to taper off gradually. So it is with drinking, with drugs and with any other substance or addiction. And so, my suggestion is this: If you are addicted to the computer, try not going on one day a week, and see if you can handle that. If that works, then perhaps you can cut back by two days.

I learned this strategy from my father, *zichrono livrocho*. My father was a chain smoker: he smoked three packs a day, six days a week. But he would never think of smoking on Shabbat. It was just inconceivable. And so he would smoke up until the moment of candle lighting on Friday night, and he would light his first cigarette from the Havdalah candle on Saturday night—but, in between, he never smoked. So let me make that suggestion to you. If you are addicted to the computer, try leaving it alone ***just*** for Shabbat, and see how that works.

* * *

And now, let me offer you a series of *Al Hets* that we should recite this year, for the sins that we have committed against God and against other people while on the computer:

*Al Het shechatanu lifanecha*—for the sin that we have committed before You by not rereading our messages before sending them out, in order to make sure that we have not written something that is cruel or rude or inappropriate. The *Amidah* says that we are supposed to guard our tongues from speaking evil and our lips from speaking guile, and if that is so, then we should surely guard the "send" button, because it has the power to send words ***much*** further and ***much*** faster than those that are spoken by our tongue.

*Al Het shechata lifanecha*—for the sin that we have committed before You by sending an email in anger, instead of waiting until we have cooled down.

*Al Het shechatan lifanecha*—for the sin that we have committed before You by sending out blind copies and not letting the recipient know that what we are telling him or her is also going to other people, as well.

*Al Het shechatanu lifanecha*—for the sin that we have committed before You by letting the convenience of email replace the enduring value of face-to-face contact.

* * *

I saw an ad the other day—an ad for a therapist who has a new website. This therapist's ad read—and, honest, I have not made up a single word—"E-advice is the latest innovation in counseling."

The ad continued:

"Are you afraid of heights? Are you having difficulties in relationships? Are you feeling tense because of the pressure you feel at the office? Are you afraid of flying?

"If so, instead of wasting precious hours traveling to and from your therapist—and instead of wasting precious time sitting in his or her waiting room—you can now submit a problem to the electronic therapist for the bargain rate of $95. You will get a professional diagnosis within an hour at the most, from a licensed counselor."

The ad didn't say whether this person is licensed or a therapist or a computer expert, but either way, I don't know about you but I am suspicious of ***any*** therapist who has so much free time that he or she can get to my inquiry and diagnose me within one hour. But, maybe …

The ad then went on to state, "You may inquire about problems such as a sense of inferiority, panic distress, eating disorders, or phobias of any kind. A full list of the phobias and problems that we are expert in treating can be found simply by clicking the "List of Phobias" link. For your first inquiry, we offer a special discount rate of $65 instead of $100. And, if you wish, you can take advantage of our special bargain rate of four phobias for just $220." That is a bargain, you have to admit.

And not only is ***your*** name and your identity protected on this site; ***the name and the identity of the therapist is also protected on this site!***

Now, why should the name and address of the therapist be kept secret? I suspect—I can't say for sure, but I suspect—that maybe the reason the identity of the therapist is being kept secret is because inquiries are handled by someone in India or in Bangladesh, just as when you call to make a plane reservation. That could be.

* * *

And now, back to my list:

*Al Het shechatanu lifanecha*, for the sin we have committed before You by being careful to stay away from people when the doctor tells us that we are contagious, in order to avoid spreading a virus—but by not being nearly as careful to stay away from the computer, even though there is a danger of spreading a virus electronically.

*Al Het shechatanu lifanecha*, for the sin that we have committed before You by sending an email to one of our friends and expecting an answer immediately, whereas in the old days, we would have sent a letter and expected an answer in three or four days at the earliest.

Have you committed any of these sins?

If so, may I suggest that you join with me today in admitting them, and in resolving to do them no more.

And, now, let me make one more suggestion:

It is easy to make resolutions when a new year begins because, as the old Yiddish proverb puts it, "*liebhoben un tsizogen kost nisht kein gelt*"—making love and making promises don't cost anything. Therefore, instead of just making a resolution not to misuse the computer today—which is easy to make and hard to keep—may I suggest that you take one of these two prayers, both of which I found on the internet, and paste them onto your computer. Every day, before you "boot up"—or, as we used to say in the old days, before you "turn it on"—that you recite one of these two prayers, either the Hebrew one or the English one.

The Hebrew one says:

*Yihi ratson milfanecha,*
*Shetichabreynu bishalom*
*Vitagi-eynu l'atar cheftseynu bishalom*
*Vitatsiley mikaf kol viyrus baderech,*
*Vitishmireynu mikol miney pritsus,*
*Ha-omdim litfoseynu b'olam havertuali.*
*Vatishlach bracha bichol maasey achbareynu,*
*Vititneynu lichen ulichesed b'eyney kol mi shenipagesh baderech,*
*Vitishma kol arnakeynu,*
*Vitishmireynu meybitul ziman.*

And the English one says:

*May it be your will, O Lord our God, and God of our ancestors,*
*To connect us to each other in peace.*
*Enable us to arrive at the websites that we desire to reach in safety and in peace.*
*Protect us from all viruses that can cause illness to our machine, and that can cause amnesia to our memory.*
*Protect us from all the kinds of pornography that lurk upon the virtual highway.*
*Send blessings upon the work of our mouse,*
*That it may remain healthy and productive.*
*Guard over our wallets so that we do not buy too many accessories that we do not really need.*
*Protect us from the sin of bitul ziman, from the sin of wasting time, which tempts all who live in the virtual world.*
*Amen.*

And then, may I suggest that you say this prayer every day:

*Ribono shel olam, whose will and wisdom connects the entire cosmos:*
*As I sit down before my computer today,*
*Let me be aware that I am about to connect*
*With many people all over this planet.*
*Help me to appreciate the endless hours of human effort*
*That went into creating this machine.*
*Help me to appreciate the complexity and the intricacy of the wiring, the circuits and the technology,*
*Within this machine that I am about to use.*
*Let me be aware of how wondrous the workings of this machine are.*
*Let me be grateful that I live in an age*
*When so much knowledge is available at my fingertips.*
*Yet let me not forget that* ***You*** *are the source of all creation.*
*Elohai, nitsor lishoni viyadi meyra,*
*O my God, guard my tongue and my hands from speaking guile,*
*And guard my lips and my fingers from spreading gossip.*
*As I prepare to use this instrument of communication,*
*let the words I type and the thoughts that are in mind*
*be a source of blessing to all those with whom I connect.*
*May the words that I send out increase the amount of understanding on this earth.*
*May my time on this computer be a source of tikkun that improves the world and brings your people closer to each other.*
*Amen.*

This is my prayer for you and for myself on this, the day when we begin the new year. In this new year that now begins, may we guard our tongues and guard our mice, and may we stay in close contact with one another, face to face, as well as by way of the machine.

May we live as human beings who are created in the image of God, and not as creatures that are made in the image of the machine.

May this be the way in which we live—online and offline. May God bless the work of our hands and our computers, in all that this new year will bring.

And to this, let us all say: Amen.

4

# Zindig Nisht

## Rosh Hashana

Before I begin, let me tell you that all of the stories that I am going to tell you today are true.

Not only are they true, but they actually happened.

And not only did they actually happen, but they happened here—in this synagogue.

I am going to disguise the names of the people involved in these stories, in order to protect the innocent (and, more importantly, in order to protect the guilty), but believe me—all of these stories are true.

In my business, I get to go to a lot of *simchas*. I get invited to weddings, to bar mitzvah parties, to special birthdays and to anniversaries. And today, I am going to tell you some of the things that I have learned from attending all of these events.

But before I begin, let me remind you, once again, of what I said previously: My sermons this Rosh Hashana are going to be very simple, very obvious and perhaps even trite. I do this because I believe that the central truths in life are always simple and obvious; I believe that the central lessons that we need to learn in life are always clichés. The reason something becomes a cliché is because it is ***so*** true that it gets repeated over and over again.

And, therefore—even though what I am going to say today is obvious and simple—I ask you to hear me well.

I want to speak to those of you who are looking forward to celebrating a *simcha* this year—and who are a little bit apprehensive about whether everything will go right and turn out the way you want it to.

I don't know if you know this or not, but *simchas* can be very complicated life events. Stuff that is usually repressed may come to the surface during a *simcha*. When you have a bar or a bat mitzvah, it means saying to your father—whether he is alive or not—"See, I have given you a new link in the chain of the generations—even though you didn't think that I could do it." When you have a wedding, it means gaining a son-in-law or a daughter-in-law, but it also means letting go of a previously held relationship with a daughter or a son—and that can be complicated. That's not to mention that having a *simcha* means dealing with the caterer, dealing with your *machetonim* and dealing with children—and none of these things is ever easy.

(By the way, does everyone here know what the word "*machetonim*" means? "*Machetonim*" means "in-laws." And do you know the difference between in-laws and outlaws? Outlaws are *wanted*.)

I want to tell you about some of the *simchas* that I have been to in this past year.

A few months ago, there was a wedding. I must tell you that I was worried about this wedding for weeks before it took place. I really was. I was worried because the parents of the groom were divorced; they had been divorced for about 10 years, and yet I knew that there was still deep enmity between them. They are not members of this synagogue, but

I have met with both of them for counseling on occasion over the years, and so I know how much anger and hostility the two of them still feel toward each other. And so I was braced: What could I do to make sure that their hatred toward each other did not spill over and spoil the *simcha*?

I met with the groom's parents a couple of weeks before the wedding, and I timidly asked: "How are you going to handle the procession? Who is going to walk down the aisle with whom?" They said to me: "What's the question? We are going to walk our son down the aisle together, just as every other set of parents does. We may have our issues with each other, but we are not going to let those issues spoil our son's *simcha*. No way!"

I must tell you that when they said that, I breathed a sigh of relief that you could probably hear a block away.

These parents had plenty of baggage that they could have carried with them as they went down the aisle. But they were wise enough and sane enough to put their *farribles* in proportion. They understood that their child's *simcha* had priority over anything that separated them from each other—at least for that day. There may have been an invisible gorilla in the room, carrying all of the "Do you know what he did to me?" and all of the "Do you know what she did to me?" questions that they felt, but they chose to put that invisible gorilla away for the duration of the wedding—and I am impressed with them for having had the strength to do that.

I must tell you that I have performed a lot of weddings over the years, but that moment—when I looked out and saw those two parents, walking their son down the aisle together—that was one of the holiest moments that I have ever seen take place in the sanctuary.

Let me tell you: In my business, I get to go to a lot of weddings and I have seen all kinds. Yet not all weddings are as nice as the one that I just told you about.

I once went to a wedding in which both Aunt Helen* and Aunt Shirley arrived wearing the same outfit. Aunt Helen was so upset by this that she walked out right after the ceremony and didn't stay for the dinner. She did this, rather than sit at a table with someone who was wearing the same dress as she was.

Another time, I attended a wedding at which someone got insulted because he was placed at the same table as a relative with whom he was on the outs. This person let that mistake spoil the whole *simcha* for him and for his family.

I have been to weddings at which 99 percent of the details went right, and the one thing that went wrong was the only thing that the family remembered and talked about for years afterward. And that is *narishkeit*!

And do you know what a ***truly*** spoiled *simcha* is? I'll tell you what a truly spoiled *simcha* is:

I was once at a wedding in which the father of the bride took his daughter down the aisle while looking like death warmed over. His face was white as a ghost, his eyes were bloodshot and you could not tell whether he was escorting his daughter to the *chuppah* or whether she was helping him walk to the *chuppah*. As they were walking down the aisle, he was crying; she was crying; I was crying; and most of the people in the room were crying. Why? Because the mother of the bride had died suddenly the day before, and the family had decided that the wedding must go on—and so it did. They had the funeral and the wedding on the same day. Now ***that's*** a truly spoiled *simcha*.

In another instance of a spoiled *simcha*, I was once at a wedding that was performed twice on the same day. Once, we did it in the intensive care unit of the hospital, because the father was too sick to come to the wedding and the family did not want him to miss it. An hour later, we did the wedding over again, in the synagogue, so that the rest of the

* Names have been changed to protect the guilty.

guests could see the service. ***That's*** what you call a spoiled *simcha*. If yours is not as sad as that one was, don't complain.

There is a wonderful Jewish expression pertaining to *simchas* that I want to teach you today. I learned it from my parents many years ago. Some of you may know it from your childhood. If not, learn it today. The expression is "*zindig nisht*."

*Zindig nisht*: If you have a *simcha*, and almost all the details go right but one or two go wrong—if you have a *simcha*, and the parents of both the bride and the groom are able to be there, and if they are both able to walk down the aisle without crutches; if you have a *simcha* in which the bride and groom look like they were meant for each other—then no matter how many details go wrong, *zindig nisht*. Don't commit the sin of focusing on what went wrong. That is what *zindig nisht* means. It means, "Don't commit the sin of burching about what went wrong instead of being grateful for what went right."

Now let me tell you about one of the nicest parties that I have been to recently. At this particular party, the couple was celebrating their 50th wedding anniversary.

The party in honor of this milestone was held at the couple's house and was sponsored by their children. Everything was lovely. The toasts were appropriate and touching. The children and the grandchildren each spoke beautifully.

But two things went wrong.

The first thing that went wrong was that the bakery somehow forgot to deliver the wedding cake.

When he realized what had happened, the 'chosen' of the wedding anniversary got up and said, "Ladies and gentlemen, there is a problem. The wedding cake has not arrived. So I am going to ask one of the grandchildren to drive to the bakery and pick up the cake. And in the meantime, until it arrives, I want everyone here to be patient and to continue singing and dancing and telling stories. Will you do that, please?"

So we did.

But then the second crisis occurred.

The cake arrived, and the container was opened. There, on the cake, was a picture of a bride and groom; underneath the picture it was written, "Happy anniversary, Fred and Louise." The only thing wrong with that inscription is that the chosen *kallah* of this *simcha* were not named Fred and Louise. Evidently, when the grandson arrived to pick up the cake, the man behind the counter at the bakery reached for the wrong cake, put it into a box and sent him on his way.

What would you have done if you were the *baaley simchah*, and that happened to you? I think that I would have called my lawyer, and sued the bakery for their mistake.

But do you know what the *kallah* at this *simcha* did?

Without batting an eye, she reached for the knife, with which to cut the cake. Before she cut the cake, she said to the people who were assembled around her, "Ladies and gentlemen: We want to wish Fred and Louise—whoever they are—as much joy at their anniversary party as we have at ours. We hope that they feel as surrounded by love as we do at this moment. And to this, will you all say, 'Amen.'"

And with that, she cut the cake and gave her husband the first piece. This was a woman who had her priorities straight.

This was a woman who understood that, if you get to your 50th wedding anniversary, and you can both still walk and talk and sing and dance; if you and your husband are still on speaking terms; if your children and grandchildren and your closest friends are all around you; then, even if the bakery makes a mistake—or even two—*nu*. It is not worth getting aggravated over, and it is not worth it to let this mistake spoil the *simcha*.

So let me make it very clear:

If your son or daughter can chant the *haftorah*, and if he or she has some idea of what it means, and if he or she has done a *mitzvah* project that helped to make the world a little bit better—then thank God and be happy. Even if your son did not sing as well as Pavarotti and even if Aunt Tillie got lost and did not show up in time to hear him.

If you reach a big milestone, and are able to celebrate a big birthday or a special anniversary, be grateful and thank God—even if the soup at the dinner is too hot or too cold, and even if the main course is too salty or not salty enough, and even if the caterer got the wording wrong on the cake and wished someone else a happy anniversary by mistake instead of you. *Nu*. Be grateful and thank God just the same. If you have to deal with any or even all of these minor snafus, *zindig nisht*—because in the total scheme of things, they don't really count. And to focus on these things, instead of on what a *simcha* is really all about, is to commit a sin.

Many years ago, I received a *bracha* from a friend of mine, and I have never forgotten it. It came from Rabbi Irwin Witty, who was a Jewish educator in Canada, who has since passed away.

I remember that I told him that we were going to celebrate a *simcha* soon, and he said to me, "May you celebrate many *simchas*—and may you celebrate all of your *simchas b'simchah*." Which means, "May you have many joyous occasions to celebrate, and may you be able to celebrate your joyous occasions with joy."

So this is my wish to you today:

If things go well for you in this new year that now begins, and if you have many *simchas* to celebrate in this new year, may you celebrate your *simchas b'simchah*. And may you not let the complaints and the aggravations and the screw-ups that are a part of every joyous occasion take away from what is truly important.

May you put away your complaints and your resentments in the time of your joy, for even though I know that that may not always be easy to do—believe me, I know—it is well worth doing.

For if you can do that, then I promise you that even if, *chas vishalom, chas vishalom*, Aunt Helen and Aunt Shirley both come wearing the same dress;

And even if, *chas vishalom, chas vishalom*, you put Uncle Irving at the same table as Uncle Charley, because you forgot that they are on the outs with each other;

And even if, *chas vishalom, chas vishalom*, the cake has the wrong people's names on it, then it will still be a great *simcha* for you and for all those whom you love.

Therefore, I have a suggestion to make to you today:

If you are planning to have a *simcha* sometime during this coming year, take these two words—*zindig nisht*—and put them on a magnet on your refrigerator. Or put them on the desk where you are going to sit when you work on the details of your *simcha*, or put them someplace where you are bound to see them—to see them when you talk to the caterer or the florist, or when you talk to your *machetonim* or to your children. For if you do, every time you see these two words—*zindig nisht*—they will set the pressures and the problems that are a part of every party into proper perspective.

I have two wishes for you today: The first is that you may have many *simchas* in this new year; the second is that you may have the wisdom and the good sense to celebrate your *simchas* "*b'simchah.*"

Amen.

# 5

# Smile! You are on Candid Camera

## Rosh Hashana

Dear friends,

I am really not sure whether I ought to give this sermon today or not, because I could get into big trouble if any of you tells someone what I am going to say today.

I thought about it for a long time, and I have decided that I am going to give the sermon today on one condition: That you promise me that you will tell no one—no one, ***no one***—what I am going to tell you today.

Do you promise?

The reason I am hesitant is because if my wife finds out what I am going to tell you today, I will be in big trouble at home; if the board of directors of this synagogue finds out what I am going to tell you today, I could lose my job.

So will you promise me that you will tell no one what I am going to tell you today?

The reason I ask this favor of you is that I am going to tell you about two of the most embarrassing experiences that I have ever had in my whole life. And if you tell anyone, I will never speak to you again. Is that understood?

The first experience that I am going to tell you about occurred this year, on the day before Rosh Hashana.

I am sure that you know that the day before Rosh Hashana is a busy time for rabbis. There is the service to prepare; the sermons to look over, *teshuvah* to do—and the phone is ringing off the hook with rabbis calling to wish us well or to ask for advice-—and in the middle of all this, my wife asked me to go out and do some shopping for her.

What do you do when your wife asks you to do something?

I do whatever she asks me to do.

What don't you do for your wife? Especially on *Erev* Rosh Hashana? And so I put down my books and I went out to do what she asked me to do for her.

So there I was, driving down Powerline Road and meditating on the state of my soul and thinking about all the *teshuvah* that I need to do, when all of a sudden, I hear a siren go off from the police car behind me.

I pulled over—figuring that the policeman probably wanted to ask my advice on how to do *teshuvah*—otherwise, why would he stop me on *Erev* Rosh Hashana?

Instead—and much to my surprise—he ***accused*** me (***me***! ***Me***, of all people!); he accused me of driving too fast ***and*** he accused me of going through a red light. And he accused me—me!—of driving 55 miles per hour in a school zone?

Now, I ask you: Those of you who know me, would I do that?

Am I the kind of person who would drive too fast?

My first reaction was to deny it. I admit that it might be possible that I was so preoccupied thinking about *teshuvah* that I may have driven a little bit too fast. It is even possible that maybe, ***maybe*** I drove 35 miles per hour in a school zone. It may even be possible that I drove 40 miles per hour in a school zone. It is perhaps even conceivable—it is unlikely, but it is conceivable—that I drove 50 miles per hour in a school zone. But would ***I*** drive 55 miles per hour through a school zone?

***Me?***

No way!

Would I drive through a red light? ***Me?*** No way! Yellow? Maybe. Pink? Possibly. But *not* red.

I started to say that to him, but before I could answer, he said to me, "Mister, would you look at the radar and see for yourself what you did?"

It was then that I realized that he had my rate of speed recorded. And to that, I had no answer. How do you argue with a radar screen? So I gracefully accepted the ticket, wished the policeman a *shana tova* and went on my way. I drove a little more slowly and a little more carefully from then on for the rest of the trip.

That was my last sin of the old year.

When I got home, I paid for the ticket—in cash—so that my wife wouldn't see the check and find out what I did. (By the way, I get so many tickets that I now keep a lawyer on retainer, just for my traffic fines.)

But if you tell my wife what happened—I am warning you, now—that if you tell my wife that I got another ticket for speeding, I will ***never speak to you again***.

So will you please promise me, that you won't tell my wife what I did?

The second sin that I committed was worse—much worse. It was beyond question the most embarrassing experience that I have ever had in my life. It was so embarrassing, in fact, that I still blush every time I think of it.

I will tell you about it, but only on one condition: Promise me that you will never tell anyone about it.

It happened a number of years ago, back when I was rabbi of a synagogue in Miami. The *chazen* and I officiated at the wedding of a lovely couple. The parents of the bride were friends of the *chazen*'s, and so because of him, I was invited to officiate, too.

It was a beautiful wedding.

A few weeks after the wedding, the parents of the bride called and invited us to come over and see the videotape. We went. We had some drinks, nashed some food, and then we sat down in the den and made ourselves comfortable. The father of the bride pressed the "play" button on the VCR, and the tape began.

We saw the bridesmaids and the ushers marching down the aisle, with soft music playing in the background. Suddenly, though, I noticed that two people were talking over the music. There were two people engaged in conversation, clearly audible, while the bridal party was going down the aisle.

I thought to myself: Who could be so crude? Who could be so ***rude***? Who could be so badly mannered that they would be talking at a time like this?

To make matters worse, the conversation was in terrible taste. These two people, whoever they were, were saying stupid and insensitive things. And then, all of a sudden, I realized: ***Oh, my God! That's me! That's me and the chazen!***

What happened was that we had been standing together under the *chuppah*. It was a long procession, and so I flipped off the microphone in front of us. We were schmoozing. I never realized that, right above our heads there was another microphone—a microphone that had been placed there for the videotaping. And so every word that we were saying was being recorded—and we didn't know it.

The *chazen* said to me, "What do you think of that dress that the mother of the bride is wearing? Isn't it a *shmate*?"

And I said—thank God, thank God, ***thank God*** I said—"I think the dress is nice." However, I continued, "But don't the ushers look silly in those tuxedos? They look like penguins."

He said, "What do you think this wedding is going to cost? I bet it will be quite a bundle."

I replied, "From what I hear, they're *ungeshtoped*. They can afford it."

And, now, here we were—sitting in the den of the home of the parents of the bride, listening to and eating the words that we had said. Can you imagine how embarrassed we were?

The parents of the bride are very nice people. They forgave us. They also promised us that before the chosen and *kallah* saw the tape, they would make sure that it was edited and that what we had said was cut out. And they did. But I have to tell you that I went home that night completely mortified. To this day, I blush every time I think of that incident. Believe me, if we had known that we were being recorded, we would have talked very differently—or not at all.

The reason I share this experience with you today is because I have the feeling that I am not the only one who has had this kind of an experience. It happened, for example, to Jesse Jackson. Do you remember the incident? Some years ago, he said something derogatory about Jews, he called New York "Hymietown," and then—much to his embarrassment—he found out that the microphone was on and he was being recorded.

It happened to Ronald Reagan once, too. He was playing with the microphone when he said something silly about the Russians and made a joke about how he was going to drop the atomic bomb on them just for fun—and then he found out that the microphone was on. That has happened to lots of people in public life.

The thesis of my sermon today is that whether we know it or not—whether we realize it or not—***we are all on candid camera, every day of our lives***. Therefore, we need to live with the awareness that we are.

Let me first give a couple of obvious examples of this truth, and then let me talk about some examples that are closer to home.

The first example comes from New York. Do you remember the incident that took place a couple of months ago in a hospital in New York? A woman came into the emergency room and asked for treatment, and they told her to sit down and wait until her name was called.

About one half-hour later, the woman fainted, landing on the floor. Members of the hospital staff walked past this woman for the next 20 minutes and didn't do a thing. Janitors went by and mopped the floor around her, doing whatever else they had to do, too, and no one even gave her a passing glance. Nurses and doctors treated her as if she was invisible.

And the whole scene was caught on camera!

The woman died, and I just wonder what kind of a defense the hospital is going to offer when her family sues them for criminal neglect. I guarantee you they won't have much of a case when the film is played in the courtroom.

This hospital won't get much sympathy from me, either—or, I suspect, from the rest of the people who watched that scene as it was played over and over again on the television, for days. I hope that the family sues the hospital for everything its insurance company has!

The second example I will give occurred some years ago, in Albany. There was a certain governor of New York state—I won't tell you his name—who evidently made arrangements to visit a certain house in Washington, D.C., while he was there.

How shall I describe this house, in *shule*? Let me just say that it was the kind of house that is not a home. This governor had arranged to pay a great deal of money in order to visit this house. That was what upset me when I heard the story. Visiting a house of ill repute is one thing, but paying

***several thousand dollars per visit***? That, it seems to me, is too much!

*Nebech*, when this governor called to make the appointment, he had no idea that his conversation was being recorded. Can you imagine how embarrassed he must have felt when the tape of that conversation was revealed for his family; his constituents; and for all the world to hear?

There was a similar case here, in Broward County, a couple of years ago. A policeman and his wife were accused of running this kind of a house. The couple was caught and the case came to court. Yet there was one gentleman who was very upset that this couple was going on trial. He tried to arrange a settlement in order to keep the case out of court, but he was unable to do so. This man was the vice mayor of a certain city in Palm Beach County. Evidently, this man understood the term "vice mayor" literally, and it seems that this man had—how shall I say this politely—he had evidently visited this house and had had an intimate, private conversation with one of the ladies who worked in the house. Much to this man's embarrassment, it now turns out that this private conversation was recorded on film! Can you imagine how embarrassed he must be? I am sure that if he had known that he was being recorded, he would have behaved very differently.

The next example comes from Washington. Do you remember the case? Some years ago, the former mayor of Washington, D.C., Marion Barry, had an intimate and private conversation with a lady friend of his in a hotel room—without a chaperone. During the course of the conversation, Mayor Barry relaxed by taking some "coke." I don't mean Coca-Cola; I mean coke. A few minutes later, the police broke into the room and accused Mayor Barry of taking illegal drugs. He said, "Who, me? We were just talking!" The police then showed him the hidden camera, on which was recorded everything that he had done. How embarrassed he must have been!

The same thing has happened to many of our political leaders in recent years.

When Barack Obama joined the Rev. Jeremiah Wright's church some years ago, could he have imagined that he would someday be running for president of the United States—and that the tapes of some of Wright's sermons would be played over and over again on television, and that they would cause him great embarrassment? If he had known, I am sure that he would not have joined that church.

And so, if there is anyone sitting here today who is planning to run for president of the United States someday, let me reassure you that I am fairly confident that my sermons are not taped; if they are, there really isn't anything that I have said in any of my sermons that will come back to haunt you if you run for president. At least, I hope not.

Do you remember what happened when Barack Obama became president and the governor of Illinois had to appoint a successor for him in the Senate? This governor made the mistake of asking how much money he could get for appointing someone to Senator Obama's seat, without realizing that his conversation was being recorded by the police. As a result, he is no longer living in the governor's mansion. Instead, he is living in a very small apartment in the state penitentiary. If he had known that he was being taped, I am sure he would not have said what he did.

And now, let me tell you the most bizarre example of being on candid camera that I know.

It happened a few years ago in New Jersey.

There was a wedding at a certain catering house in South Orange. The father of the bride brought a great deal of cash with him with which to pay the caterer, the orchestra and the waiters. The money was in an envelope that he kept in the inside pocket of his tuxedo jacket. The wedding was *freilich*. Everyone danced enthusiastically and, as the evening went on, they began to feel warm. The father of the bride took off his jacket and draped it over a chair. When the party was over, he put on his jacket and reached into his pocket—and the money was gone!

The father had no choice. He had to sit down and write checks to the caterer, the orchestra leader and the waiters. And then someone remembered. Someone said, "Wait a minute! The camera has been on all night. Who knows? Maybe it recorded the theft!"

They played back the recording and, sure enough, they saw it—the ***father of the groom*** had reached into his *mechutan*'s inside pocket, taken out the money and put it into his own pocket—and it had all been caught on camera!

To put it mildly, the marriage got off to a very rocky start.

Why do I tell you these stories? Simply to make two points: First, that all of us would behave much better if we thought we were being videotaped; and second, that we ***are*** on candid camera every moment of our lives, whether we realize it or not.

Isn't that what *Unitaneh Tokef* says? That there is a God, and that this God is "*sofer, umoneh, v'ed v'yodea, umochicach, vikotev, vichotem*"—that God sees, hears, knows, testifies, records, counts and judges all that we do? That is what *Unitaneh Tokef* says. How do you feel about that prayer? Do you believe it?

I confess that when I was a child, I pictured God as the great Scorekeeper in the Sky: an inspector who was always watching our behavior and who knew all our secrets. I pictured God as one who runs the great computer in the heavens that is even more efficient than that of the IRS.

But now I am older. Now I realize that if you take this prayer literally, it is gross. But if you take this prayer seriously, it is true.

Now I share the view of God that is expressed in this poem by James Cavanaugh:

Once I believed some grey and giant judge
Kept careful records of all the deeds of men,

That with some black and lasting kind of pen,
He carefully recorded every petty crime—
And most of all, of mine.
But now I know there is no judge with angry pen
Who keeps track of deeds and time.
Instead, every face records what life has been about
And sculpts a memory into every crack and line—
And most of all, on mine.

Now I know that it is not only God who watches and records all that we do; my face does, too. And my ulcers do, too. And my children do, too. Now I know that our children are walking tape recorders and, whether we realize it or not, they are "on" all the time.

How much *tsedaka* do you give? Ask your children. They know.

Do you complain when the bill for the *shule* dues comes in the mail? Ask your children. They know.

Do you make snide comments behind the others' backs about what your friend wore at a party? Ask your children. They know.

Do you respond to Israel's call for help? To the synagogue's? When the president makes his appeal for the synagogue this year, will you respond generously—or will you tune him out? Ask your children. They will know.

When you tell them on Monday, "Never tell a lie!" and then tell them on Tuesday, when somebody with whom you don't walk to talk calls you on the phone, "Tell them I am not home!"—they hear that, too. And they record what you say.

Our children are walking tape recorders. All that we do and are, they see and hear—and record. If you don't believe me, read some of the books that have been written in recent years by the children of the rich and famous. Read that nasty book by the daughter of Joan Crawford, called "*Mommie Dearest*." Read the biography written by Yael Dayan, the daughter of Moshe Dayan. Read the book that was written by Maureen Reagan, the daughter of Ronald Reagan. Read these books and you will see that these children recorded internally all the faults and foibles of their parents; and then, when they grew up, they vomited them up into print.

It is not only the children of celebrities who "record" parents' words and actions. What we do—what we talk about at the table, what we stand for, what we fall for—is all recorded by our children. And it affects them for the rest of their lives.

That is the bad news.

Now let me give you the good news. The good news is that the good we do is also recorded on the memories of our children. And that lasts, too.

I have given you some examples of embarrassing moments that got recorded on film, but now let me give you some examples of good things that have been recorded on life's "candid cameras," as well.

Story No. 1: My friend and teacher, Rabbi Arnold Turetsky (*zichrono livracha*), once told me this story:

There was a woman in his congregation who attempted to commit suicide. You couldn't really blame her. Her husband had walked out on her for a younger woman. Her children had rebelled and left her, each in a different way. She wasn't able to find a decent job, and she had very few friends. She had very little self-worth, and as a result, she did what she did.

Rabbi Turetsky went to visit this woman when she was in the hospital. They were talking, and she was going on and on about how ugly she was and about how worthless she felt. For some reason—he didn't know why—he said to her: "Tell me, what did your grandmother call you when you were a child?"

She smiled and said: "My grandmother used to call me *sheyne ponim*," which means a beautiful face.

He said to her: "Were you a *sheyne ponim*?"

She said: "Oh, no. I was a clumsy, awkward, ugly kid then—just as I am now."

He said: "Really? Was your grandmother a liar?"

She said: "Oh, no. My grandmother wouldn't lie. Never!"

She was silent for a moment, and then she said: "I guess that's what she thought I was."

Rabbi Turetsky saw her a few weeks later. He asked her how everything was going. She said, "It's still pretty rough, but I have to tell you that at least once a day, I say to myself: If my *bubbie* thought that I was a *sheyne ponim*, then maybe I am."

This woman's *bubbie* has been dead now for probably 30 years, and yet her granddaughter is still living off her words today. She is still being nourished by the words of praise that she got in her childhood. What a great gift it was that her *bubbie* gave her—better than stocks or bonds, by far! Words that her grandmother may have said casually got recorded onto the soul of her grandchild, and they are still there today—and they are literally helping to keep her alive!

The second example I will give comes from my own life. Many of you know that we have lots of kids in my congregation. When I go around with the Torah on Shabbat morning, I always carry candy with me, which I give to the kids as I go by. I have been doing that for many years, in whatever *shule* I am in. Smart kids already know to sit at the end of an aisle so that they can stick out their hands and get candy as I go by. Some of them even used to greet me at one end of the aisle and then scoot over to the other side in order to greet me again. The kids love it—and so do their dentists.

Do you know where I got this custom from? I got it from Dovid Tepper, *alav hashalom*, who sat in the row behind us in the old Galitsianer *shule* on Wylie Avenue in Pittsburgh, where I grew up.

Dovid Tepper was a baker. He was not a very rich man. God forgive me for saying so, but I don't think that he was a very learned man. He was not, as we used to say, "*boki in de kleine osiyos*." He was not a man who was very versed in the commentaries. But Dovid Tepper loved children. And so every Shabbat, when he came to *shule*, he came with a big bag of Hershey bars. I have to confess to you that when I was 6 years old, I did not go to *shule* in order to hear the rabbi's sermon; I did not go to *shule* in order to hear the *chazen daven*. I went to *shule*, at least in part, in order to get a Hershey bar from Dovid Tepper.

And when I grew up and became a rabbi, I did what he did. I don't think that I ever planned it this way, but somehow the example of what he did registered with me. Now, when I go around behind the Torah on Shabbat morning, kids know to get to the aisle so that they can get a Tootsie Roll from me. No wonder the dentists in this congregation love me so much. It was because of Dovid Tepper that I now do this. And who knows? I have had three young people in my time who have gone on to become rabbis. Someday, one of the rabbis who grew up in my *shule* may grow up to be the candy man for the kids of the next generation, because of me. Who knows in what city, in what country or even on what planet that will be, but it could happen. And if it does, then Dovid Tepper, who has been gone now for over 50 years, will still be affecting kids—50 years from now. That is how long the tapes inside of us can last, and how wide and deep their influence can be.

One last example: A couple of years ago, I went to see one of the members of our synagogue who was in the hospital. This man had sent word that he wanted to see me, and so I went.

I arrived at the door to his room and braced myself, mustering up my courage before walking in. (That's what I do whenever I have to go into the hospital room of someone whom I care about who is very ill.) The man said to me, "Thank you for coming, Rabbi. I think you know that I have a serious surgery scheduled for tomorrow. I hope that I will make it. The doctor says my chances are fairly good. But just in case I don't make it, I don't want to leave any debts behind me. So here is a check to cover what I owe you for the Kol

Nidre campaign—just in case." And he gave me a check, written in an almost illegible scrawl, to pay his pledge.

I have to tell you that that experience and those words are recorded in my mind, and they are recorded indelibly on the memories of this man's children, who were there that day as well. This was a man who did not want to leave a single debt behind when he left this world, and who taught me and his children to live in the same way.

When he said that, I also understood a childhood memory that I had not thought about for a long time. I remember how my father, *zichrono livrocho*, used to sit down at his desk on *Erev* Yom Kippur with his checkbook, writing out check after check after check to all kinds of charities and causes. We kids used to tease him about it. We used to say, "How do you know that all these appeals are legitimate?" And he would answer, "Either they are legitimate or they are not. And if they are not, the crook who sent them has to make a living too."

Now I understand why he did it. Yom Kippur is Judgment Day. It is the day when we think about the preciousness and the precariousness of our lives. It is the day when we focus on our mortality. It is the day when we say *Yizkor* and we wear a *kitel,* so that we will realize our mortality. My father was teaching my brothers and me a lesson by writing those checks . He was recording for us a message, which was that *tsedaka* is the rent we pay for the space that we occupy on earth, and that no one should be so vain or so arrogant as to not pay the rent owed for the privilege of living. No one should be so naïve as to think that he has time to do it tomorrow, either. For tomorrow may not come.

The bad news is that we are on candid camera, and that all of the vain and the dumb and selfish and stupid things that we do are recorded, whether we know it or not. The good news is that we are on candid camera and that all of the good and the noble deeds that we do are also recorded, whether we know it or not.

And the very good news is that if we don't like what we have recorded in a past year, we can do what the parents of the bride did for me when I was embarrassed by what I had said at that wedding in Miami. We have the power to "edit the tape" of our behavior. We can go back and, though we can't edit or splice out what we did, we can change its meaning. We can turn our words or actions from a sin into a stepping stone toward growth: from an *aveyra* into a turning point that makes us realize the error of our ways and that enables us to change. We have the power—if we really want to—to make of our sins lessons from which we can learn. If we do that, and we edit the tape in this way, we can live differently in the new year than we did in the year that has just ended.

And so these are my two wishes for you today, as the new year begins:

No. 1: May you remember the customs and practices that were good in your parents' home, and may you continue them.

No. 2: May you realize and understand that whatever you do, whether it be something good or something bad, is always being recorded—not only by God in heaven, but by your children and grandchildren, by your friends and by your family here on earth.

Therefore, be careful what you do. And if you do something bad, edit the tape and delete (or at least, repent) all the things that embarrass you, and learn to live better from now on.

And, remember: You promised me that you won't tell anybody about the two dumb things that I did that I told you about today.

And may God bless you for keeping my secrets. Amen.

## 6

# What Should You Do When Your Time Is Almost Up?

## Shabbat Shuvah

Before I begin, I must tell you that I have a problem.

I have written two sermons for today, and I don't know which one to give.

One is a short sermon: It is only 84 pages long. The other is a little bit longer: It is 135 pages long. The first one is funny and light and entertaining, and I am tempted to give that one because every rabbi likes to be liked—and if I am entertaining, perhaps you will like me. The other one is grim and serious and forces us to confront the reality of our mortality.

And this is Shabbat Shuvah, which is the Sabbath on which we are supposed to think about serious things. This is the time when we are supposed to think about our mortality. This is the main theme of these Days of Awe. This is why we wear a shroud (a plain, simple gown that has no pockets) on Yom Kippur. This is why the focus of the prayers at this season of the year is on the preciousness and the precariousness of life—and on the reality of death. And so this is the theme that I should really talk about today, is it not?

Perhaps I should give one sermon, and if it bombs, I can give the other one to make up for it. Or perhaps I should give one sermon, and if it is well received, then I can give the other one as an encore.

In the end, I came up with this compromise: I will give one sermon now, and then we will *daven* Mussaf and have Kiddush. And then everyone can come back here, and I will give the other sermon.

Is that a fair compromise?

Do you agree to this arrangement?

If so, let me begin:

I want to raise a question with you today that I suspect that all of us think about at some time in the quiet of the night, but that we very seldom talk about in public. The question is this: What would you do if you found out that your time on this earth was almost up? What would you do if you found out that you had only a few more weeks or a few more months at the most left in which to live?

I am sure that you all know the old Jewish joke about this question: What would you do if the doctor told you that you have only six more months to live?

The joke goes that the Catholic would say, "I would spend my last six months praying and repenting so that I can be accepted into heaven." The Protestant would say, "I would like to spend my last six months arranging for a smooth settlement of my business affairs, so that my children will not need to quarrel over my estate". And the Jew would say, "I would like to get a second opinion."

I like this joke, because it makes the point that we should not surrender to death until and unless we have to: that as long as we have life, we should fight to stay alive. But the truth is that there comes a time when each of us must face the question of what we should do with the last days of our lives. And all the jokes in the world will not help us when that time arrives.

And so, let me share with you three answers to this question today. One comes from the Talmud. One comes from my wife, who is really much smarter than I am. And one comes from a great scientist and a great writer who died this year.

The Talmud tells a story about how one of the sages met the Angel of Death in the marketplace. The angel says, "I have come to collect your soul, for this is the day when you are due to die." The rabbi says to the angel, "Do me a favor, will you please? Give me a week more in which to get ready. I don't want to die in the marketplace, like a stray dog or like a homeless beggar. Let me go home and give me a week in which to arrange my learning—*lisader et torati*—so that when I come before the Court on High, I will be able to show what I have accomplished in my life."

The Angel of Death agreed, and gave the rabbi another week. When the week was over, the angel comes knocking on the rabbi's door, and says, "Time's up. Let's go." And the rabbi says to him, "Can I please have another week?"

The Angel of Death said no.

I like that Midrash, because it is realistic. Everyone would like another week, and if we got it, we would want another one after that. But the reality is that some of us get advance notice of our death and some of us do not.

I had a good friend in Riverdale whose name was Rabbi Abraham Karp. He was the rabbi of Temple Beth El in Rochester for many years, and he lived in Riverdale when he retired. He set out to go to the grocery one day, in order to buy some things for his family. He started to cross the street, to get to the grocery store, but he never got to the other side. He died in the middle of the street.

So some of us are fortunate, like the rabbi in the Talmud that I told you about, who got a week's notice. Some of us are not. Some of us meet the angel who has come to collect our soul on the street; on the bus; on a plane; at the clubhouse; or at home. For some of us he comes too quickly, with no advance notice, no time to prepare and no time to say good-bye; for others he comes too slowly, and his coming is long and lingering and seems to go on forever.

I knew a rabbi once who lived in Woodmere, Long Island. His name was Rabbi Irving Miller. Rabbi Miller was fanatic about taking care of his health. He watched what he ate very carefully. He exercised every day. And once a year, he would go to the Mayo Clinic for a complete checkup. One year, he went to the clinic and stayed there for three days, going through a whole battery of tests, just as he always did. When he finished his checkup, they gave him a complete bill of health. He said, "Thank you very much," and paid the bill. He left the clinic, hailed a taxi to take him to the airport—and he was halfway into the taxi when he dropped dead of a heart attack.

So, some people get advance notice and others do not. For some people, if I dare say so, the Angel of Death comes too quickly; for some, if I dare say so, the angel comes too slowly. For some people the *Malach hamavet* comes little by little, hour by hour, inch by inch; and for other people, the angel of death comes too suddenly—*keheref ayin*—in the blink of an eye. And whether or not we get advance notice of his coming is up to the angel, and not to us.

My wife says that she would like to have at least some notice before she dies. She says that she would like to have at least a couple of weeks' notice, if not more.

Why?

Because all her life, she has had to be careful about what she eats. She has had to be careful that she does not eat too much sugar, and she has had to be careful not to eat too much of other tempting foods, because she is hypoglycemic. She has had to be careful about how much ice cream and how much cake she eats. But she says that if she knew that she was going to die in a couple of weeks anyway, regardless of what she ate—boy, would she eat! She says that she would eat everything that had been forbidden on her diet, and then she would have seconds, and maybe even thirds, and if she did so she would go out happy.

This morning, I want to tell you about someone who faced this question this year: What should you do when you find out that your time on earth is almost up?

To be honest with you, I am not sure that I agree with everything that this man said. His answer is a bit too secular for my taste. But the Talmud says that you should not judge anyone until you have walked in his shoes, and so I am not going to pass judgment on what this man said. I will leave it to you to decide for yourselves what you think of his answer.

Oliver Sacks was professor of neurology at the New York University School of Medicine, and he was also a well-known writer. He was a man who combined two careers: he was both a great doctor and a great writer.

Dr. Sacks was 81 years old, and up until last year, he was in very good shape. He proudly boasted that he swam at least a mile every day, and that he worked out in the gym every day as well! Up until a few months ago, he felt that he was in very good health. But then, a few months ago, he went to the doctor for his annual checkup—and he was told that he has cancer of the liver. The prognosis was just plain bad. The doctor told him that the progress of this kind of cancer can sometimes be slowed down, but that once it has gone as far as his had, it cannot be stopped. He was told that he had only a few more months, at the most, left to live.

He walked out of the doctor's office and went home, and thought about his situation for a few days. He brooded, as you or I likely would, if we got such news. And then he sat down and wrote a column for the op-ed page of the New York Times. This is what he wrote:

"It is up to me now to choose how to live out the months that remain to me. I have to live in the richest, deepest, most productive way I can. ***When*** I go is not up to me, but ***how*** I go—and what the angel will find me doing when he comes knocking at my door—***that*** is up to me."

Dr. Sacks continued:

"Let me say these things:

"First, that I have the manuscript of a book on my desk that is nearly finished. And I am determined to get it done if I can, before my time ends."

I must say that when I read that last sentence, I was impressed, because blessed is the person who dies while at work on a task that is not yet finished. Whatever it is—a book, as Dr. Sacks had; a symphony, as Beethoven had; or whether it is a paid job or a volunteer job, helping the *shule* or teaching grandchildren—whatever it is, blessed is the person who is in the midst of an unfinished task when the angel comes. I think that that is the way to live and that is the way to die.

When I read that line, I thought of my teacher, Dr. Louis Finkelstein, who worked on his commentary on a rabbinic midrash up until the day he died. I remember what he said to someone who came to visit him. He said that he was grateful that he was dying from the feet up and not from the head down, so that he could work on his book until the very end.

Dr. Sacks also wrote:

> *Over the last few days, I have begun to see the world as if from a great altitude. I now look at the world the way that the passenger on an airplane does, when he looks down from the sky. Everything*

*seems smaller than it used to. Everything seems more connected than it used to. And some things seem less important to me than they used to.*

*I now feel that there is no time left for me to do anything that is not essential. And so I no longer listen to the national news on television every night, the way that I used to. I no longer pay much attention to politics, or to global warming, or to many other such questions that I used to be deeply concerned about.*

*It is not that I am indifferent to these things. But they are no longer my business. They will be solved, if they are solved, by the next generation, not by mine.*

*I have confidence in the next generation, I really do. They are bright, and talented, and caring, and the world will be in good hands when they take over from us. I am impressed whenever I meet young doctors nowadays—even the young doctor who diagnosed my illness. He may look like a bar mitzvah boy to me, but it is clear that he knows his stuff. And so do many of the other young people whom I meet nowadays. And therefore, I believe that the future is in good hands.*

*The third thing that I am now aware of is how many of my friends and how many of my contemporaries have died in recent years. My generation is on the way out. And each time I lose a friend, it feels like a ripping away of a part of myself.*

I remember Louis Finkelstein said something like that when he gave the eulogy at the funeral of his teacher, Louis Ginzberg. He said that a person does not die in one moment.

He dies little by little. He dies, in part, each time he loses a friend.

And that is what I think Oliver Sachs meant when he said that it feels like a ripping away of a part of yourself each time you lose a friend.

In the article, he goes on:

> *"There will be no one like us when we are gone, but then, there is no one who is like anyone else, ever. When people die, they cannot be replaced. Each one leaves a hole that cannot be filled, for it is the fate of every human being to be a unique individual, to live his own life, and to die his own death. All we can do when they leave us is remember them. We cannot bring them back.*
>
> *"The fourth thing that I feel is that I have things to do in whatever time I still have left. I have friends to say goodbye to. I have broken relationships that I need to heal. I have new levels of knowledge and insight that I still want to achieve. I even have a few places that I would like to visit, if my strength holds up. And I even hope that there will be time in which to have some fun."*

"I have friends to say goodbye to, and I have broken relationships that I need to heal." Think about those words. Too many of us cheat those who are at the end of their lives by not letting them say goodbye. We say to them, "Oh, you are looking much better," or we say other lies, and they catch the signal. They understand that we do not want to hear the truth. And so they accommodate us, and say nothing that we do not want to hear. But inwardly, they feel cheated of the chance to say a real goodbye. Oliver Sacks wanted more than lies at the end of his life. He wanted the chance to make up with those from whom he was estranged and he wanted the opportunity to bid farewell to those whom he loved … and so do most of us, at the end of our lives.

Oliver Sacks ended his reflections with these words:

> *"I cannot pretend that I am not afraid. Of course I am. But the predominant emotion that I feel right now is gratitude. I have loved and I have been loved. I have been given much, and I have given something back in return. I have read and I have written. I have travelled and I have thought. I have studied and I have taught. And therefore, I feel that I have been a productive human being, and I have tried to be a mentsch. I have lived for a while on this beautiful planet, and that has been an enormous privilege, and a great adventure.*
>
> *And therefore, when the angel comes, I hope that he will give me time to say two words, if not more. I hope that he will give me time to say with a whole, even if not with a completely happy heart: thank you.*
>
> *For if I can leave the world with these two words—thank you—on my lips, what a good way to go that will be."*

I love that last line, don't you? "For if I can leave the world with these two words—'thank you'—on my lips, what a good way to go that will be."

And so, these are my wishes for you—for you and for me—as the new year begins:

My first wish is that the angel who comes to take us away finds us doing our job—whatever it is—to the very end, for if we can do that, then we will be alive for as long as we live and we will not have shriveled up and died spiritually or mentally before we die physically.

Second, my wish for you and for myself is that we may leave this world with trust and confidence that those whom we leave behind will be wise enough and strong enough to be able to carry on the work of the world that we will leave behind. May we leave with confidence that the world we leave behind is in good hands.

And third, may we all have the *zichut*—the privilege—of being able to end our lives with "thank you" on our lips: Thank you to God, thank you to the world and thank you to those whom we love. For there are no better words with which to leave the world than these.

May you and I be able to look back over our lives, when the end comes, and may we be able to say with a whole heart: "Thank you." For if we can say and if we can feel these words in our heart at the end, how blessed our lives and our deaths will be.

## 7

# Adam Greenberg at the Bat

## Shabbat Shuvah

Let me warn you before I begin that I am going to do two strange things in my sermon today—two things that I don't usually do.

The first is that I am going to take my text not from today's Torah reading, and not from the Machzor, which is what rabbis usually do on this day; instead, I am going to take my text from the *sedra* of BiHa'alotcha.

The second strange thing that I am going to do today is speak about a lesson that I learned a few years ago, from something that happened in baseball. I am going to do this not because I am not an expert on baseball, nor because I am the son of an expert on baseball. Rather, I am going to do this because I believe that this incident teaches a lesson that all of us need to learn when a new year begins.

And so, if this is clear, let me begin:

The title of my sermon this morning is *"Adam Greenberg at the Bat."*

Now I am sure that when you heard this title, all of the baseball experts in the congregation must have thought that I made a mistake. Or they will tell me that the name of the famous poem that I must be thinking of is "*Casey at the Bat*," and not "Greenberg at the Bat." They will tell me that if I am going to give a sermon about a baseball player named Greenberg, I must surely mean Hank Greenberg: the player for the Detroit Tigers who brought honor and credit to his people and who respected the Jewish religion by going to *shule* instead of to the baseball field when Yom Kippur occurred during the World Series.

But trust me, I know who I am talking about. I want to talk to you today not about Casey, and not about Hank Greenberg, but about another Greenberg—a Greenberg whose name was Adam Greenberg. Adam Greenberg had a lifetime battering average of .000. And yet I consider him to be one of the most outstanding athletes of any year and I believe that there is much that we can learn from him.

Before I explain why I am so impressed with Adam Greenberg, I need to tell you about a holiday that has almost completely disappeared from the Jewish calendar. It is a holiday that hardly anyone knows about anymore. I would wager that there are probably very few people here today who have even heard of this holiday, and yet it is one of my favorite holidays. I really wish that we could bring it back again.

The holiday that I have in mind is Pesach Sheni.

How many of you have heard of it?

It is mentioned only once in the entire Torah, in the *sedra* of Biha'alotcha.

The Torah says that the Israelites shall observe the holiday of Passover by bringing a sacrifice on the 14th day of the first month. And it says that they did as they were commanded to do. But then the Torah says that some people came to Moses and asked him a question. They said: "We were unable to offer a sacrifice on that day—either because we were too far away and could not get back to the sanctuary on time, or because we were ritually impure on that day and so we could not enter the sanctuary. Does that mean that we are debarred from offering the Paschal sacrifice?"

They said: "*Lama nigra?*" Why should we be deprived?

You can feel from their question how much the festival must have meant to them. You can tell that they felt deprived that they could not offer the Paschal lamb the way the rest of the House of Israel did. And so Moses said: "Stand here, and I will take your question to the Lord, and we will see what he says." And so he does.

The answer of the Lord comes back quickly. God said: "Whoever was unable to offer the Paschal sacrifice at the proper time may do so one month later—on the 14th day of the following month. Just like the rest of the Israelites, they shall eat it with unleavened bread and with bitter herbs. Just like the rest of the Israelites, they shall not leave any of it over until the morning. Just like the rest of the Israelites, they shall eat it broiled, and not baked, and just like the rest of the Israelites, they shall not break a bone of it."

That is the law of the Pesach Sheni. It provides that those who were unable to observe Pesach at its proper time are given a second chance, one month later.

I love this law, I really do, because I often wish that I could have a do-over or a mulligan in my life. I don't need a do-over or a mulligan in golf. In fact, if I got a do-over in golf—golf is *mir goonisht giholfen*—it would not help me very much. But I wish that I could have a do-over for some of the decisions that I have made in my life that did not turn out very well. For example, I wish that I had a second chance at being a better parent. Perhaps that is what grandparenting is. You don't have time to pay attention to your children when they are small, because you are too busy making a living. But by the time your grandchildren come along, you are not so busy, and you get a kind of second chance in being able to teach them.

I am sure that if you are like me, you can think of many other examples in your life when you wish you could have a Pesach Sheni—a second chance—to do what you should have done right the first time, but for whatever reason didn't.

And this brings me to the story of Adam Greenberg.

Adam Greenberg grew up in Connecticut. It was the great dream of his life, from childhood on, to someday be a player in the major leagues. I don't know if you realize what a difficult goal that is to achieve. There is so much competition. Only a few get to realize this dream, but Adam Greenberg did. After being a star player in college and playing for a few years in the minor leagues, Adam Greenberg was called by the Chicago Cubs in mid-season.

This was the greatest day of his life. This was the day that he had waited for and worked for for so long! He flew down to Miami for a series that the Cubs were playing against the Miami Marlins. His family came down from Connecticut to watch him play his first game in the major leagues, and to cheer him on.

The first game came and went—and Adam Greenberg sat on the bench. The second game came and went the same way. In the third game, in the ninth inning with the score tied and with one man on base, the manager put Adam Greenberg into the game as a pinch hitter. This was his big moment. The whole game would depend on what he did or did not do. If he hit a triple, his team would win; if he struck out or popped up, they would lose.

Greenberg took his place at the bat, crowding the plate so that the pitcher would not be able to throw an inside curve. That turned out to be his big mistake.

The Marlins pitcher was a lefty named Valerio de los Santos. Greenberg stood at the plate, waiting for the first pitch, hoping that he could hit it out of the park and win the game.

Santos looked him over and threw a fastball. The machine that records these things later showed that this pitch went from the mound to the plate at a speed of 92 miles per hour. It hit Adam Greenberg right in the head. Part of it caught a bit of the helmet, but most of it went smashing into his skull. The sound of that ball hitting his head was a horrible sound to the catcher, as well as to the umpire who was standing nearby. You could hear the gasps and feel the shock that came from the crowd in the stands.

Greenberg went down like a tree that had been struck by a bolt of lightning. He was sure that his skull had been split open, and so he grabbed his head with both hands, hoping that he could keep his brains from falling out.

"Stay alive! Stay alive!" he remembers telling himself, over and over again, as he lay crumpled on the ground. He heard the catcher telling him that he would be all right, but he did not believe him because the pain that he was feeling was so intense. He could hear the trainers and the team doctor come running out onto the field, and he could hear them talking to each other. He noticed that they did not ask for a towel, and that gave him a little bit of hope: if they didn't ask for a towel, that meant that he was not bleeding. If he was not bleeding, that meant that his skull had not split open. And if his skull had not split open, that meant that he might not be dying after all.

The fear subsided, and in its place, Adam Greenberg felt a terrible sense of embarrassment and shame. He thought to himself, Here I am. It is my very first time at bat—it is the very first pitch that I have ever received in the major leagues—and I have to be carried off the field on a stretcher! And in front of my parents, yet!

The next day Greenberg felt well enough to go out to the ballpark, but he could not keep his eyes open during the game. In next few days, he had blinding headaches and a terrible case of vertigo. The Cubs sent him back to the minor leagues. For the next seven years he wandered from one minor league team to another. He went from the farm team of the Cubs to the farm team of the Royals, and from there to the farm team of the Reds … until he ended up playing for the Bridgeport Bluefish, which is not exactly where the major league teams go when they are looking for talent.

Can you imagine having to live in Bridgeport, Connecticut, and having to play for the Bridgeport Bluefish in order to make a living? *Nebech.*

During those seven years, as Greenberg wandered from one minor league team to another, he suffered almost every day from severe vertigo and blinding headaches that lasted for hours on end. But all during those seven years, Adam Greenberg held on to his dream. He held on to the hope that he could someday have a do-over. He held on to the hope that maybe some team would give him a second chance. He held on to the hope that if he ever got a second chance, he would do better the next time.

There was one man—a man named Matt Liston—who shared Greenberg's dream. Matt Liston just did not believe that it was right for someone to work so hard to get to the major leagues and then be knocked out on the first pitch, and so he organized a write-in campaign that urged some team to give Adam Greenberg a second chance.

Twenty thousand people signed the petition that Matt Liston posted on his website. The Marlins decided to give Greenberg a second chance. Maybe it was because they were in last place anyway, so they figured that it couldn't do any harm. Or perhaps it was because they felt a little bit of guilt, since it was their pitcher who had thrown that ball that hit Adam Greenberg in the head in the first place.

Anyway, for whatever reason, the Marlins decided to give Greenberg a second chance—a kind of Pesach Sheni. But this time they decided that they were not going to take any chances or risk any liability if something happened to him. They wrote him a contract that had two special clauses in it. The first clause stated that if he got hurt again, they would bear no liability for his medical expenses. The second clause stated that this was a one-day contract, with no guarantee that it would be renewed.

Would you sign a contract that gave you no medical insurance, in a game that could be so dangerous? And would you sign a contract for one game, with no promise of renewal? Adam Greenberg signed this contract without any hesitation. He did so because he wanted an opportunity to make up for what had happened to him the first time. He wanted to have a Pesach Sheni.

Adam Greenberg's dream came true. He stepped into the batter's box and waited for the first pitch. The ball came right across the plate—and the umpire called it a strike.

Greenberg waited for the second pitch.

This time the pitcher threw a curveball. Greenberg swung with all his might—and he missed it by a mile.

The count was now 0 to 2.

The pitcher wound up and threw the ball again, and this time Greenberg swung with all his might—and missed again.

Three pitches; three strikes. So ended Adam Greenberg's baseball career.

I watched that game on television, and I watched Greenberg's press conference after the game. And I must tell you that I had two reactions.

My first reaction was sympathy and disappointment that, *nebech*, after waiting so long for a second chance, he struck out when he got it. How sad that was—for him and for all those rooting for him.

But at the same time, I must tell you that I was impressed by the way he handled it. Adam Greenberg handled this moment like a true pro. There was a press conference after the game, and he told the reporters that he was glad that the pitcher did not lob the ball to him or give him an easy pitch. He said that that is not the way you are supposed to play the game in the big leagues. He said that he was pleased that the pitcher had treated him just like any other player on the team, and had cut him no slack.

And these were the closing words of the interview—read them carefully:

> *"Life sometimes throws you curveballs, and it sometimes throws you fastballs. And you don't get to choose what kind of a pitch it is going to throw at you. Life threw me a fastball that went 95 miles an hour the first time I batted in the big leagues. It hit me in the back of the head and it knocked me down. But I got up from it, and that is really all that counts. My life is good, because I was able to get up again after life knocked me down. Anything else that happens after that is a bonus, and so I have no complaints—none at all."*
>
> *"Life's going to throw you curveballs, or fastballs to the back of your head. I got hit by one of them. It knocked me down, and I could have stayed there. I had a choice, and I could have said, 'Poor me, that's horrible.' But I chose to get up and get back in the box.*
>
> *And that's kind of the message to everyone: No matter what is going on in their own personal life, or anything, get back up, keep going. If you do that, good things do happen. Sometimes it takes seven years. But you know what? Anything is possible."*

I must say that I think that is a remarkable statement, isn't it?

If I had my way, I would paste Greenberg's words onto the locker of every player in the American League and the National League of baseball, and I would paste them onto the locker of every player in the National Football League, as well. I would do so because we are just beginning to become aware of how many athletes—in baseball and football, in high schools and colleges, in the major leagues and on football fields—are being injured during games. We are just beginning to realize how many players are suffering serious brain damage because their helmets are not good enough, or because the opposing tacklers or pitchers are hitting too hard and too fast. Therefore, we need Greenberg's words as a reminder to every athlete to be careful and to never purposely harm another player.

Do you know what else I would do, if I could? I would post Greenberg's words on my mirror, and on your mirror, and on the mirror of every single person who has been knocked down by life. And who among us has not been knocked down at some time in life?

I would give the words of Adam Greenberg to every person who has ever had a crippling illness and who has recovered, and to every person who has ever failed in business and started over again. I would give these words to every person who has ever had a bad marriage and survived it, and then has gone on to marry again. I would give these words to every single person who has ever been knocked down by life and been able to get up and start over again, for we all need to hear these words and to take them to heart.

I would tell you, I would tell myself and I would tell all the other people we know who have been knocked down by life and able to get up and start over again one more thing: I would tell them that ***it is not true*** that Pesach Sheni has disappeared from our calendar.

I would tell them that Rosh Hashana has come along and has taken the place of Pesach Sheni, because every time a new year begins, it brings us the same message: Even if the past year has been a living hell, and even if you have been knocked down and defeated by life many times during the last year, the new year is a new year! You can get up and you can begin again. The first day of the new year can be the first day of the rest of our lives, and we can start over again—no matter how hard or hurtful the past year had been.

It means, as Adam Greenberg put it, that if we can get up after life has knocked us down, anything else is a bonus—and therefore, we should have no complaints.

And so my wish for you, in the new year, is not that we will have a year with no defeats. For if I wished that for us, that would be a naïve wish, because no one gets through a whole year of life with no defeats—at least, not very often.

My wish for you, for me and for all those we love is that if life knocks us down in the new year, may we have the strength and the stamina and the courage and the resiliency to get up again. I pray that God will bless us with the ability to get up, off our knees, after we have been knocked down—and to go forward again. For if we can do that, then it will be a good year for us and for those whom we love.

The gift of resiliency—the ability to get up and start over again after a defeat—is something for which I have no secular explanation. The gift of resiliency is, to me, proof of the goodness of God. If life knocks us down in this new year, may God give us the ability to get up and to begin over again.

For if we can do that, then regardless of our batting average, we will be—like Adam Greenberg, whose lifetime batting average is .00—we will be heroes in God's record book forever.

And to this, let us all say: Amen.

8

# Dancing with Alzheimer's

## Kol Nidre

This is the holiest night of the year, and therefore, I want to speak to you tonight as honestly and as openly as I can about a subject that I am not very eager to talk about—and that you are not very eager to hear about. However, I believe that we all need to talk about it at some time in our lives.

I want to talk to you tonight about a question that some of us are dealing with today, and that some of us had to deal with yesterday, and that some of us will probably have to deal with tomorrow. The question that I want to talk to you about tonight is: What are our duties? And, further: What are the ***limits*** of our duties, when someone whom we love becomes old and weak, and frail and helpless?

I confess that at first, I hesitated about whether or not I should give a sermon on this topic tonight. I hesitated for three reasons:

One is that it may be a downer, and I did not want to depress you. But then I realized that Yom Kippur is supposed to be a downer. It is supposed to be a day for thinking about the most serious questions in our lives. So the fact that a topic is serious or even grim is not a reason to avoid talking about it on Yom Kippur.

The second reason I hesitated is because I was afraid that this topic might only apply to a few people. But then I realized that almost everyone I know is either dealing with this question themselves, right now, or else knows someone who is dealing with this question. I read that, according to the American Association of Retired People, there are 80 million people in the United States who are dealing with this question ***right now***.

Eighty million people? That is a pretty big percentage of the population of this country!

I realized that, if that figure is even half right, then this is a real question that concerns a great many people. This is an issue that we need to face up to and think about. If there are 40 million people in this country struggling with questions like how and how much to care for someone, or what the care limits are for those who are old and weak and helpless, then we surely want to know if the Torah has any wisdom or guidance to offer.

The third reason why I hesitated about giving a sermon on this topic tonight is that I knew that, if I started on this topic, it might turn out to be a long sermon. But that didn't hold me back at all, because I know that this is a congregation that ***loves*** long sermons. People kept coming up to me after Rosh Hashana and saying: "We loved the service, but we have just one complaint—it wasn't long enough." And they said to me: "Would you please try to make the services a little bit longer, if you can, next week?" So the fear that this might turn out to be a long sermon did not hold me back at all.

Therefore, let me speak to you tonight about the question concerning what you should do and what the limits are to what you should do when someone whom you love becomes old and weak, sick and helpless.

My sermon tonight is dedicated to three people. The first person lives in Washington, D.C.; the second lives in Chicago; the third is a part of this congregation.

The first person, the one who lives in Washington, D.C., is Justice Sandra Day O'Connor, who retired from the Supreme Court several years ago. Do you remember what happened when Justice O'Connor announced that she was going to retire? Immediately there was a great deal of discussion in the media about who would take her place, and whether the court would now move to the right or to the left. There was hardly any attention paid, though, to the reason ***why*** she had decided to retire. In her letter of resignation, all she said was: "Dear Mr. President: I am resigning from the court for personal reasons ..." But she did not say what those personal reasons were. Her son did, though. When he was interviewed by the press, he said: "My dad is now in the early stages of Alzheimer's. And therefore, my mom has decided that she wants to devote her remaining years to caring for him."

When I read that that was the reason why she had decided to resign, I was struck by a question: Would a male member of the Supreme Court have done that?

I don't know. My guess is that if a male Supreme Court justice had a wife who was stricken with Alzheimer's, he probably would have arranged the very best kind of medical care for her. He probably would have chosen the best medical facility that was available for her. But would a male Supreme Court justice have resigned from the court in order to care for her himself? I don't know. I don't think so.

Hardly anyone has ever resigned from the Supreme Court in all of American history.

But that is what Justice O'Conner did. And I think that she deserves much respect for the decision she made. May God bless her and her husband with strength in the coming years.

The second person to whom my sermon is dedicated is a woman who lives in Chicago. She has been married for many years to a man who is a mover and a shaker in the Chicago Jewish community. Until recently, this woman has basked in her husband's glory. But now, he has Parkinson's—and so this former mover and shaker barely moves at all, and when he does, he shakes, and so when he walks, he leans on her with every step. Anywhere they go, she lifts the wheelchair out of the trunk of the car and assembles it before buckling him in. Whenever I see them now, I marvel at the change that has taken place in their relationship. They have moved, in just a few short years, from being a celebrity and a helpmate to being an invalid and a caregiver. And what a bewildering change that must be—for both of them.

The third person to whom my sermon is dedicated may be one person, or it may be more than one—who has slipped away from her duties and responsibilities at home for a few minutes so that she can be with us at services tonight. This woman—and my guess is that it is probably a woman, though that is not necessarily so—my guess is that this woman is sitting here right now, weary and worn out, bone-tired and exhausted, but with the hope that maybe, ***maybe*** the prayerbook or the Torah or the rabbi will have some words of wisdom that will give her the strength to continue in her difficult, frustrating and seemingly never-ending task.

Let me ask you this question: If a soldier were to walk into a synagogue wearing the Congressional Medal of Honor or wearing the Purple Heart, how would he be greeted? My guess is that he would be welcomed with open arms. This person would be given a seat up front, as well as an *aliyah* or an ark opening, or any other honor that he wanted. And rightly so! For any person who wins a medal for bravery in action is a hero, and any person who receives the Purple Heart deserves our respect. Is that not so?

And yet, without taking anything away from the achievement of that soldier, God forbid, let me suggest that his bravery probably lasted for only a short time. He probably demonstrated courage under fire for an hour, or maybe for a couple of hours at most—whereas the bravery of caretakers goes on, day after day, week after week, month after month, perhaps year after year and, sometimes, with no end in sight. Therefore, these people deserve at least as much respect and at least as much honor as those who have shown bravery for a brief time in battle.

Yet for some reason—I am not sure why—these people get very little recognition. Nobody gives them a badge or a medal. The *shule* never gives them a plaque. They get no tribute dinner and they are never chosen as the person of the year. Their names never appear in the synagogue bulletin or in the daily newspaper.

I believe that these people, the caretakers amongst us, are truly heroic people. For they carry out the enormously challenging and sacred task of caring for people who are afflicted with dreadful diseases that ravage their bodies and consume their souls, that strain and drain and warp and spoil and shorten the lives of those who care for them.

I want to talk about these people tonight for two reasons.

One is that this is the night when we recite *Sh'ma Koleynu*, the prayer in which we ask God not to abandon us when we grow old, and not to leave us when our strength wears out. These caretakers are the people who do the work of God. These are the people who do not abandon the old when their strength wears out. These are the people who do not throw the old and the weak away when their minds and bodies give out.

I must tell you that this prayer, *Sh'ma Koleynu*, speaks to me with ever increasing power every year, and I suspect that it speaks to your hearts as much as it does to mine. We say this prayer ***four times*** on Yom Kippur. We will say it tonight, and then we will say it again at Shacharit in the morning, and then again at Mussaf, and then again at Minchah. Four times we open the ark; four times we rise; and four times we say these awesome words: *Al tashlicheynu l'et ziknah, kichlot kocheynu al ta-azveynu.* Do not abandon us when we grow old, O God. When our strength gives out, do not abandon us. I must tell you that every time I say these words, I shiver. And so do many of you.

I remember when I was a child and people used to cry when they said these words. Even those people who didn't cry when they said *Al Chet*; even those people who didn't cry when they said *Ashamnu*; even those people cried when they said *Sh'ma Koleynu*. Because the fear of growing old, and the fear of becoming helpless, abandoned and weak is terrifying to us all. It gets a little bit more frightening every year of our lives. It gets a little bit more frightening to say these words every time we get a little bit closer to old age.

I remember that when I was a child, I thought: They have found a cure for polio. By the time I grow old, they will find a cure for old age, too.

But they didn't. And they won't.

I remember how I used to get annoyed when they introduced me as the "young rabbi." Now I get annoyed that they don't. I remember how I used to think that middle age was two years older than however old I was. Now I know better. Middle age is when your middle begins to show your age—and I'm past it. And that is why *Sh'ma Koleynu* speaks to my heart as powerfully as it does.

There is one more reason why I have chosen to speak about this topic of caregiving, and the limits of care giving today. And that is because I found a poem on this subject this year that moved me very much. I found it in the New Yorker. It is by a poet named Galway Kinnell. This is what it says:

While spoon-feeding him with one hand
She holds his hand with her other hand,
Or rather lets it rest on top of his hand,
Which is permanently clenched shut.

When he turns his head away, she reaches
Around and puts in the spoonful.
He will not accept the next morsel
Until he has completely chewed this one.
His bright squint tells her that he finds
The shrimp she has just put in delicious.
Next to the voice and the touch of those we love,
Food may be our last pleasure on earth. …
She strokes his head very slowly, as if to cheer up
Each separate discomfited hair sticking up
From its roots in his stricken brain.
Standing behind him, she presses her cheek
To his, kisses his jowl, and his eyes seem
To stop seeing, and do nothing but emit light.
Could heaven be a time—after we are dead—
Of remembering the knowledge
Flesh had from flesh?
When picking up a cookie he uses
Both thumbtips to grip it
And pushes it against an index finger
To secure it so that he can lift it.

Do you feel the power of that poem as much as I do?

I don't know who the narrator is—perhaps a husband—is watching while this woman—perhaps his wife—spoonfeeds her old father, as best she can, slipping a bit of food into his mouth whenever he opens it. Or else reaching over and putting the food into the side of his mouth when he turns away, waiting patiently until he finishes one spoonful before she offers him the next. His bright eyes tell her that he finds the food she gives him delicious, for he no longer has the ability to speak to her in words.

And then, the poet says:

She takes him to the bathroom …
When they come out, she is facing him,
Walking backwards in front of him,

And holding his hands, pulling him
When he stops, reminding him to step
When he forgets, and starts to pitch forward.
She is leading her old father into the future,
As far as they can go,
And she is walking him back into her childhood,
Where she stood in bare feet on the toes of his shoes,
And they foxtrotted on this same rug.
I watch them closely; she could be teaching him
The last steps that one day she may teach me.
At this moment, he glints and shines
As if it will be only a small dislocation
For him to pass from this paradise into the next.

I must tell you that when I read this poem, I feel as if I was there—in that living room, watching this daughter feeding her father. I marvel at how kindly and gently she feeds her father. I marvel at how she helps this old man find some bit of happiness: a happiness so real that he glints and shines; a happiness so deep that it will only seem like a small dislocation when the time comes when he will pass from this paradise into the next one.

And as this man who is her husband watches how this woman cares for her father, he wonders to himself, Will she someday ever have to feed ***me*** this way? Or will I someday have to feed ***her*** this way? And if it will be me who has to feed her, will I be able to do it for her as gently and kindly as she is doing it right now, for him?

When I read this poem, I thought of all the people whose mates or parents or children suffer from illnesses like the one that this man has. I thought of all the people who are caretakers to their husbands, wives, parents or children, and I wondered: When they stood underneath the *chuppah* many years ago, did they ever imagine then that it would someday end up like this? When they exchanged rings and promised each other undying love, did they ever imagine that this is what undying love would look like? When they said to each other, "I will be there for you in sickness and in health," did they ever imagine—***could*** they have ever imagined—that it would end up like this?

A friend of mine told me recently that he had purchased long-term nursing care. I asked him why, because my friend is fairly young. And he said, "Because if I have to. I am willing to take her to the bathroom, but I sure don't want her to have to do that for me."

I wonder: When you and I were small children and our parents seemed to us to be so all-wise and all-powerful; when they fed us with a spoon while we sat in a high chair; could we have ever imagined that someday the roles would be reversed? That someday, ***we*** would be the ones who would feed them and that ***they*** would be the ones who had to be fed?

When I read that poem, I thought of the old Yiddish proverb that says, "When parents feed children, they both laugh. When children feed parents, they both cry." How true, how terribly true, that proverb is!

It is hard—almost unimaginably hard—to be a caregiver. For when you are a caregiver to someone whose mind has become clouded and whose body have been diminished by illness, so much of your life is consumed by caregiving. There is so little relief, so little respite, and, sometimes, so little appreciation from the one you are caring for, that the task sometimes seems to be beyond your strength to continue.

When you are a caregiver, you have to struggle against exhaustion, self-pity, resentment, anger and a host of other emotions that no one who has not gone through what you are going through can ever even begin to understand. Eventually, your strength wears out. You become weary and worn out. And you can't help yourself—you won't say it to anyone else, you don't even dare say it to yourself—but deep down inside, you sometimes wish that it would end already!

You can't help feeling that it's ***enough*** already—enough for the patient and enough for you. You can't help thinking that you wish that it were over already—and then Yom Kippur comes, and you realize that what you had thought was a sin. You feel guilty and ask God to forgive you for having had such a thought.

Other people may tell you how good you are. They may say that you are saintly. But in your own eyes, you are simply doing what you have to do. It is not a life that you would have chosen, but you cannot imagine doing anything else in the situation in which you find yourself.

But the truth is that what you are doing ***is*** heroic. For you do have an alternative! You could quit. You could give up. You could abandon the one for whom you are caring. And therefore, because you ***do*** have an alternative, mustering up the physical and emotional stamina that caregiving requires—day after day, week after week, month after month and sometimes year after year—***is*** heroic. To hold on to your task, even when the person you love is no longer able to say or feel gratitude for what you are doing—when the person you are caring for no longer knows who you are or even who he is—this is heroism: heroism of the highest order.

My parents had a wonderful expression. Perhaps yours did, too. They used to say "*Mir zol nisht divisen vifel mir ken dilayden,*" which means, "No one should ever find out how much they can stand. No one should ever find out how much we are capable of enduring." And it is true. None of us can ever really know in advance how much pain we are able to endure, and how much love we are capable of giving, until we are tested.

If the Yiddish expression is to go through *shivah medurah gehenem*—to endure seven levels of hell—I know a woman who, it seems to me, has gone through at least *tisha midrey gehenem*—at least nine levels of hell, and maybe more. This woman cares for a husband who has been sick the entire time I have known them, and long before. She cares for a husband who is in line for a third kidney transplant, who is possibly losing his sight and who has many, many other things wrong with him—and she is still standing! I won't say that she is still smiling—that would be beyond the strength of any human being in her situation—but she is still standing, and that, to me, is an incredible wonder. May God bless her with the strength to continue.

There are very few, if any, tasks in life that are as draining, as exhausting and as all-consuming as caretaking is. Especially if it is for someone who is no longer capable of saying—or even of comprehending—the words "thank you."

And so the question I want to study with you tonight is this: Does the Torah have any wisdom or guidance to offer to those who are facing this challenge today? Or to those of us who may have to face this challenge tomorrow? For if it does, we surely want to know what it is.

I have searched the sources of Jewish wisdom long and hard, in preparation for this talk tonight, and I think that I have found three lessons within the tradition that I want to share with you.

First, you should know that, according to Judaism, you have the moral right and the halachic right to follow the advice of Maimonides. Maimonides is very clear. He says that there are limits to what a human being can do. And if you reach that limit, you are allowed to hire help; you are allowed to bring your loved one to an agency that is set up to care for people like him or her, and you are allowed to share the task with them. For if you don't, then you will collapse. And why should there be two who are ill instead of just one?

We were sitting at dinner a few weeks ago, and someone at the table told us about a case in his family in which the caretaker worked for years, caring for a loved one who was ill, and in the end the caretaker dropped dead of exhaustion—and the sick person lived on.

I am sure that you know stories like this one, too. Therefore, Maimonides says that you are allowed to turn over the care of one who is seriously ill to someone else who can do it better than you; more objectively than you. Do not misunderstand: Maimonides says that the decision to turn over the responsibility for the care of a sick one does not absolve you from the duty to visit, and it does not absolve you from the duty to care—by no means! But it does absolve you from being consumed with the task until you, yourself, becomes ill as a result.

This is my first word of guidance to you: Know that there are limits to human strength and that there is no point in self-destruction. Therefore, according to the Rambam, there is a time when it is permitted and there is even a time when it is a *mitzvah* to share the care of someone whom you love with others.

The second point I would like to make is that if you refuse to take the permission the Rambam gives you, then the second thing the Jewish tradition has to say to you is that, as the Talmud puts it, "*Hashchinah shruyah al mitato shel hacholeh*"—the presence of God hovers over the bed of one who is sick.

What does that mean? It means that, when you look upon the face of someone who is ill, frail and impaired by disease, you must remember—you must remember and never forget—that this person is, even in his or her time of illness, dementia or nearly comatose state—this person is still, nevertheless, ***made in the image of God***.

Nothing, ***nothing***—nothing whatsoever—not even the loss of his mind, his sight, his hearing or anything else—can ever destroy someone's dignity as a human being, made in the image of God. Whether this person can still speak or think or not, whether this person knows who you are or not and whether this person knows who he is or not, he is still made in the image of God. And therefore, this person is still deserving of our care, compassion and respect.

What does that mean?

It means that no one is ever allowed to refer to him as "the lung case in room 503," or "the heart problem in room 561."

For it is not a lung case that is in room 503, and it is not a heart problem that is in 561—it is a ***human being*** who has a lung problem, who is in room 503, and it is a ***human being*** who has a heart problem and who is in room 561. Therefore, no one is ever allowed to treat this person roughly or disrespectfully.

It means that no one is ever allowed—God forbid, God forbid, ***God forbid***—to mistreat this person who is in their care. It means that no one is allowed to talk in their presence as if they were not there. I have heard doctors talk to each other about a diagnosis over the bed of someone who is ill and ignore him, using big words in his presence as if he was not there: as if he could not hear and as if he did not want to know what they were saying.

I have heard families talk in the presence of someone who is in coma as if they did not know that all the medical authorities agree that hearing is the last sense to go, and that the sick person may be able to hear what they say—as if they were no longer conscious, or as if they were no longer alive. No one is ever allowed to treat them as if they are not fully human. For the *Shechinah* hovers over the bed of the one who is sick, and we must never, never forget that!

It is the claim of Judaism that up to, at and after the moment of death, the human being is still a human being. Therefore, in the immortal words that Arthur Miller wrote and put into the mouth of Willy Loman's wife in "*Death of a Salesman.*" Do you remember that play? It is kind of a Yom Kippur experience to see that play. The scene that I remember best in that play is the moment when Willy Loman—Willy "Low-man,"—what an appropriate name that is—is falling apart. He can no longer keep up with his route. The boss's son has taken over the business and is thinking of firing him. Willy Loman is scared, and everyone else is too busy to notice. Then Willy Loman's wife comes center stage.

She loves him. With all of his faults and all of his shortcomings, she loves him. And so she comes center stage and she says: "Willy Loman is having a breakdown! *Attention must be paid!*"

Nobody hears what she says. They are all too busy with their own lives. But I remember that line, and it has stayed with me since the first time I heard it. If you want a four-word summary of Jewish medical ethics, this would be it: Up to, at and after the end of life, ***attention must be paid***!

There is a wonderful midrash that I would have you learn tonight if you do not already know it. It is the midrash that says that when Moses came down from Mount Sinai and saw the people of Israel dancing around the Golden Calf, he smashed the two tablets of stone on which God had inscribed the Ten Commandments. Then, after God forgave the people for their sin, Moses went back up the mountain and brought back a second set of tablets to replace the ones that he had broken.

The Midrash asks: What did Moses do with the broken pieces of the first set of commandments—the ones that he had broken? And the answer is "*luchot vishivrey luchot, munachim ba-aron*"—both sets, the intact ones and the broken ones, were put into the Ark. Why? In order to teach us that that which was once holy remains holy—even in its broken state. In order to teach us that broken people, senile people, people with Alzheimer's and people with Parkinson's are still holy: that people who were once holy remain holy, even in their broken state. This is the second lesson that the Torah teaches to those who are caretakers: Know that the people whom you care for are holy people, and that the presence of God hovers over them; therefore, care for them as kindly, gently and as tenderly as you can.

For you have the power—not necessary to cure them, but at least to care for them. You have the ability to send a message to them with your words and deeds—the message that ***you matter to me***. In my eyes, ***you are still precious***. You may not know who you are anymore, but ***I know who you are***, and ***I care about you***. And despite the damage that life has done to your body and mind, ***you are still beloved to me***.

If you are able to send this message—I care about you, and you are precious to me, even now, and even in this state—what a blessing you can be to that person. I think that this is what the poet means in that poem that I shared with you in which the narrator speaks of the old man whose eyes still gleam, and who will someday make the small transition from one paradise to another. Because if you are in the care of a person who values you that much—even at the end—then you live in a paradise of sorts even if you cannot speak or stand or walk, or do anything else. That is the second lesson that the Jewish tradition offers to caretakers: Know that *shechinah shruya al mitato shel hacholeh*—that God's presence dwells on the bed of the sick person, and therefore treat that person with loving care.

And now, the third lesson that I want to offer you tonight. This lesson I want to address not to the caretakers, but to the rest of us.

How many of you know someone who is struggling to care for a husband or a wife, a father or a mother, a sibling or a child who has cancer, Parkinson's, Alzheimer's, Downs Syndrome or some other such debilitating disease? If so, then let me ask you on this, the holiest night of the year, to resolve to do whatever you can to care for the caretakers in our midst, so that they do not collapse. Let me ask you tonight on this, the holiest night of the year, to resolve that at least once every couple of weeks you will call and say to this person, "I am going to the supermarket today. Is there anything that I can pick up for you?" Let me ask you on this, the holiest night of the year, to resolve that at least once in a while you will call this person and say, "I am going shopping for a dress. If I see something that is in your size and that I think you might like, can I buy it for you?" And, "If you don't want it, you can return it, but won't you please at least try it on and see?" Let me ask you, on the holiest night of the year, to resolve that at least once every couple of weeks you will call and say to the caretaker whom you know, "Would you like me to cover for you for a couple of hours, so that you can take a break and maybe go to a movie or a play or a concert?" Let me ask you on this, the holiest night of the year, to resolve that at least once every couple of weeks you will call and say, "Does your son need any help with his homework?" Or, "Does your daughter need chauffeuring to her ballet class?" And, if so: "Can I do it for you?"

If we will ***just do this***, can you imagine the boost in morale that you can bring about? Can you imagine the sense of not being abandoned that you will be giving to these caretakers? Can you imagine the strength and the relief that you will be bringing to these people who feel so alone, so neglected and so forgotten?

Let me finish by telling you about a very simple experience that I had this summer. It was a simple experience, and yet it moved me so much that it is the reason why I am giving this sermon tonight.

I had an appointment for a checkup at the doctor's office several months ago. I was waiting in line at the receptionist's desk, to sign in, before I sat down. There was a man in line in front of me, an old man, and I couldn't help overhearing the conversation between this man and the receptionist. He said to her: "Could you please do me a favor? I see that the doctor is running late. Could you please do whatever you can to get me in as soon as possible? Because I have to leave in a few minutes. I have an appointment—a very important appointment—and I can't be late."

The receptionist said that she would do her best. But then, for some reason—I don't know why—maybe her curiosity got the best of her—she asked this old man: "What's your rush? What is this appointment, and why do you have to leave so quickly?"

The man said to her: "It's my wife whom I have to meet. She is at the JARC, which is the home in Boca for people who suffer from Alzheimer's. And I have to get there in time to have lunch with her. I do that every single day."

The receptionist said: "But if she has Alzheimer's, will she really know whether you are there on time or not?"

And the man said: "Oh, no. She doesn't know who I am anymore. She hasn't for a long time."

The receptionist said: "Well, if she doesn't know who you are, then what is the big rush to get there in time to have lunch with her?"

The old man replied: "You don't understand. She may not know who she is, ***but I do***."

At that point, the receptionist got up and went into the doctor's office, and said something to him. When she came out, she took this old man by the hand and walked him into the doctor's office. And then, she turned to me and she said something that has stayed in my mind ever since. I can't say this for sure, but I think that, if I am not mistaken, her eyes were moist, as she said to me, "That's the kind of love that I would like to have in my life someday."

I don't know if this nurse was single or married, but I was moved by what she said: "That's the kind of love that I would like to have in my life someday." If you marry somebody for their looks, good looks don't last a long time. If you marry somebody for their money, you find out afterward that that is an expensive mistake to make. But if you marry someone who loves you ***as much***, as this man did, then you are really fortunate, and you are really blessed.

And ***that*** is the meaning of caregiving.

So I pray today:

May God bless Sandra Day O'Conner, in her new task in life.

May God bless my friends in Chicago, as they face together this last test of their lives, in partnership and in harmony.

May God bless the people in this room who are struggling to carry out the *mitzvah* of caregiving as lovingly and as loyally as they can. May God teach us how to help them, and how to encourage them in every way that we can.

In this new year that now begins, may God bless each one of us with much good health, for health is *takeh,* the greatest of all the blessings. I must tell you that when I was young, I never understood it when people would say "*abi gezunt*"—if you only have your health. Now I understand. Therefore, I wish for you and for me, and for all those whom we love, much good health in the new year.

But if someday in the future—if someday, in one of the years to come—either we or the one whom we love, becomes old and weak and infirm, may God bless us with the kind of a caregiver who is able to do this holy work with love. And if it should turn out that our lot is to be the one who must be the caretaker, then may God help us do this sacred task as carefully, as lovingly and as patiently as we can.

Amen.

9

# Four Phrases to Live By

## Yom Kippur

The older I get, the more my attitude toward the prayerbook changes.

When I was younger, I thought that the prayers in the prayerbook were outdated, and that we needed new prayers that would be about the issues of our time and in the language of our time.

And so I wrote beautiful prayers about Biafra—which no one uses anymore. I wrote beautiful prayers about Vietnam—and no one looks at those prayers anymore.

Today, when I come back to the High Holy Day prayerbook after having been away from it for a year, I am re-impressed with how powerful and how accurate a document it is.

Most of the prayers that I wrote five or ten years ago are outdated by now. But these prayers, some of which were written a thousand years ago, are still fresh and still on target.

And I must tell you that, of all the prayers in the Machzor, the one that seems to me to be the most accurate and the most insightful is the *Al Het*.

This list of 44 sins—two for every letter of the Hebrew alphabet—hits me, and hurts me every time I say it because it is so true. What amazes me about this list is that, even though it was written many centuries ago, I can't think of a single sin on this list that we do not commit—and I can't think of a single sin that we commit that is not on this list. It is an accurate X-ray of the human psyche, is it not?

It says that we are gluttons. Aren't we?

It says that we envy. Don't we?

It says that we gossip and that we lust, and that we are proud and arrogant and inquisitive. Aren't we?

It says that we drink too much, and that we eat too much, and that we give too little. Isn't that true?

It says that we are too competitive, and that we are too conformist. Aren't we?

Is there a single sin on this list that we can deny? I can't think of any. Can you?

If you look at this list carefully, you will notice another thing about them: more than one-third of the sins on this list are sins of speech.

"For the sin that we have committed before You by gossiping."

"For the sin that we have committed before You by slandering."

"For the sin that we have committed before You by talebearing."

"For the sin that we have committed before You by boasting."

Etc. Etc. Etc.

More than ***one-third*** of the *Al Hets* are sins of speech.

Why? Because the tongue is the part of the body with which we sin the most, isn't it? I don't think that I have hurt anyone with my fist even once during this last year. And I don't think that I have hurt anyone with my foot even once during this past year. But I am sure that I have hurt many people with my tongue. Isn't that true of you, as well?

And so the Machzor is right in reminding us that the tongue is a powerful and dangerous weapon. Therefore we must be careful in how we use it, and we must atone for how we abuse it.

The *Al Het* is a powerful list. Yet I would like to suggest to you today that there is one sin that is missing from the *Al Het*; one sin that ought to be included. If I had my way—if I were the editor of the Machzor—there is one sin that that I think ought to be added to the *Al Hets*, because it is at least as harmful and at least as destructive as any of the sins of speech.

And that would be the sin of silence.

The sin of silence is usually understood in a political sense: we think of it in connection with keeping quiet while evil is being done in our society. It is a phrase that is used, in connection with the Holocaust, or in connection with the people who are starving in central Africa, or in connection with some cause like that. It usually refers to people who sit on the sidelines and don't speak out as they should when evil is being done. But that is not what I have in mind today. That is an important sin to talk about: there is no denying that. There is an obligation on every human being to speak out when he sees injustice being done. But that is not what I have in mind today.

What I have in mind today is the much more insidious, the much more widespread and the much more destructive sin of silence that goes on within our homes and within our lives.

What I have in mind today are the many homes in which husband and wife sit side by side in front of the television set every night for hours and never say a word.

What I have in mind today are the homes in which kids come back from a date and the parents say "What did you do?" And the kids say "Nothing. And the parents say "Who did you see?" And the kids say "No one." And the parents say "What's new?" And the kids say "Not much."

What I have in mind today is the invisible iron curtain that separates many of us from each other as we go through life. For that kind of silence can warp, and mar, and strain, and stain and spoil our lives. That kind of silence can hurt us and harm us at least as much as angry words can—and maybe even more.

Divorce statistics are easy to compile. We have all seen the figures. But God only knows how many homes there are in which people stay legally married while being emotionally divorced. God only knows how many homes there are in which people are officially married and yet have so little that they can communicate to each other. For these homes, there are no statistics available, and yet we know that there are many—perhaps even more than there are homes that are officially broken up. These are marriages that are just as dead as those that have been officially dissolved and buried. For a home in which people do not speak to each other, or in which they only talk about trivia, is a cell—or a hell—or a motel—or a watering station—or something else—but it is not a home!

Do you remember the old limerick that we used to sing when we were kids?

Sticks and stones
May break my bones,
But words will never hurt me.

You know something? It's not true!

Now that I am older, I realize that that limerick is inaccurate. Words ***can*** hurt. Words can hurt even more than sticks and stones. And ***silence hurts the most***. Silence can hurt even more than words. So let me offer you what I think is a more accurate version of that old limerick, one that I once learned from Rabbi Sidney Greenberg:

Sticks and stones are hard on bones,
Aimed with angry art,
Words can sting like anything—
But silence breaks the heart.

Silence breaks the heart. Silence hurts a thousand times more than sticks or stones, or even angry words. And therefore the sin that we ought to face up to on this holy day, the sin with which we hurt each other perhaps more than any other, is the sin of silence.

So let me make four specific suggestions to you tonight—four suggestions which I first heard from Rabbi Arnold Turetsky.

I think that if you want to measure the worthwhileness of your life; if you want to measure the amount of health and happiness that you have given to others during this past year; and if you want a program by which you can learn how to become more of a *mentsch* in this new year, then I suggest that you make this simple resolution:

"I resolve that in this new year, I will learn to say these four phrases more often than I have in the past:

Thank you,
I'm sorry,
I love you,
And How are you, and what do you need?

These are four simple phrases. And yet I tell you that I cannot overemphasize the importance that they can have in our lives, and in the lives of the people with whom we live.

I don't care how big your vocabulary is, or how many languages you know. If you cannot say these four phrases, you are emotionally crippled. And if you cannot say these four phrases, you impoverish the lives of those with whom you live.

Thank you.

I love you.

I'm sorry.

How are you?

And what do you need, and what can I do for you?

These are phrases that have the power to transform our lives. And they have the ability to give power and purpose, dignity and zest, spirit and value to the people around us.

When was the last time you said "thank you" to your wife for a meal? Do you take it for granted that you are entitled to a good meal when you come home? Or do you take the time to say, "Thank you. I noticed what you did for me. I appreciate it."

If you do that, the meal will taste better—to you and to her.

When was the last time you said "thank you" to the synagogue for enriching your life?

And when was the last time you said "thank you" to God for your many blessings?

What is the first prayer that a Jew is supposed to say when he wakes up in the morning? It is *Modeh Ani*, which means, "I thank you, God, for giving me a new day."

What is the prayer that we are supposed to say after every meal?

It is the *Birkat Hamazon*, the grace after meals. The reason we are supposed to say that prayer after every meal is because for Jews, to eat and not say "thank you" is vulgar! For Jews to eat and not say "thank you" is a perversion.

And just as we must say "thank you" to God, so must we say "thank you" to those with whom we live and through whom we live.

And so it is with the other three phrases.

"I love you"—I don't think that John Wayne or Clint Eastwood or Bruce Willis ever said those words in a movie. It would have been considered kind of unmanly if they did. Tough guys don't cry, and tough guys don't say "I love you" in cowboy movies, because they would seem kind of weak if they did. But in the Jewish tradition, there is nothing unmanly about saying "I love you." On the contrary, it is the manly—or at least the *mentschlich*—thing to do.

And so it is with these other phrases.

To say "I am sorry" is not easy. The words sometimes stick in our throats. We end up saying silly things like, "things happened," instead of saying what we ought to say, which is, "I did it, and I am sorry."

It is a *mitzvah* of the highest importance to say, "How are you?" To say it—and then to ***listen to the answer***, and not just say it in a perfunctory way, with half a head, while your mind is on something else.

I remember I was on the receiving line one year on Kol Nidre night, and everybody that went by was saying, "How are you?" And I was answering, "Fine, thank you. How are you?" Neither I nor they were thinking about what we were hearing and what we were saying. And so, one year, just for the fun of it—just to see what would happen if I did it—when someone asked me, "How are you?" I answered, "Fine, thank you. I just murdered my uncle."

And the woman in front of me answered without missing a beat. "That's nice. I hope you do it again next year."

That is not what it means to say, "How are you?"!

To say "How are you?" means to ask and then to listen—to *really* listen to the answer.

It is a *mitzvah* of the highest order to say to someone whom you love, "What do you need?" And, "What can I do to help you?"

Because if we said that often enough to our children, if we said it and meant it, then perhaps there would not be such a wall between us.

Then perhaps when we asked, "Where did you go?" they wouldn't say, "Nowhere." And when we asked, "What did you do?" they wouldn't say, "Nothing."

Let me finish with two stories that mean a great deal to me: Two stories that I hope will touch you as much as they do me.

The first story comes from the Russian writer, Turgenev. I read it years ago, and it has stayed with me ever since.

Turgenev wrote:

> *I was once walking in the street when a beggar stopped me. He was a frail old man with inflamed eyes, with chapped lips, with filthy rags and disgusting sores. Oh, how poverty had disfigured this repulsive creature!*
>
> *He stretched out to me his red, swollen hand, and whispered for alms. I reached into my pocket—but no wallet, no coins, no money did I find. I had left them all at home.*
>
> *The beggar waited, and his outstretched hand twitched and trembled slightly. Embarrassed and confused, I seized his hand and pressed it, and I said, "Brother, please don't be angry with me. I am sorry, but I have nothing to give you. I left my wallet at home, brother."*
>
> *The beggar raised his bloodshot eyes to mine. His blue lips smiled, and he returned the pressure of my fingers. "Never mind," he stammered. "Thank you, thank you for this, for this, too, was a gift.* ***No one has ever called me 'brother' before.****"*

I love that story, and I hope that you do, too, for it makes the point that a kind word is also a gift—a real gift. You can make a person's day, and even his life, brighter with a kind word.

The second story that I want to tell you is, beyond question, the most powerful story that I have heard this year. I heard it from a man that I met in Syracuse. Usually, when someone comes over to me and says that they have a story for me, I wince, because it is usually either a story that my great-great grandfather would have considered old or else it is a story that I can't tell from the pulpit. But this story is different. This is a story that has haunted me ever since I first heard it.

The rabbi I met there told me that he had officiated at a funeral over the summer. At this funeral, he said the required prayers. He performed the proper rituals. And then, when the service was over, he asked the people to form two lines and to give comfort to the mourners as they passed by. But much to his surprise, when the service was over and it was time to leave, one mourner would not leave the grave. The rabbi tried to lead the man away, but he wouldn't go. The rabbi said: "The service is over now. You have to leave." But the man shook him off, and said: "You don't understand. I loved my wife." The rabbi said: "I'm sure you did, but the service is over now. You have to leave." The man shook him off again, and said: "You don't understand. I loved my wife—and ***once, I almost told her***!"

Can you imagine the pain there must be?

Can you imagine the shame there must be?

If you have to stand at a grave and bid farewell, and realize ***then*** what you didn't say when you could have—when you should have—when there was still time?

Can you imagine having to live the rest of your life with the knowledge that you loved someone, and that "once, you almost told her"?

May none of us ever have to live with that kind of regret in our heart. Let none of us hold back the words of love, the words that can help and heal. Let none of us keep these words bottled up inside ourselves, where they can do no good, until it is too late.

My friends, if you remember nothing else from all of the many words that you have heard from the pulpit during these holy days; if you remember nothing else from all the many words that you will say from the prayerbook on these holy days; I ask you to remember the four phrases. Remember them and say them, not just once, but many times during the coming year.* Say them not just today, when it is cute and funny to say them, but all during this new year:

"Thank you."

"I love you."

"I am sorry."

And, "How are you? What do you need?"

Say them to your spouse.

Say them to your children and to your grandchildren.

Say them to your God, and to your people, who have given you so much and who need you so much.

Say them, and mean them.

May you say them and hear them many times in this new year.

For if we do, then it will be a good year, a holy year, and a blessed year: for you, for me, and for all those whom we love.

Amen.

---

* With thanks to the blessed memory of Rabbi Arnold Turetsky, who taught me the significance of these four phrases.

10

# The Man Who Created the Jewish State

## Neilah

Dear friends,

This is it.

This is the closing hour of the day. One more service, and it will be all over, and we will go back to our regular lives. So what should I say to you—what should we think about, whose words of wisdom should we study—in this, the moment before the Neilah service?

I am not going to study with you the words of Maimonides or Isaiah, Rav Kuk or Martin Buber. I am not going to study with you the lives of any of the great and famous heroes of our people. Instead, all I want to do in these, the closing moments of the day—the moments before we separate, to go our different ways—is to study with you the life of a very ordinary man: a man who I am sure you have never heard of, a man who sold insurance for a living in Boston many years ago.

His name was Max Alpert. You have probably never heard of him, but perhaps you know the name of his son, Carl Alpert, who was for many years the public relations director of the Haifa Technion. When his father died, Carl wrote a tribute to him, which he entitled, "*The Man Who Created the Jewish State*." This is what he wrote:

> *My father set for himself two goals in life, though at the time he set them, both seemed impossible. And yet Papa's life was an enormous success. Let me tell you what he did. Perhaps there is something that you can learn from him.*
>
> *Not long ago I received formal notification from the lawyer who was the executor of my father's estate. He listed the modest assets that my father had left behind: a few Israeli bonds, the practically worthless shares of the Jewish Colonial Trust, which my father had bought many years ago and held on to, and a few stocks and bonds. The lawyer's letter summed up the financial value of the estate of the late Max Alpert, and it was very modest indeed. There were no buildings, no real estate, no artwork and no personal belongings of any great financial value.*
>
> *My father had to deal with economic difficulties, business reverses and occasional bouts of bad health that dogged him, so that by all the usual ways of measuring achievement, it would appear that he was a failure. And yet I believe that my father was a great success in life.*
>
> *Let me explain why I think he was a success:*

*My father had two great causes that he believed in: Zionism and Jewish education. Every program that looked toward creative Jewish survival commanded his moral, financial and physical support.*

*He once told me the story of how they used to promote attendance at the old cheder in the West End of Boston. There was no tuition fee. On the contrary, every child who had a good attendance record for the week got a bag of candy. The method may not be considered very good pedagogy today, especially not by the dentists, but it worked. It encouraged many kids to come to Hebrew school when there were lots of other things that they could have been doing, like playing ball or doing their public-school homework.*

*At Zionist meetings in those early days, he would be the first one to arrive in the hall. He got there early in order to see to it that the chairs were properly arranged, that the lectern was set up and that the refreshments were in order. The program required some entertainment besides the guest speaker, and so my father always volunteered my cousin, Sylvia, to play the piano and to lead the singing. To this day, I still remember the songs we sang at those meetings. They were all about how someday there would be a Jewish state in Palestine.*

*Pop insisted that I go to Hebrew school at a time when all my childish desires for play and recreation rebelled against spending those precious afternoon hours inside. He insisted that I stay at least until my bar mitzvah, and I can still remember his pride when, at that age, I chose to continue going to cheder.*

*Pop was what we used to call, in those days, a "meeting goer." Whenever there was a meeting devoted to a Jewish cause, Pop was there. Whether it was a meeting of the shule, or the Dorchester-Mattapan Hebrew School, or the Mattapan Zionist District, Pop was there. He was there because he had work to do there. He would keep the records, or send out the meeting notices, or remind the members of their obligations. He would talk Jewish education to skeptical parents. Since he was never able to make big financial gifts, he did his share by rendering services—by doing the mundane, prosaic, routine things that are needed in order to keep an organization going.*

*I sometimes wondered to what extent his constant soliciting of people on behalf of his causes affected his ability to sell them insurance policies. If it did, the cause came before business, as far as he was concerned. Papa had set certain goals for himself in life. He was determined to achieve them. And now, when we look back, we realize that he did. My father was a success.*

*My father was a success in life because, with the help of lots of other people in Boston and in Palestine and elsewhere, he created the Jewish state! And he built synagogues in America. And he revived Jewish education. To be sure, he didn't do it all by himself, but his shoulder was always at the wheel. He knew the pain and the fatigue of the effort, but when success came, he felt great fulfillment.*

*I remember how, shortly before he died, my father visited Israel for the first and only time in his life. He traveled the country from north to south*

> *and from east to west. He saw the trees that he had planted. He saw the cities that he had built. He saw the villages that he had established. For Pop, they were all personal achievements, and he looked upon them with delight. It was for these that he had devoted his life.*

And then Carl Alpert finished his tribute to his father, which he wrote while he was sitting *shivah* for him, with this:

"I hope it is not sacrilegious of me to say that Papa looked over all that he had created, and behold—it was good. And Papa was satisfied. And he rested."

I share this memoir with you, at this holy moment, for several reasons.

The first is so that you and I may realize how much love and sweat and strain and effort and devotion and love went into building this Jewish state that we now have. Most of the people who are here today were born after the State of Israel was established, and so they take the state for granted. What is Israel? Big deal! It is a country that is 10 or 12 hours away by plane, a place where you can go on vacation in order to snorkel at Eilat or to hike in the Galil. But if you are old enough to remember what it was like before the State of Israel was born, or if you were fortunate enough to have had a father or a mother or a grandparent like Max Alpert—or like my father and mother who did so much and cared so much and worked so hard so that there would be a Jewish state—then you cannot ever take it for granted. And so the first thing that I want to say to you is: Cherish Israel! Never, never, ***never*** take it for granted! Let it be the apple of your eye! Guard it and protect it with your love and your devotion and your means, for if you do, you will be continuing the legacy that your father or your grandfather left behind.

And the second thing that I want to say to you today, at this sacred moment before the sun goes down, is this: What is your *mishegas*? What is your cause? What is the dream by which you live? What is it that you work for, after hours—after you have done the work that you get paid for? What is the cause that gives meaning and purpose to your life?

It need not necessarily be the State of Israel; it need not necessarily be Jewish education—although those are both surely very, very worthy causes that need and deserve our support. It can be any one of many other worthy causes—health care, education, the welfare of the poor in our community, aiding the suffering of the people who live in Darfur, the making of a better America, or the enhancement of Jewish life—whatever it is, is there some cause in your life that you believe in passionately and that you care about with all your heart and soul and might?

For if there isn't, then your life is dull and drab and empty, no matter how much real estate you own and no matter how many possessions you have. For ***the purpose of life is to live a life of purpose***, and if you have no central cause in your life—no dream that possesses you and that will not let you rest—then your life is poor, much poorer than the lives of our grandparents who lived in poverty but who built the Jewish state and who created American Jewry.

So these are the questions that I ask you to think about in these, the closing hours of the day. Before the gates swing shut, and before we go back to our ordinary lives, let us ask ourselves these questions:

First, do I appreciate and do I carry on the dreams of those who came before me? If so, will I demonstrate that I do, by my support of the Jewish state and by my efforts on behalf of Jewish life here, in this land, in the year that now begins? Or do I have a dream and a cause of my own that give meaning and purpose to my life? And if so, will I demonstrate that I do—by my efforts on behalf of this cause, in the new year that now begins?

Someday, the lawyer will send our children a letter in which he will tell them precisely what we have left them in material things. He will tell them precisely what stocks and what bonds and what real estate and what works of art we have left behind for them. But he will not be able to tell them in that letter whether we were a success or not.

That will depend not on how much of a material legacy we leave behind, but on how we lived and for what purpose we gave our time and our strength. Our grandparents did not leave their children much cash, but they built the Jewish state and they created the Jewish community that we inherited, and so I believe that they lived successful lives.

And what about us? Will we live successful lives, as they did?

The answer to that question is in our hands. Let us think about how to answer it, as we prepare ourselves now for the closing service of the day.

## 11

# *Siz a Rachmones off der Goy* (It Is a Pity on the Gentile)

## A Story for Sukkot

We have been through a lot in the last six weeks, you and I. We have gone through the month of Elul, and then *Selichot,* and then Rosh Hashana, and then the Aseret Yimey Teshuvah, and then Kol Nidre and then Yom Kippur. It has been a series of ever more intense confrontations.

We have been forced to struggle with the basic questions of human existence: Who am I? Why do I live? And: Why have I sinned so often in this past year? And how will I change in this new year?

Now it is Sukkot, and the tradition provides us with a change of pace. Instead of confronting the grim and serious questions of life, the tradition tells us to go outdoors and eat in the sukkah, and to celebrate the harvest and to have joy. It is a wonderful change of mood from the Days of Awe to the Season of our Rejoicing.

And so all I want to do today is just tell you one story. It is a story that I love, and that I hope that you will love, too. But first, let me tell you a little bit about the man who wrote this story.

His name was Abraham Reisen. Do any of you know that name?

Abraham Reisen was the poet of Jewish poverty. First in Europe, and then in America, he wrote songs, stories, poems and parables describing the lot of the poor people. One of my favorites is the lullaby that he wrote about the man who has to go to work very early in the morning, before his little child wakes up, and who comes home from work very late at night, long after his little child goes to sleep. Reisen pictures the man bending over the crib in which his sleeping child lies and apologizing to the child for never being around when the child is awake. The man explains to his child why he works such long hours. And he promises him that, with the money he earns, the child will be able to go to college when he grows up; and he will be able to see his own child, and to play with him, when he comes back from work.

Most of Reisen's stories and songs take place in America. But I once found one that takes place in a small town in eastern Europe. In summary, here is the story—see if you like it as much as I do:

> *Antosh cracked his whip and urged his old mare to move faster. It was already nearly noon, and he was only on the outskirts of the town. But the poor horse just plodded slowly along. Anton lifted his whip again and threatened the horse:*

*"Please, move!" he said, although he could not bring himself to hit the animal again. The horse whinnied, and it seemed that she was laughing at Antosh. But what could he do? Everyone else whom he passed on the road that day laughed at him. Everyone.*

*Antosh wondered: Why were they laughing at me? What could be wrong?*

*It had all begun a few weeks ago.*

*The days in eastern Europe were gradually growing shorter, and the nights were growing longer. Antosh, who was a peasant who lived in a small village, would have liked to have a lamp, but the kerosene jug was empty and he had no money with which to buy more. His supply of salt was running low. He had only a small piece of soap left. There was not a tea leaf left in the pot, and there was not a single pinch of snuff left in the jar.*

*"Things are tough," Antosh said to himself. "No salt, no tobacco, no soap—nothing."*

*Antosh had no job and no way of earning money. He had only one hope: to load his wagon with the green branches that the Jews used to cover their sukkahs, to take them into town, and to sell them.*

*And so right after Rosh Hashana, he began to pester the only Jew who lived in his village. "When will you Jews celebrate your Sukkot holiday?" he asked each day. And each day, the Jew would answer, "I dunno. But I think it is a long way off yet."*

*"But when?" Antosh would ask him, again and again.*

*Finally, one day, the Jew—just to get rid of Antosh's pestering, and ashamed to admit that he didn't know—said, "One week from today."*

*Actually, it was only five days to Sukkot, but the Jew did not know that. So Antosh planned to come to town with his merchandise two days before the holiday. Little did he know that that was actually the first day of Sukkot.*

*On that day, Antosh arose early, hitched up his wagon, took his ax and drove into the forest. There, he cut down branches and put them into the wagon. He chose the longest and thickest branches he could find. Good merchandise sells better, he thought. The load continued to grow until at last, the wagon was full.*

*Now Antosh drove slowly and carefully, and as he drove, he kept thinking of the soap, the tobacco, the flour and all the other things he would buy with the money he earned from selling schach to the Jews for their sukkahs.*

*When he reached the outskirts of the town, he saw—much to his surprise—that the sukkahs were all covered with schach already. His heart skipped a beat, and his head began to whirl. He steadied himself, and thought, It is the same every year. Some Jews cover their sukkahs early and others do so later.*

*He rode on. Two women were standing in front of a sukkah. When they saw him, they pointed at him and started laughing.*

*"Why are you laughing at me?" Antosh asked.*

*"Because you brought your branches so early," they laughed.*

*"What do you mean, early?" Antosh asked, not understanding why they were making fun of him. He was answered with peals of laughter. Antosh spat angrily and rode on, thinking to himself, How can it be? If I counted right, today is two days before the holiday.*

*He broke out in a cold sweat, because it occurred to him that he might have made a mistake. Perhaps he was too late. All the sukkahs were covered. He would have no money with which to buy salt or tobacco or anything else.*

*Sadly he drove on, and his horse, who seemed to sense his master's misfortune, pulled the wagon with a bowed head.*

*At last, he reached the village square.*

*"I have twigs and branches for sale," he called out in a weak voice. "Who wants to buy roof coverings for Sukkot?"*

*His voice echoed back. Except for a goat or two ambling down the road, the square was empty.*

*And then, suddenly, the doors of the synagogue in the center of the square swung open and the people came streaming out. Jews in well-brushed black coats and fur-trimmed hats, little boys whose side curls had barely begun to grow, women in their holiday dresses—they all came out. The services had just ended.*

*Ah, here they were, thought Antosh. Now he could sell his wares. He cried out, "Jews! Antosh, the woodchopper, is here with twigs for your sukkahs. I have branches, I have twigs, I have ..." Antosh stopped.*

*The crowd had surrounded Antosh and his wagon.*

*"Thank you for coming," said one man. "Only, you are a little bit late. Can't you see that it is already Sukkot?"*

*"Everyone's sukkah is already covered," said another.*

*Antosh the woodchopper cried, "But—but—but—I need salt. I need tobacco. I need soap. I need soup. I need so many things."*

*The crowd that was gathered around Antosh stopped laughing. The people saw his sad face, and they felt sorry for him.*

*Just then, the rabbi of the village came out of the synagogue. He saw what had happened, and he understood what was going on. "Wait a minute," he said, and he made his way through the crowd and climbed aboard Antosh's wagon.*

*"Antosh has worked hard to gather all these twigs and branches," he said. "He meant well, and so it is our duty to help him. S'iz a rachmones oif der goy—it is a pity on this poor non-Jew. And therefore, as your rabbi, I command you to open your stores immediately, even though it is yontif!"*

*"But rabbi, it is yontif. How can we sell merchandise on the holiday? It is forbidden to handle money on this day," said the people.*

*"Who said anything about handling money?" asked the rabbi. "I command you to open your stores and to give Antosh the things that he needs, and not to charge him any money."*

*Everyone was quiet for a moment. They had never heard of anyone opening their stores on a holiday.*

*But then Jonah, the baker, said in his deep voice, "The rabbi is right. I'll open my bakery and give Antosh six loaves of bread."*

*Then Reuven, the grocer, said, "I will give him five cans of kerosene."*

*And David, the fish dealer, said, "I will give him two pickerel and seven carp."*

*Then all the rest of the people chimed in. This one offered tobacco, that one offered barley, and this one offered rice; and soon, Anosh's wagon was full of all kinds of good things.*

*Antosh had never known such kindness in all his life. He was beside himself with joy. He did not know whether to laugh or to cry. Slowly, he stood up in his wagon.*

*"Dear people," he stammered, "I cannot make speeches. All I can say is that I am grateful—very, very grateful." And he sat down.*

*As he was about to drive away, someone gave him a big piece of hallah.*

*"Here, take this home—in honor of the holiday," he was told.*

*"Here's another piece," said someone else. Then everyone began bringing hallah for Antosh. He was so moved that he could only murmur, over and over again: "Thank you, thank you, thank you so much."*

*Everyone was happy. Mordechai, a jolly Jew who was celebrating the holiday and who had a future son-in-law visiting him, brought out a glass of whiskey for Antosh. "Here," he said. "Drink this in honor of the holiday."*

> *Antosh swallowed the whiskey and then took a bit of hallah, and cried out, "I'll never forget this day. Never!" And he hit his horse and started back home again, eager to tell his wife all about this experience.*

This is the story, as Abraham Reisen tells it. Do you like it as much as I do?

I like it because it tells about a community that managed to shower a well-meaning peasant with all the gifts he needed without violating the law that forbids doing business on *yontif.* They opened their stores, and more important, they opened their hearts, to the poor man who had meant well but who had mixed up the day on which Sukkot starts. They showed compassion to this man, even though he was not a Jew.

We don't have too many such stories in Jewish literature. The people among whom the non-Jews of eastern Europe lived were not very friendly to the Jews, as a rule, and so the Jews lived in fear of them—and not with love or trust or compassion. But at least in this story, the rabbi teaches his people that compassion should be shown to every human being—even to the peasant—and that it is a *mitzvah* to help someone who is in need even if he is not Jewish.

And is that not a nice lesson to learn on the holiday of Sukkot?

The sages say that on Sukkot, 70 sacrifices were offered by the people of Israel on behalf of the 70 nations of the world. This story demonstrates that that spirit of caring for all people continued down through the centuries.

May it continue in our time, too.

Amen.

12

# When Should You Listen to Your Wife and When Should You Not Listen to Your Wife?

## Sukkot

I want to tell you a story today. It is the story of a man who put up a sukkah one year, even though his wife told him not to do it.

But first, before I tell you this story, let me ask both the men and the women who are here today the same question.

The question is this: When should you listen to your wife and when should you not listen to your wife?

What do the women say?

The answer that the women gave was: "All the time."

Now let me ask the men the same question. When should you listen to your wife?

What do the men say?

"Sometimes."

Who is right? Let me tell you a story that I think provides the answer to this question.

The reason I begin my sermon by asking this question is because of an essay that I read recently by a man named Marc Silver. Marc Silver is an editor at U.S. News and World Report, and he is the author of an important book called *"Breast Cancer Husband: How to Help Your Wife (and Yourself) Through Diagnosis, Treatment, and Beyond."*

Marc Silver tells the story of how, about five years ago, his wife, Marsha, told him not to build a sukkah for Sukkot. She had a good reason to say that. In early September of that year, she had been diagnosed with bilateral breast cancer. That means a tumor was found in each breast. And therefore, she was not exactly in the mood for shlepping food from the kitchen to a shack outside, or for eating out of doors—or for eating altogether, for that matter.

Cancer had just about completely taken over their lives. They were visiting doctors almost every day, looking for more opinions, as Marsha tried to settle on a team of doctors whom she could trust. They looked for appropriate treatments. And by the way, they were also a little bit busy planning for the bat mitzvah of their youngest daughter, which was coming up soon.

So Marsha was right. How could her husband be expected to find a couple of hours of spare time in which to gather up the 2-by-4s that sat in the garage all year and transform them into a sukkah? They surely had more important things on their minds than that, in such a busy and stressful time! And so Marsha said to her husband, "Please don't put up a sukkah this year."

And yet Marc Silver says that this time, he didn't listen to his wife. Years earlier, it had been Marsha insisting on their having a sukkah. It meant a lot to her to erect this fragile shelter, where the family would eat their dinners while fending off the bugs. With no experience in sukkah building, he was the one who had been reluctant. It seemed like an awful lot of work for just one week of dinner al fresco. But eventually he came around to liking it. He began to feel that it was fun having their own intimate backyard hut, with echoes that harked all the way back to biblical times.

Building a sukkah had become a family tradition, and Marc said to himself that he did not want to let the cancer take it away from them. And so, with the help of his two daughters, he put up the sukkah. That night, as they sat in the rickety hut looking up at the stars through the boughs of green, they felt as if they had found some temporary refuge from the breast cancer that was consuming their lives.

When the week was over, Marc Silver said—and his wife agreed—that it was a good thing that he didn't listen to her.

But, he confesses, there were other times when he didn't listen to his wife during her battle with breast cancer and, in those cases, not listening to his wife had been a big mistake.

Like the time she called him at work to tell him that a blunt radiologist had looked at her mammogram, and said, "Sure looks like cancer to me, lady"—as rudely and as stupidly as that! Marc says that when Marsha called him at work to tell him about this experience, he somehow didn't catch the anguish in her voice. He heard the words but missed the pain. So he pretended, to her and to himself, that everything was all right and that there was no reason to worry. He stayed at work until quitting time. When he came home, he still wasn't sure how to listen. His instinct was to try to cheer her up with words instead of paying attention to what she was really feeling.

As the weeks went by, Marc says, he eventually learned to hone his listening skills. In the doctor's office, he learned to take notes so that he could read them back to his wife afterward, for Marsha was not certain that she would be able to absorb all of this technical and scary information that they were being given. Having a second pair of ears at an appointment was a big help to her.

Gradually, Marc Silver learned that listening can be more complicated than you would think. What does it mean when your wife says to you, "You don't have to come to the doctor with me"? Does it mean that she doesn't want you to come to the doctor's with her? Or does it mean that she wants to spare you the inconvenience of taking time off from work if you don't want to come? Or does it mean, perhaps, that she thinks you are not very smart when it comes to medical matters and that she would rather have her sister, who is a nurse, go with her instead? Or is she really saying: "I love you, and I need you to know what's going on and that we are in this together—but I don't want to say so because that would be putting a burden on you, and if you don't know that I really want you to go with me, then you are a very stupid dodobird"?

Learning to listen, says Marc after some years of training, means letting your wife speak and not cutting her off if she wants to talk about how scared she is. Many people think that optimism is a cure for cancer. Unfortunately, it's not. But studies have shown that patients who let out all of their emotions cope better with the stress of treatment than those who do not. So telling your wife that everything is going to be fine may make ***you*** feel better, but it probably won't make ***her*** feel any better. Sometimes, the patient just feels lousy, or scared, or depressed, or miserable or angry, and all she wants to do is talk about it. And if that is how she feels, who better to listen to her than you?

Maybe, Marc says, that's why the cancer doctors told him that the motto of husbands of breast cancer patients ought to be "Shut up and listen." Marc says that by following that motto, he was able to help his wife get through a lumpectomy, chemotherapy and radiation treatment. Today, five years after her diagnosis, she is, *baruch Hashem*, doing well.

Marc Silver also relays that he found out afterward that he could have learned the same lesson in the importance of listening from the Torah! In the story of Abraham and Sarah, which is read in the *sedra* of Vayera and then again on the first day of Rosh Hashana, Sarah is upset with Hagar and cannot stand the sight of her or of her son, Ishmael. She says to Abraham, *"Girash et ha-ama hazot v'et bina"*—Get rid of that woman and of her child. Notice that Sarah calls her "that woman"; they have lived together for many years, their children have grown up together, and yet she is so upset that she cannot pronounce Hagar's name. She is so angry that she cannot think of her as a person with a name and a face, and so she calls her "that woman." She cannot stand the sight of the child. She cannot bear to think of the child inheriting with her own child. And so she does not call Ishmael by his name. Instead, she calls him "***her*** son."

Abraham is caught in the middle. He cares about Sarah and Isaac, but he also cares about Hagar and Ishmael. He does not know what to do. And so God says to him: "Whatever Sarah tells you to do—*sh'ma bikola*." "*Sh'ma bikola*" is usually understood to mean "obey her." I am married to a woman whose Hebrew name is Sarah, and so I have put these words from the Torah on a magnet on our refrigerator door: "Whatever Sarah says—listen to her."

But I don't think that that is the real meaning of this verse. "*Sh'ma bikola,*" literally, does not mean "do what she says"; "*sh'ma bikola*" means, literally, "listen to her *voice*." What God is saying is that if you listen to her voice, and not just to what she is saying, you will see how upset she is. You will understand that Sarah is on the edge of a breakdown. And you will realize that these two women can no longer live in the same kitchen; that they have to be separated. If you just listen to her words, you can argue as to whether Sarah is right or wrong; but if you listen to her voice, you will realize how desperate she is and you will understand that you have no choice but to separate them—for Sarah's sake, for Isaac's sake, for

Hagar's sake, for Ishmael's sake and for God's sake, because the situation as it is now simply cannot continue.

And so what Marc Silver learned from his experience as the husband of a cancer victim you and I can learn by paying attention to the Torah reading. If you want to be a sensitive husband, you have to learn to listen not only to the words that are being said, but to the tone of the words—to the frustration, to the anger and to the anxiety that is lurking underneath the words. If you can do that, then you can be of enormous help to your partner when she is going through a difficult time.

So this is my answer to the question with which I began today: You should listen to your wife when she needs a listening ear and a listening heart.

You should listen to your wife's words, but also to the pain and the fear and the anxiety and the anger that sometimes lies underneath the words. You should listen to your wife when she is in pain, and not deny her the right to these feelings by telling her: "Don't worry. Everything is going to be fine." For that kind of talk only vitiates what she is feeling and does her no good.

And when should you not listen to your wife?

When she tells you not to build a sukkah this year, when you know that deep down that she really wants you to.

13

# The Last Eight Lines ...

## Shemini Atzeret

No one ever preaches on the last *sedra* of the Torah, because it is only read on Simchat Torah, and nobody is in the mood to give or to hear a sermon on that joyous day. But let me speak about the last eight lines of the Torah today, because I believe that they contain some wisdom that we need to hear—especially in the moments before we recite *Yizkor*.

For 51 weeks of the year, the Torah gives us guidance in how to live. Now, in the last *sedra,* the Torah gives us guidance in how to die. And so join me now and let us study together the way in which the Torah ends.

The Torah states that Moses went up from the plains of Moab to Mount Nebo, to the top of the summit, facing Jericho. And the Lord showed him all the land: the Gilead until Dan, Naftali, the land of Ephraim and Manasseh; all the land of Judah until the western sea, the south, the plain, and the valley of Jericho; the city of palm trees, and all the way until

Zoar. And the Lord said to him: "This is the land I swore to Abraham, to Isaac, and to Jacob, saying, 'I will give it to your offspring.' I have let you see it with your eyes, but you shall not cross over there."

That is such a poignant passage, isn't it? Moses has worked so hard for so many years. He has put up with so much. Moses has had to deal with enemies both outside and inside the community. And now? Now, just when he is within sight of the land and almost within touching distance of the land, God tells him to climb Mount Nebo and to look at the land from afar—but that he cannot actually enter the land.

Can you imagine how Moses must have felt at this moment in his life?

Can you imagine how heartbroken he must have been?

And then comes the last lines of the Torah.

Moses, the servant of the Lord, died there, in the land of Moab, by the mouth of the Lord. This can mean either "at the command of God" or "by the kiss of God." And God buried him in the valley, in the land of Moab, opposite Beth Pe'or. No one knows the place of his burial to this day. Moses was 120 years old when he died, and his eye had not dimmed, nor had he lost his freshness. The People of Israel wept for Moses in the plains of Moab for 30 days, and then the days of weeping for Moses came to an end. Joshua, the son of Nun, was full of the spirit of wisdom, because Moses had put his hands upon him. And the People of Israel obeyed him, as they did as the Lord had commanded Moses. And there was no other prophet who arose in Israel like Moses, whom the Lord knew face-to-face, as manifested by all the signs and wonders that the Lord had sent him to perform in the land of Egypt: before Pharaoh and his servants and before all the land; all the deeds that he performed with a strong hand and with great awe Moses performed in the sight of all Israel.

With these last words, the Torah ends.

Ever since Ibn Ezra and Spinoza, biblical critics have said that Moses could not possibly have written these last words.

They say: How could Moses have described his own death and his own burial?

How did traditional readers of the Torah answer this question? There are at least two explanations that are found in the Talmud.

One explanation is that up until this point in the text, Moses wrote; the last eight lines, Joshua wrote. That makes sense. But the other explanation found in the Talmud is that, up until this point, God spoke and Moses wrote what he was told to write, but these last lines God spoke *umoshe katav bidema*—and Moses wrote in tears. According to Rabbi Meir or Rabbi Shimon, in another source, Moses performed one last, heartbreaking mission before he died: He recorded his own death, and he did so while crying.

"*Katav bidema*" can be understood in two ways. It could mean that Moses wrote while crying, or it can mean that he wrote with tears instead of with ink.

Either way, the last picture we have of Moses in the Torah, according to this midrash, is of a broken-hearted man doing what he has been told to do and writing what he has been told to write, but doing so with anguish and with sorrow and with heartache.

If that is the last scene in the life of Moses, it is a scene from which all of us can learn a lesson. The lesson is this: It is all right to cry. It is normal and it is natural to cry at the end of life. Moses may have cried with sorrow that he would not enter the land but would only see it from afar. Moses may have cried with heartache and worry over what would happen to his people after he was gone. Who would care for them and defend them, if he was no longer there? Or Moses may have cried simply because he was a human being, and therefore he cried when he faced the end of his life.

Let me consider this explanation of why Moses cried, because it is an explanation that I believe we need to hear in our time. For we live in a culture in which crying is considered somehow inappropriate.

Are any of you old enough to remember the funeral of John F. Kennedy? If so, what do you remember about that sad day? Do you remember the carriage in which his body was carried? Do you remember the crowds that lined the streets, so somber and silent? Do you remember the scene of young John-John proudly saluting as his father's cortege went by? Or do you remember, as I do, the sight of Jacqueline Kennedy—dressed in black and with a veil over her face, so that if she cried, no one could tell?

Perhaps that is where we got the idea that it is wrong to cry, even at the saddest moment of your life.

If that is where the tradition of not crying or not being seen to cry at a sad moment in your life comes from, I think it is wrong. If ever anyone was entitled to cry on that day, surely Jacqueline Kennedy was. One moment she was the First Lady; an instant later, she was leaning over the body of her husband, blood spattered all over her lovely pink dress, and she was a widow. Surely if anyone was entitled to cry on the day of his funeral, she was. And yet, perhaps to protect us—or perhaps because she had been trained from childhood that crying is improper and undignified—she walked with stately grace. If she cried that day, we did not see it.

I have seen that happen more than once. I have officiated at funerals where a grieving widow's children meant well, but they did not want her to spoil the dignity of the service or to interrupt the rabbi's eulogy with her cries—and so they persuaded the doctor to dope her up with tranquilizers. And the next day, when I came to pay a *shivah* call, she would say to me: "Tell me, rabbi, was I there?"

I believe that the children may have been well-meaning, but they did their mother no favor when they narcotized her in this way. And I do not believe that Moses, who wrote the last words of the Torah with tears in his eyes, would have approved.

I have seen this happen in hospital rooms many times. Well-meaning friends come into the room of a terminally ill patient, and they mouth platitudes. They say: "Oh, you're looking much better today!" And the patient reads their body language and understands that they do not want to face up to the truth of what is going on. And so they go along with the charade and pretend to believe what they are being told.

Every time that happens, the patient is cheated of the opportunity to deal with what is really happening. The patient is cheated of the opportunity to say goodbye. The patient is cheated of the opportunity to look back over his or her life and to atone for what he or she did that was wrong, and to surrender his or her soul to God in trust. I believe that we do the dying person no favor if we try to hide from them what they surely know, and if we keep them from the opportunity to cry or to pray or to teach at the end of their lives.

Jewish tradition is more realistic than that. The Jewish tradition says that if someone is fortunate enough to have some advance notice that he or she is dying, that we are supposed to encourage them to say the *Vidui*—the last confessional which is supposed to be said at the end of our lives. We are reminded that saying the *Vidui* is not a death warrant. We are told that many have said the *Vidui* and lived, and that many have not said it and died, and so we need not be afraid to say it and we should not be afraid to hear it.

The *Vidui* is a powerful prayer. It says:

> *Dear God, I want to live, but if this is Your decree, then I accept it from your hands. I ask You to care for my family, whom I love so much. I confess the sins that I have committed before You. And I place my spirit in Your hands. May You redeem me, O God of truth.*

And then it ends with the recitation of the *Shema.*

Blessed are those who are conscious at the end of their lives, and who are able to recite this prayer. And blessed are those who cry with them and for them at this sacred moment.

And so, the lesson that I believe that we should learn from the midrash on the last few lines of the Torah is that if Moses could cry when he contemplated that his days on earth were about to end, then so can we.

There is a custom that is found in every synagogue that I have been to. When the time for *Yizkor* comes, the young people who do not have to say *Yizkor* leave the room. The kids go out to play. The teenagers go out to stroll and socialize.

Why do they do it? I can't prove it, but I think that I know the origin of this custom. I think that parents cried when they recited *Yizkor*. Parents cried when they thought of those whom they had lost who meant so much to them. And parents were embarrassed to have their children see them cry. They thought that it would diminish them in the eyes of their children, if they saw them cry. And so they ordered them out of the room before *Yizkor* began.

And every year, in every synagogue that I have ever been in, the rabbi announces that there is no need for children to leave before *Yizkor* begins. And in every synagogue—including this one—as soon as the rabbi finishes making this announcement, the children leave the room.

I tell you this midrash about how Moses cried at the end of his life, and I tell you this passage that says that all the House of Israel cried when this leader was lost, so that you may know that crying is not a sign of weakness; crying is not a disgrace in the Jewish tradition.

This is the lesson that Moses taught us when he wrote the last words of the Torah at God's command, but with a tear.

Let this be the lesson that all of us learn and that all of remember when a tragedy occurs in our lifetime and we are moved to tears.

And let this be the lesson that is in our hearts as we now begin the recital of the *Yizkor* service.

14

# Announcing the Formation of a New Organization

## Parshat Shemini

This morning, I would like to announce that I am forming a brand-new organization, and that I am inviting you to join me.

But before I do, I want to share two news items with you—and then I want to ask you a trick question.

Let me begin with the two news items. I am on a great many mailing lists, and so I get news items from all kinds of different organizations. Two announcements came across my desk recently that each said something about the state of *kashrut* in our time. One of these announcements, I believe, constitutes good news; the other, I believe, is sad news.

The first announcement came from the *kashrut* division of the Union of Orthodox Jewish Congregations of America. I don't know if everyone here knows this or not, but the Union of Orthodox Jewish Congregations of America is the largest supervisor of *kashrut* in the world. It has supervisors in China, Vietnam, Africa, Asia, all over Europe and wherever food is raised or manufactured. It is estimated that probably half of the products in your supermarket, and maybe more, are under the supervision of the Orthodox Union. Not only Jews, but others, as well, look for the "U" when they buy products—perhaps because they believe that food that is kosher is cleaner or healthier, or perhaps for another reason. And one of the reasons why the Union of Orthodox Jewish Congregations of America is able to sponsor so many worthwhile programs for young people and for adults is because of the success of its kashrut program.

At any rate, the *kashrut* division of the Orthodox Union sent out a press release just before Pesach (Passover). In this release, it was proudly announced that they are now the supervisors of *kashrut* at 18 different stadiums where Major League Baseball teams play their games. And what is even more impressive, they reported that a great many of these places will not only have kosher food, but that they will even have kosher *l'Pesach* food for sale.

The press release named the stadiums, and told you at which location you can find the kosher booth at every one. It even told you something about the menu at each place. And I must tell you that when I read this list, I was impressed. I said to myself: God bless America—where you can go to a ballgame, and you don't have to pack and take your kosher food with you. You can buy it there! And God bless America, where *hol hamoed* consists of only three days—the other days are either *yontif* or Shabbat—and yet you can buy kosher *l'Pesach* food at a ballgame!

As the Russian-Jewish comic Yakov Smirnoff used to say: "What a country!"

My guess is that the reason why those stadiums now sell kosher food is that there is a market for it. It may be a niche market, and it may not include everyone who goes to the ballgame, but it is evidently big enough to justify the companies that manage the food courts at these places to arrange for kosher food. And I believe that the existence of this market is a testimony to the success of Orthodox Judaism.

There was a time when either you were an observant Jew or you went to the ballgame: nobody I knew did both. And the fact that we now have these booths at the stadiums, where you can buy kosher food, is a testimony to the existence of a new kind of Jew. We now have Jews who not only belong to Orthodox synagogues, but who live Orthodox lives. And just as we now have observant lawyers and doctors, we now have observant Jews who go to a ballgame. That is the good news to be found in the first news release. Orthodox Judaism has succeeded in producing Jews who live comfortably in both worlds, who work in the secular world and who are observant Jews, at the same time.

And this is a mighty achievement. All of us should admire this accomplishment, and perhaps we should even be a little bit envious of it, too.

But the second news release is not such good news—at least, not in my opinion.

I got a news release this week from Rabbi Shmuel Yankelovitch, who is a graduate of Yeshivat Chovevei Torah and whom, I believe, is one of the brightest young voices in Jewish life today. Rabbi Yankelovitch sent out a news release in which he announced the formation of a new group called Torat Chayim. This group calls upon the broader Jewish community and the rest of the Western world to consider the moral, ecological and health-related dangers that are associated with meat consumption. In this statement, the members of Torat Chayim call upon all Jews—whether they be Orthodox, Conservative, Reform, Reconstructionist or nonaffiliated—and upon non-Jews as well, to consider the dimensions of *halachah* and the Jewish ideal of reducing meat intake in order to create a healthier, safer and more ethically vibrant world.

The statement relays, in part:

> *We, the undersigned, are committed to the observance of kashrut, and to its continuance as a vehicle toward just, healthy living and the service of God. We encourage the community to consider the research on livestock raised in the factory farming system and to question whether food prepared in this manner meets the reverence-for-life standard on which kashrut is based. A substantial body of research suggests that there is significant and unnatural pain caused to animals during their raising and their slaughter for human consumption, that factory farming is one of the leading contributors to carbon emissions, and that the consumption of meat is a leading contributor to cardiac disease, gastrointestinal ailments, and certain types of cancers. Therefore, it behooves the Jewish community and all the people of the world to have spirited and respectful conversations about reducing meat intake and about coming together to find solutions for this global concern.*

Notice that this resolution does not say that we should all become vegans, or even vegetarians. All it says is that we should come together across all the lines that divide us to study the question of whether eating meat is healthy, whether it is good for the planet, and whether it is in keeping with the concepts of limiting pain to animals and respect for all creatures, which are at the heart of the *kashrut* laws.

So why do I say that this is a sad resolution?

For this reason:

How many Orthodox rabbis would you guess there are? My guess is that there are probably somewhere around a thousand Orthodox rabbis in this country—give or take. And how many Orthodox rabbis would you guess signed this resolution? Can you guess? Five hundred? Three hundred?

Twenty-five.

Among them are some of the tried and true liberal voices within Orthodoxy that we know: Yits Greenberg, Danny Landes of Pardes, Mel Gottlieb of Los Angeles—and that is about all. I could not identify most of the others who signed this resolution.

And I think that that is sad. How can you explain that the overwhelming majority of Orthodox rabbis did not sign this statement, which simply asks that we discuss, consider and examine the moral, health-related and *halachic* issues in *kashrut* today?

Evidently, there is a chasm within Orthodoxy today, as well as a chasm between Orthodoxy and the other groups within Judaism: a chasm in which Orthodox rabbis will not sign a resolution that seems so uncontroversial simply because it comes out of a group within Orthodoxy that they are unwilling to recognize or to grant legitimacy to. That is sad.

Have we reached a stage in which we no longer talk to one another or listen to one another? If so, then we may end up doing more harm to ourselves than all our enemies could ever do to us.

And so I think it is sad when a request—a request for discussion of what is surely a real challenge to *halachah* in our time—is simply ignored, just because of the group that raises it.

Do you agree?

And now, let me ask you a question. And let me warn you, in advance, that this is a tricky question.

What group in Jewish life do you believe is the most insular and the most isolated? What group in Jewish life would you say is the least likely to listen to and to learn from the other groups?

I am pretty sure that most of you would say the Haredim, the ultra-Orthodox. We think of them as being isolated from the rest of us. We think of them as not wanting to and not willing to learn from any other group, because they feel that they already have all wisdom within themselves. Isn't that so? Pirkei Avot says: "Who is wise? The person who is willing to learn from everyone." But we say that the Haredim behave as if this was not a rule for them. Isn't that so?

And yet I would say that that is a stereotype. The truth is that we are just as isolated from them as they are from us. The truth is that we all live in separate siloes, and that we are no more open to listening to or learning from them as they are to listening and learning from us. The truth is that we seldom meet Haredim, and if we do, we assume that we know what they think without ever asking them.

To prove my point, let me tell you about one Haredi rabbi from whom I learn every week. His name is Rabbi Avi Shafran, and he is the public affairs director of Agudath Israel of America, which is a prominent Haredi group in America, in Israel and elsewhere. Rabbi Shafran, contrary to what we would expect, is a graduate of an Ivy League university; the column that he writes every week is erudite and sophisticated and elegantly written, and I learn from it every time I read it.

Rabbi Shafran recently wrote a column based on the findings of a research project that was published in a journal of sociology. The study divided people into two groups: One group was given chocolate every day, and the other was given chocolate only once a week.

Can you guess which group liked chocolate more, at the time of the interview, after a few months on this diet?

The group whose members ate chocolate once a week enjoyed the taste of chocolate. The group that ate it every day reported that its members were bored with it, and that they wanted something else for a change.

That led Rabbi Shafran to point out that in our society, we are swamped with a host of choices. If you go into a supermarket, you will find five different brands of tuna fish to choose from. If you go into a restaurant, you will find more than half a dozen different items on the menu. And that is why we become bored by all these choices, and that is why we keep looking for something new or someplace new to eat.

It was not like that in the ancient world. There, bread was the staple: you ate it every day, perhaps with a vegetable, perhaps with some gravy, and perhaps without either. That is why the term for a meal in the ancient world was "breaking bread." That was the legal and the social definition of a meal, because that is what most people ate every day.

Because meat was expensive, and because it was not readily available, meat was reserved for the Sabbath in many Jewish homes. And that leads Rabbi Shafran to speculate on what it would be like if we took meat off the menu during the week, and only ate it *likoved shabbas*—in honor of the Sabbath.

He suggests that, if the findings of the study about chocolate are correct, then meat should taste better if we only ate it once a week.

Rabbi Shafran also suggests that in an age in which obesity has become a major issue, eating less meat would be beneficial to our health. If the studies that have been conducted by the ecologists are correct, then eating less meat would be good for the planet, as well.

Which brings me to the new organization that I am thinking of creating, and that I would invite you to consider joining.

I must confess that I have not had much success up to this point in creating new organizations. I once wanted to form a Pessimists Club—but I quickly realized that it probably would not work, so I dropped that idea.

And then I thought of forming a new organization that I was going to call the Boca Raton Sitting Club. It was meant to be a counter to the Boca Raton Running Club, which is very popular in this community. I thought that we could get together for brunch at a club every Sunday morning, and as the runners went by, we would lift our glasses to them and call out, "*Meshugeners*!"

I thought that that would be a good idea because, as some of you may know, I am thoroughly against exercise. And so I really intended to form this group. But much to my shock, my two grandchildren are now runners. They now run five, 10 and even 15 miles every Sunday! I tell them that if they want to go that far, they ought to take a bus. But what can I do? They don't listen to me. And so I have decided not to form the Boca Raton Sitting Club, after all.

But the organization that I ***do*** want to form, now, is called The MOOSHY Group. "MOOSHY" stands for "Meat Only On Shabbat and *Yom Tov*." This is a group that I believe can add to the beauty of our Shabbat observance, and this is a group that I believe can add to both our personal health and to the health of our planet. This is a group that can help us avoid *tsar baaley hayim*—the pain to animals—and to strengthen the reverence for life, which is at the heart of the laws of *kashrut*.

And so, if you agree with me—and if you would like to join as charter members of my group—will you please see me after services.

15

# An English Critic and a Yiddish Poet Raise the Same Question

## *Yizkor*, Shemini Atzeret

I chanced across two documents recently that raise the same question.

One is a story that appeared in the New York Times; the other is a poem that appeared in a Yiddish newspaper many years ago. One concerns the famous literary critic, Frank Kermode, of Harvard; the other comes from an unknown Yiddish poet. Somehow I think that, even though I am pretty sure that these two men never met in person, these two documents raise the same question. And I believe that it is

***the*** *Yizkor* question, and so I want to share it with you this morning.

The story about Frank Kermode is this:

Kermode was once moving from one apartment to another. He gathered the books and papers that he really cared about and put them in one pile, for the moving company to take. He took those books and papers that he no longer needed and put them in another pile, for the trash man to take. Somehow, the trash man came first and, by mistake, took the wrong pile. Kermode says that he was not very upset, and that he wondered if perhaps the trash man hadn't made the right choice, rather than he.

Compare that story with this Yiddish poem. I don't know who wrote it, but I imagine that it expresses the sentiments that many in the immigrant generation felt. They came to a bewildering new world in which they were looked upon as "greenhorns." I wonder where that expression comes from? And soon their children, who spoke English better than they did, began to look down upon them and upon the world from which they had come. That is the background for this poem, which captures some of the pathos and poignancy of the Yiddish original:

My dear little boy,
What will you do, when my time comes?
And I belong to the grass
And will not be here to kiss and fondle you—
What will you be?
A *homo novus*—a new kind of Jew?
And what will you do with the bequest
Which I will leave you here on these bookshelves?
Jewels for the weekday, pearls for the Sabbath;
Generations stored a treasure here.
What will you do with these old brown folios?
"*The Chovos Halevos*," "*The Chayey Adam*," "*The Kav Hayashor*,"

And "*The Eyn Yaakov*,"
And these thin books of verse—gifts to me
From Yiddish princes, kings, the writers.
My heart tells me that you will not need them
Even though (of this I am sure),
The treasures they contain exist in other tongues.

And one day the junkman will come by—a Jew with
sidelocks
Who (after a bath) looks like the King of Spades,
And he will fill the streets with his old cry:
"Any rags? Any bottles? Any old things today?"
Call him in and ask him this:
"Do you have a good supply of strong rope?"
"And do you not (God forbid) have a rupture?"
"Can you carry a heavy load of culture?"
Then show him your inheritance—my books—
And don't forget the souvenirs in the cellar—
Your *zeidi's tallis* and *tefillin*,
(So musty now that even the cats will not deign
To play with the tassels or toy with the ribbons);
Give one last caress to the smooth silk,
As if you were closing my eyes,
And help the junkman load his wagon.

But before he goes, if you wish,
Tell him in a few words—
Like ginger that sweetens the air—
That you are the descendant of princes:
That your grandfather was a scholar and a savant,
And your father was a poet and a recluse,
And their inheritance is in this wagonload
That will now go through fire to God.

Can you feel the pain in this poem, and can you feel the sense of abandonment?

Here is a man who once knew Yiddish poets, and who once received autographed copies of their work. Here is a man whose father knew the basic books by which Jews live: the ethical works and the legal works; the books like the "*Eyn Yaakov*," that contains the legends and stories of the Talmud; the "*Kav Hayashar*" and the "*Chovos Halevovos*," that contain the moral teachings and the values of our people; and the "*Chayey Odom*," that contains instructions on how a Jew should live. This is a man who has inherited a rich legacy of books and yet who knows that his children will not need them or want them—or even be able to read them. This man foresees that these books will someday end up being given to the junkman.

There is a painful irony in the last line. What will the junkman do with the books? After he is paid a couple of dollars for hauling them away, he will take them to some dump, and there they will be burned. As he says, "[They] will now go through fire to God."

That line is ironic. Once, books like these were burned at the stake in auto-de-fes. Once, they were seized by the enemy and burned by those who were filled with hated. And now they will be burned again—but this time, not with hatred, but with indifference; not by the enemies, but by the inheritors who do not realize how precious they are.

Frank Kermode told the story of how the junkman confused the two piles, the one that contained his precious papers and books and the one that contained the ones he wanted to throw away. He told of how the junkman took the wrong pile by mistake. He tells his story with rueful humor. The unknown Yiddish poet tells a very similar story, but he tells it with pain and anguish. For him it is no laughing matter when his heritage goes up in smoke. For him, it is painful when his heritage is of no interest to his descendants.

That poem expresses what many early immigrants to this country felt when they saw their children and grandchildren growing up utterly indifferent to the books and values that they had brought with them. They had an inheritance to give them—not in stocks or bonds or real estate, but in books and pamphlets, poems and legends, laws and ideas and ideals. Many of them died with much pain in their hearts because they felt that their way of life was going to go into the grave with them.

But the pain and disappointment that these Jewish immigrants felt may have been premature. In the immortal words of Yogi Berra, "It ain't over till it's over"—and the eulogy to Judaism and Jewish books that this unknown poet wrote may yet turn out to be a poem that his grandchildren and their children will study and appreciate in class, and will refute by the way in which they live.

When that poem was written, everyone—including the immigrants themselves—felt that traditional Jewish life was over: that it would only last as long as the immigrant generation and then it would be finished. Everyone believed that America was a *trefe medinah*, and that there was no way that the tradition could survive here.

And today?

A friend of mine bought a refrigerator recently. This refrigerator came from one of the biggest manufacturers and—because my friend is a compulsive reader, as I am—he read through the book of instructions that came with it. When he got to page 17, he found this instruction: "For those who are Sabbath observers, this is the way to disconnect the refrigerator light…" What would that unknown poet have said if he could come back and read that refrigerator manual?

And what would that poet who wrote with such despair think if he were to come back today and find that there are now two ovens that come with Star-K supervision, so that they can be used without violating the Sabbath?

And what would that poet who wrote with such despair think if he were to come back today and find that some of the Campbell soups—and soon, perhaps, all of them—are now produced under the supervision of the Union of Orthodox Jewish Congregations of America?

And what would that poet who wrote with such despair think if he came back and found that a Jew—an observant Jew, at that—ran for the vice presidency of the United States, and that no one thought that his religion was an issue either way in the campaign?

And what would that poet who wrote with such despair think if he came back and found that not only are there still Jewish men who put on *tallis* and *tefillin* regularly, but that there are now Jewish women who do so, too?

And what would that poet who wrote with such despair think if he came back and found that there are now classes in Jewish studies in almost every single university in America: that there are now over a thousand professors who belong to the Association for Jewish Studies, which is the professional organization of those who teach Jewish studies at American universities? What would he think if he saw that many of those poetry books that he thought his children would throw away, and many of those classic Jewish books of ethics and *halachah* that he thought his children would throw away, are now taught on college campuses?

And what would that poet who wrote with so much despair think if he came back and found that there is now a treasured house of Yiddish literature in western Massachusetts, located near the campus of Amherst? What if he knew that there are people all over America who serve as scouts for this "treasure house," who rummage through cellars and attics in every city, in order to find Yiddish books to send to this Yiddish culture center, where they can be repaired, preserved and shared with those who want to know more about the world from which they came?

If he came back and saw these things, would he still call America a *trefe medinah*? Or would he understand that America is a land of opportunity—not only for Jews, but for Judaism, as well?

There was a social scientist named Hansen who wrote, many years ago, that "that which the children throw away, the grandchildren rummage in the wastebaskets of history to rediscover." This is what we may be seeing happening in our time.

Abraham Joshua Heschel lived through those years in America when the Jewish tradition was being literally thrown away. America was a land that worshipped newness, and no one had the time, room or interest for old things. And yet he wrote, in part:

"Without solidarity with our fathers, the solidarity with our brothers will be feeble. The vertical unity of the Jewish people is essential to the horizontal unity of the Jewish people. … We are either the last generation of Jews or those who will hand over the heritage to those who come after us."

By now many of us are the fourth generation of Jews in this land. For many of us, the author of that Yiddish poem is our great-grandfather—not our father. For many of us, the heritage has been lost or abandoned—not by us, but before it got to us. And yet *Yizkor* time is a moment to think about those books that got carted off by the junkman and those values that ended up on a trash pile. *Yizkor* is a moment for thinking not only about our own individual losses, but for thinking about our collective loss—the loss of those books, insights and values that made us a precious and a holy people.

*Yizkor* is a moment in which to think about supporting those institutions of Jewish learning—the synagogue, the department of Jewish studies at our local college, the day school, the yeshiva, the kollel, the center at Amherst and all the other places that perform the *mitzvah* of rescuing Jewish books and teachings from the hands of the junkman. Frank Kermode could smile at the fact that his trash man could not distinguish between his good books and the ones he wanted to throw away. But for Jews, it is no laughing matter when a book gets lost. For Jews, it is a painful thing when books that somehow survived the book burnings by our enemies end up being burned by the indifference of our descendants.

This is the *Yizkor* that marks a transition between the somberness of the holidays that have passed and the frivolity and the hilarity of Simchat Torah that will soon begin. Let it be a moment in which we resolve to reconnect, not only with our parents and our grandparents who are gone, but with the inheritance that they have left to us. For "they are our life, and the meaning and the measure of our days and in them we should meditate day and night"—and we should treasure them, from generation to generation.

Let us guard the books that we have inherited, for they are indeed the meaning and the measure of our lives.

And to this, let us say—not only with our lips, but by our deeds, as well—amen.

# 16

# Can We Grow Old and Still Stay Young?

## Shemini Atzeret

Rabbi Jonathan Sacks of England tells the story of how, when Queen Elizabeth celebrated her 75th anniversary as sovereign, she and her husband, Prince Phillip, hosted a great party. At this party, some of the leading people in England toasted her and wished her well. One of the dignitaries who spoke that day was Vivian Wineman, head of the Board of Deputies of British Jews. When it came time for him to speak, Wineman lifted his cup and made a toast to the queen. And what did he wish for her? He gave the queen the traditional Jewish blessing for such an occasion. He said to her: "Your majesty, may you live to be one hundred and twenty."

The queen was kind of puzzled when she received this wish, for she had never heard this expression before. And so, after the ceremony was over, she asked him what this blessing meant and where it came from.

Wineman explained that this wish comes from the last chapter of the book of Devarim. The Torah says that Moses was one hundred and twenty years old when he died, "*v'lo kahata eynav, v'lo nos lecho*"—that his eyes were still undimmed and his strength was still undiminished. And since no one can be expected to live longer than Moses did, this is the wish that we make for each other: "May you live to be one hundred and twenty—as Moses did—and when you grow old, may your eyes be undimmed, and may your strength be undiminished—as his were."

For most of human history, that was just a pious wish: it was not attainable. Until a century or so ago, very few people lived to be seventy, and only those with special strength could dream of reaching eighty. But in this last century, life expectancy has climbed up and up and up. Today, there are many people who reach ninety years of age, and there are some who reach a hundred and some who reach even more. So the idea of reaching a hundred and twenty does not seem as far-fetched as it once did. And who can predict? In another century, it may become common for people to reach a hundred and twenty years of age.

But the real question is this: ***If*** they do, will that be a blessing or a curse?

That depends on how they live. If they live like Moses, with their eyes undimmed and with their strength undiminished, it will be a great blessing; if not, if their bodies deteriorate and if their minds wear out, then it will not be a blessing—not at all. And so the question that confronts us all is this: How do you grow old and yet stay young?

I think that the answer can be found in this obituary of Moses that we are going to read tomorrow. What does it say about him? It says that when he grew old, his eyes did not dim and his strength did not diminish. I used to think that these were two unrelated blessings: his eyes did not dim, and his strength did not diminish. But now I think that they are really one two-part blessing. Moses had a good old age, and not just because he lived for many years. He had a good old age because, even when he was old, he kept his eyes focused on the future. He kept his eyes focused on the task that he still had to do, and that was the reason why his strength did not diminish.

It would have been easy for Moses to retire. He could have moved to Florida and taken social security, as so many people do today. Or he could have focused his last days on nostalgia. He could have spent those days looking back over his life, thinking of his many achievements. We all know people who do that. Give them half a chance and they will tell you, in detail, what they did back when they were in the army or when they were in the Boy Scouts or at some other time in their lives. Moses could have spent his old age brooding over the things that had gone wrong in his life and the mistakes that he had made. He could have spent his last days lamenting, "if only I had done this," or, "if only I had not done that." But Moses did not do either of these things. Instead, he spent his final days on earth teaching the next generation what they should do when they arrive in the Promised Land. He talked about how to create a just society. He told them how to be kind to the widow and the orphan and the stranger. He told them how to live in the land that they were going to inherit. And then, at the very end, he gave them his blessing. And by doing these things, he left behind a legacy that outlived him. Moses spent the last days of his life focused on the future, and not on the past. He spent his last days looking into the future and teaching the next generation and the ones after that how they should live.

And that, I would suggest to you—and to myself, as well—is the secret of how to grow old and still be young. Cast a line as far into the future as you can, and if you do, you will live for as long as you are alive.

We say *Yizkor* four times a year: on Pesach, on Shavout, on Yom Kippur and on Shemini Atzeret. But I confess that the *Yizkor* service that has the greatest impact on me each year is the one that we recite on this holiday, on Shemini Atzeret. Because this is the day when we feel our age the most. You look out the window and you can see the leaves beginning to fall off the trees. You look at your calendar for the candle-lighting time, and you realize that the days are beginning to get shorter and shorter. You look at the thermostat and you realize that the weather is getting cooler and cooler, and that winter will soon be here. And you read that powerful and painful chapter of *Kohelet,* with its description of the gradual encroachment of old age, and you come to those words that shake you: "Then there will come those days when you will say, '*Eyn li cheyfets bahem*'—I have no desire in them."

That is the shortest, simplest definition of old age that I know. It is the time when *eyn li cheyfetz bahem*—when you no longer have any desires: not for food, not for drink, not for work, not for travelling, not for anything. Old age is the stage when *eyn li chetfets bahem*—when you no longer want or need or care about anything.

My friend and teacher, Rabbi Sol Landau, used to tell a story that illustrates what it is like to be old. He used to talk about the four retirees who meet at a party. The first one says proudly, "I was a doctor." The second one says smugly, "I was a lawyer." The third one says boastfully, "I ran a big business." And then they turn to the fourth man, and they say: "And who did you use to be?"

"Who did you use to be?" is a question that leads you nowhere. Moses understood that. That is why he focused not on the achievements of his past, and not on the mistakes of his past, but on the work that he still had to do and on the new generation that he still had to teach.

And so it is with many people in our time. We now live in a fast-changing world, and therefore there are people who make enormous success at an early age. Rabbi Sacks points out that Mark Zuckerberg, Bill Gates, Sergey Brin and Larry Page, for example, all became multi-multi-millionaires in their 20s or in their early 30s. But did you know that each one of these prodigies chose an older person to be their mentor? They did so because they felt that they needed advice—not on how to make money—they already had more money than they knew what to do with—but because they felt that they needed guidance on how to live with so much money.

And by doing that, they not only brought blessing to their own lives, but they brought blessing and purpose to the lives of those whom they chose to be their mentors.

Let me tell you about the day when I learned what old age is and what it can do to a person. When I was a child, we knew a family that lived nearby. The husband and the wife were bright people, and they were deeply involved in the world. One of the signs of their involvement was the fact that they got three newspapers every day. They got the local paper, they got the New York Times and they got a Yiddish paper, every single day.

The years went by, and they became old. I remember coming home from rabbinical school one day and going to visit them. They were sitting out on the porch, and all around them the newspapers were piled up, unopened. There must have been at least two weeks' worth of newspapers on the porch, still in their wrappers. I asked them why they no longer read the newspapers, and one of them answered with words that have stayed in my mind ever since. She said to me: "*Vos ob ich difin*?"—"What benefit will I have from reading them?"

That was the day when I learned what old age means. It is when you no longer bother reading the paper because, what do you need it for? It is what Kohelet meant when he said: "*Ma yitron ha-adam mikol amalo sheyaamol tachat hashamash*?"—What's the use of all the work that a person does under the sun?

Fifty-one weeks of the year, we learn from Moses how to live. In the last pages of his book, we learn from him how to age and how to live at the end. He tells us, very simply, to keep looking forward. He tells us, very simply, that we still have work to do. He tells us, very simply, that there is a new generation coming up and that they need to learn from us how to behave in the years that lie ahead. And therefore, for as long as we live, we have work to do. We have people to teach. We have experience and lessons to share.

There is something very moving about seeing Moses at almost a hundred and twety years of age still looking forward, with his eye undimmed and with his strength undiminished. When the curtain came down on his life, he was still teaching, still sharing his wisdom, still busy, still inspiring those who will come after him to carry on the tasks that he will not be able to finish.

That is the way to grow old and still stay young.

Let me finish with just one last story. I tell you this story in memory of my dear friend, Rabbi Morton Liefman. Morton did not live as long as Moses did, but he did live until he was almost 90 years of age, and he was able to teach his children and his children's children until almost the very end.

At his funeral, Morton's younger colleague and friend, Shay Held, told this story. Held did his doctorate at Harvard on the life and thought of Abraham Joshua Heschel, and by the time he finished it, he knew about as much about Heschel as anyone ever did. He met Morton one day in the seminary cafeteria, and Morton called him over and said: "I've been meaning to call you. Would you please do me a big favor? Fritz Rothschild, who wrote the first book about Heschel and his thought, is now a very old man. He sits at home all day and the phone never rings. He feels abandoned and unnecessary. Would you please think of a question about Heschel's thought, and call him and ask him for his opinion? Even if you already know the answer, would you call him and ask him the question anyway? For if you do, I promise you that you will make his day."

And so Shay Held did that.

When Morton went to visit Fritz a few days later, Fritz told him what Shay had done and how grateful and excited he was to have been asked a question.

Let this be the way we treat the old people in our lives. Let us not only care for them, but learn from them. Let us not only take care of their physical needs, but of their spiritual needs, as well. And let us understand that one of a human being's greatest needs—as great as the need for food or drink—is ***the need to be needed.***

For if we do that, then—like Moses, our teacher—we and they will be able, with God's help, to grow old and still be young.

Amen.

17

# Did a Miracle Really Take Place in Los Angeles This Year? If So, What Was It?

## Hanukkah

There was a lovely story that appeared on the front page of the Los Angeles Times some time ago. It impressed me very much, and so I want to tell you about it today.

It is the story of a man named Michael Goldberg, who lives on Wilshire Boulevard in Los Angeles. Goldberg has a menorah that means a great deal to him. It has been in his family for more than four hundred years. It has traveled with the family in all its wanderings, from Poland to Paris to New

York to California. The menorah is so precious to this family that they keep it in their vault at the bank, and they take it out only once a year, on Hanukkah.

This year, as always, they took it out a few days before Hanukkah. Michael's wife, Ellen, teaches at the Wilshire Avenue Temple, and so she took it to class one day to show the children. Afterward, she wrapped the menorah in newspapers and brought it home in a paper bag, and put it in her study. She closed the door, and she figured that no one would go in and disturb it.

Sunday, while the rest of the family was watching television, Ellen went to the study to unwrap and polish the menorah. Much to her shock, ***it was not there***! She looked in all the other rooms in the house, and then she went back and looked in them again. She went from closet to closet, from cupboard to cupboard, from room to room. Nothing. The menorah was gone!

Only then did she realize that the cleaning woman must have thrown it away. Tearfully, she broke the news to her husband.

"Well, then, I will have to take the day off and go to the dump," Michael told his wife. She thought he was joking, for the trash had been picked up two days earlier, and the menorah must be buried under tons of garbage and dirt by now. But he was not joking.

"It's been with us for four hundred years, and I am not going to let it go just like that," he said. And so it was that this kitchen cabinet designer, whose usual mode of dress is a three-piece-suit, called the West Los Angeles Sanitation Department on Monday morning.

At first, his plight fell on deaf ears. The person on the other end of the line told him to forget about it. The man said to him: "You must be kidding! Do you really think that you can find something that has been buried in a garbage dump for two days?"

Goldberg figured that if he could find a Jewish person who worked in that office, he or she might be more sympathetic to his problem. So he asked if they had a Mr. Cohen working there. But for some strange reason, there was no Mr. Cohen in the garbage collection department. He asked for Mr. Levy, and then for Mr. Schwartz, and then for Mr. Ginsberg. But there was no one by any of those names who worked in the garbage department.

Finally, in desperation, he grabbed a phone book and looked through it for some Jewish-sounding names. He found Ackerman, and so he called back and asked if there was a Mr. Ackerman there.

They didn't have any Mr. Ackerman there, but they did have a Mrs. Ackerman, so they put him through to her.

Mrs. Ackerman was sympathetic. She checked with her supervisor, whose name was Edward O'Neal, and he checked his records. O'Neal found that the trash collection had been delayed one day that week, from Friday to Saturday, because of Thanksgiving. Then O'Neal checked his roster and discovered that, for some reason, truck number 840—which collected for the Goldbergs' neighborhood—had not arrived at the dump yet.

O'Neal told Michael Goldberg that truck 840 was on the way, and that it would probably be dumping its eight tons of garbage at the Sepulveda landfill within the hour. Goldberg slammed down the phone, changed quickly into his oldest clothes, and headed for the Sepulveda landfill as fast as he could go.

When Ray Brown and R.C. Clayborne, the two garbage collectors, drove truck number 840 into the landfill an hour later, Michael Goldberg was there waiting for them.

"They were very cooperative," Goldberg said later. "They made a long, spread-out discharge and then they jumped right in to help me, when I explained to them what had happened."

The bulldozer operators plowed a dirt wall around Goldberg so that no other trucks would dump more garbage on top of him as he sat amidst the garbage. Eventually, Brown and Clayborne said that they had to get back to their work. And so they excused themselves, and left Goldberg to dig through the garbage pile by himself.

Goldberg says that he was looking through every bag and going through the stuff with his bare hands. There were bags that had broken open and loose garbage had fallen out. Yet while he was wishing that he had a shovel, he suddenly saw the handle of a shovel sticking up from the garbage. It was not only a shovel; it was ***his*** shovel! The previous week, he'd been cleaning some stuff out and found an old shovel they had brought from New York. It was rusty, and so he threw it out with the trash—and now, here it was! Goldberg says. If that shovel wasn't a sign from heaven, he says that he didn't know what was.

Goldberg dug a path right through the trash with his shovel and dug down through the dirt, looking through every bag. He was sitting down, with garbage bags on his lap, ripping each one open and going through it. He was whistling while he worked. If someone had seen him, Goldberg says, they would have thought he was crazy.

Finally, Goldberg ripped through the right bag and found the menorah! He returned home and showed it to his wife. He called Mrs. Ackerman to thank her. "I felt it was worth doing whatever little bit of tracing I did to help him," she said.

"Something that valuable was worth looking for," added O'Neal, the supervisor.

On Thursday afternoon, the menorah was sitting on the kitchen counter in the Goldberg house. Michael Goldberg said that his first thought was to bring it to a silversmith immediately, but he decided to wait until after Hanukkah. He and his family wanted it with them during the holiday. "The symbolism was incredibly apt," he said.

Goldberg paused for a moment, reviewing all the twists and turns of the quest: the day's delay in pickup, his being the only truck that came late, the finding of the shovel. "Tell me that all that can just happen," he said. "This is the season of miracles against all odds."

And the reporter who interviewed Goldberg for the Los Angeles Times had to admit that he just might be right.

And with that line, the newspaper story ends.

That is a lovely story, isn't it? It was a delight to read on the front page of the Los Angeles Times. I just have one concern about the last sentence: I am not sure that he is right. Goldberg is a kitchen cabinet designer, not a rabbi, and so I am not sure that he is qualified to say what a miracle is—any more so than I am to say anything about kitchen cabinets.

What is a miracle? This may have been one, perhaps, but it very well could have been a series of coincidences. It could have very well just been good luck. Who can say for sure which it was?

I don't know about you, but I must say that I find it hard to conceive of God as being involved in garbage collections being late, or in shovels happening to turn up in the right pile, or in delivery trucks being late. Somehow, that is a conception of God that I find hard to relate to. It sounds more like the Hollywood version of God, like something that George Burns would do, in that movie "*Oh, God!*" in which God proves his reality by doing all kinds of magic tricks.

Somehow, people have been trying to prove God's existence by means of tricks and magic for years, and yet it has not worked, because any trick that one group can do, another group can do better.

When Moses tried to convince the pharaoh of God's reality by doing wonders with his staff, Pharaoh turned to the magicians of Egypt, and they did the very same tricks. So I am dubious that Michael Goldberg had a miracle. It could be, but it could also very well be a coincidence: a bit of luck; or a lot of luck; but still luck.

And yet I believe that there was a miracle in what happened—a real miracle, a miracle for which there is no secular explanation. Do you know what that miracle was? The miracle was that Goldberg cared, that he cared that much, and that he was willing to do all that—to call and run and dig in the garbage like that, in order to retrieve his menorah. The miracle is that his family kept that menorah with them all of those years, in all their wanderings. Had any one of them let it go—had any one of them decided not to carry it along as they moved from land to land, had any one of them opted out of Jewish existence and said, "Who needs it?"—it would have been all over. That this family held on to this menorah with such love and such determination through so much for so long—***that***, to me, is the miracle.

And that the Jewish people have held onto the Hanukkah story—that they have held onto it not just for 400 years, but for 2,100 years, transmitting it from generation to generation, in one country after another, when they had had so many opportunities to abandon it; when they were offered both the carrot and the stick, rewards if they gave it up and threats if they did not; that the Jewish people have held onto this holiday for 2,100 years—***that*** is the miracle. And that we still have it now, that we are ***right now*** transmitting it to the next generation, to those who will come after us—***that*** is the miracle.

Let me finish by telling you one of my favorite stories—a story that I believe explains what a miracle really is, at least as we Jews understand it.

I have a dear friend, Rabbi Arthur Hertzberg, who lives in Englewood, New Jersey. His father was a Hassidic rebbe who lived in Baltimore. The story is that there is a classical Reform synagogue in Washington, not too far from Baltimore. One year, the sisterhood of that temple got a program kit from the National Office of the Reform movement. The program said that this was "Hassidism Year," the 200th anniversary of the death of the Baal Shem Tov, and therefore they suggested that it would be good to have a program in each sisterhood on Hassidism.

The sisterhood's program chairman thought that that would be a good idea, and so she called up Rabbi Hertzberg and asked if he would speak at their temple. The rebbe said that he didn't speak or travel, but that if they liked, they could come and visit him at his *shteibel*. This sounded even more intriguing—a field trip! So the sisterhood chartered two buses, and they went to visit the rabbi at his *shteibel*.

The rebbe showed them around and told them some stories. He told them about some of the miracles that the Baal Shem Tov did. He told them some of the miracles that Rebbe Elimelech of Lizinsk had done, and he told them some of the miracles that Rebbe Naftali of Ropshitz had done. Then there was a question-and-answer period.

The first question that was asked was: "Do you really believe that the Baal Shem Tov did miracles?"

The rebbe answered: "Yes."

The next question was: "Do you really believe that Rebbe Elimelech of Lizinsk did miracles?"

The rebbes answered: "Yes."

The next question was: "Can you do a miracle?"

The rebbes answered: "***You're here***!"

It is a miracle that more than two centuries after the Baal Shem Tov's death, such a sisterhood is visiting in a Hassidic *shteibel*. It is a miracle that, more than 20 centuries after the Hanukkah story happened, we are still here, still telling the tale, still transmitting it to a new generation which, in turn and with God's help, will tell the tale to those who will come after them.

So, mister Goldberg was right, after all. This is the season of miracles. And what he did, as well as what happened to him, is one, too.

Therefore, let us celebrate Hanukkah together tonight, with a whole and a happy heart.

And to this, let us all say: Amen.

# 18

# How Come Jews Are Always Late?

## Tu Bishvat

Tu Bishvat is a great holiday in Israel. It celebrates the arrival of spring and the beginning of the blossoming of the flowers. If you were to travel in Israel on this day, you would see the land in full bloom. If you were to drive through the Galilee at this season of the year, you would see two flowers that have the same name: the Lotem. One is a beautiful, white, silky flower, and the other is an amazing, wrinkled, purple one.

How come two flowers have the same name? And if they are related, how come they look so different? Why is one white and silky and the other wrinkled and purple?

I am glad you asked.

In honor of Tu Bishvat, let me tell you a story that answers these two questions. I learned it from Liat Ben-David, who was a *shlicha*, a representative of Israel. Ben-David was in Palm Beach, Florida for some years and later she was director general of the Israel department of the Jewish Agency for Israel. I think that it is a very important story because it not only explains why there are two Lotem trees in Israel—one white and the other purple—and why they look so different, but it also explains a mystery that scholars have struggled to explain for many, many centuries. This mystery is: How come Jews are always late?

Here is the story:

Once upon a time, King Solomon decided to have a party. He decided to invite all the people of the kingdom to the party. He sent out a special invitation, with beautiful gold letters and decorated with silver and gems. The invitation weighed so much that it took ***five*** 37-cent stamps to mail it! But the king did not mind because he could afford it, and he wanted everyone to come to this party. And on the invitation, he wrote, "Black tie only." When everyone got the invitation, they understood that it did not mean that you were supposed to wear nothing but a black tie. They were very sophisticated people, and so they understood that when an invitation says "black tie only," what it really means is that you are supposed to dress up in your fanciest clothes. And so they all went out and bought tuxedos and evening gowns; they all went out and went to the beauty parlor or to the barber shop; and they all went out and bought new shoes. Because when King Solomon invites you to a party—you go! And when he says "black tie," you wear something as fancy as you possibly can.

Now, in a small village in the Galilee, there lived two brothers: the Lotem brothers. As sometimes happens in families, these two brothers were opposites—opposites in every way.

The older brother was neat and organized. Everything on his desk, everything in his closet, everything in his room, was perfectly organized. And when he made an appointment with you for 3 o'clock, he was there at 3 o'clock. Not 3:05; not 2:55; if you invited him for 3 o'clock, he was there at precisely 3 o'clock.

The younger brother was the very opposite. His room was always a mess. His desk was a *hekdesh*. Papers were strewn all over the room, and it was impossible for him to find one when he was looking for it. He was careless and easygoing. And if you invited him to meet you at 3 o'clock, he might get there at 4 o'clock, or even—it sometimes happened—at 5 o'clock. And sometimes, he ***would*** get there at 3 o'clock—but, at 3 o'clock the next day.

The two brothers lived together, though it was not easy for two such different personalities to coexist in the same house. They would argue a lot, but they loved each other, so they stayed together in spite of the differences in the way they lived.

When they got their invitations to the king's party, they were both very excited. They hastened to send in their RSVPs. (Does everyone here know what "RSVP" stands for? The acronym is French, and it stands for, "Remember Send Vedding Present.")

When the day of the king's party arrived, the older brother carefully laid out two beautiful suits: a white one for himself, and a purple one for his brother. Do you know why he chose a purple suit for his brother to wear? Just in case—it shouldn't happen, but ***just in case*** his brother should spill some wine on his suit, it wouldn't show. And do you know why he chose a white suit for himself? Because he knew that he was a careful person and that he would not spill any wine on his suit. He never did.

Then he chose a black tie for himself and a black tie for his brother. The black tie fit very well with his white suit, but he wasn't so sure that it fit so well with the purple suit that his brother was going to wear. But if the king wanted everyone to wear a black tie, who was he to argue with the king?

He chose a pair of shiny black shoes for himself and a pair of shiny black shoes for his brother. He made sure that both suits were clean and pressed.

Then he called his brother and told him that it was time to get dressed for the party. They both got dressed, one in his white suit and the other in his purple suit. They both put on their black ties and their shiny black shoes. Then they looked in the mirror, and both were pleased with how they looked.

But the younger brother said, "It's too early to go. We still have plenty of time. I would like to sit down for a few minutes."

The older brother said, "OK, but be careful that you don't wrinkle your suit!"

The younger brother went to his room and, instead of sitting down, he stretched out on his bed, and soon he fell asleep. When the time came to leave for the party, the older brother tried to wake him up, but he couldn't. He was sleeping so soundly that his brother simply couldn't arouse him. The older brother was angry, and he did not want to be late, so he decided to leave him behind. Half an hour later, the younger brother woke up, realized what had happened, and ran after his older brother, calling, "Hey, wait for me!"

The younger brother reached the palace just as his older brother was being introduced to the king. When the king saw the young man rushing in and taking his place next to his brother—huffing and puffing and out of breath, with his suit all wrinkled, as if he had slept in it (which he had), and with his eyes bleary from sleep and his shoes scuffed from running and his hair mussed by the wind—he demanded an explanation. And when he heard the story, the king decided to punish both the brothers. He punished the younger brother for being so careless and disorganized, and he punished the older brother for not having taken better care of him.

And so the king turned them both into flowers: the white and silky Lotem which, just like the older brother, always blooms precisely on time; and the wrinkled purple Lotem, which always blooms just a little bit later.

That is why we have two kinds of Lotem flowers in the Galilee. And that is why the smooth white one always blooms right on time and the wrinkled purple one blooms a little bit later every year.

And that is why the Jews are known for always being late. In case you have wondered what the origin is of the Jewish custom of coming late, this is it. We are descended from the younger of the Lotem brothers, who lived in the Galilee.

The truth is that not all Jews are always late. German Jews are famous for being punctual. Eastern European Jews and those who come from the Sephardic countries are not so punctual. And to illustrate this truth, let me tell you one of my favorite stories. This story is not only true—all my stories are true—but it actually happened! And I know because I was there.

Many years ago, the daughter of Dr. and Mrs. Ernst Simon of Jerusalem married the son of Dr. and Mrs. Simon Greenberg of New York. Dr. Simon was a professor of education at Hebrew University; Dr. Greenberg was the professor of education at the Jewish Theological Seminary. The wedding took place in the backyard of the Simon home on Ben Maimon Street, in the Rechavia neighborhood of Jerusalem.

The Simons were German Jews, and so they wanted the wedding to begin exactly on time. They scheduled the wedding for 6 o'clock. They invited their German-Jewish friends and their British friends for 6 o'clock. They invited their Arab friends for 7 o'clock. They invited their Jewish friends for 5 o'clock. ***And everyone came on time.***

So the next time you visit Israel, may I suggest that you do so in the spring. Try, if possible, to schedule your visit for Tu Bishvat, the holiday of the trees and the flowers and the season of the year when nature comes alive and the flowers begin to blossom in Israel. And if you can, try to make sure that you schedule your visit to the Galilee for the 15th day of Shvat. And try to be on time. Don't be late. Because if you are late, you may miss the blossoming of the white silky Lotem and only get to see the blossoming of the wrinkled purple one.

A good Tu Bishvat to you all. Let me invite you to the Tu Bishvat seder that the children of our school will be holding tomorrow. We are not going to send you a fancy invitation, the kind that has gold letters and is decorated with silver and gems, because we are not quite as rich as King Solomon was and we therefore cannot afford to send out invitations that require five stamps to mail. But please come if you can. You don't have to wear a black tie. You can wear a white suit if you want to, because we will not be serving wine and so there is no danger that you will spill any on your suit. And you don't have to go to the beauty parlor or buy new shoes or purchase a new suit for this event. It will be "semi-formal," which means that clean jeans are fine.

But do try to come on time. Because if you don't, everyone will know which Lotem brother you are descended from.

19

# Search Committee Report to the Congregation

## By Rabbi Purim Dreamer, Secretary

The search committee, under the leadership of Paul Erbstein, has been working night and day in order to find the perfect rabbi for our congregation. We asked the committee to give us an update on how the search is going, for the readers of the Purim issue of the Hakol, and this is what they told us:

The chairman felt that he did not want to have too big a committee since that would be inefficient, and so he has limited the committee to only those people who are learned, pious, intelligent and modest. So far, he has carefully chosen 450 members of Temple Anshe Shalom who meet all these criteria.

The committee began its deliberations by determining the kind of rabbi that we feel would be right for Anshe Shalom. After much discussion, we decided that we want a rabbi who will bring in the youth while devoting all of his time to the old. We want a rabbi who will be active in the general community while being available at all times in his office. We want someone young who has many years of experience. And above all, we are looking for a strong rabbi who will take orders.

With these criteria in mind, we began interviewing candidates. Since Anshe Shalom is a traditional synagogue, we thought we would begin by considering applicants who came from the Bible. Some of them seemed quite promising, but in each case we found some flaw, and since we want the rabbi of our synagogue to be flawless, we have rejected them.

The first candidate we interviewed was a man named Noah. He came with good references from God himself, who told us that he was really outstanding in his generation, a genuine *tsadik*. We felt that, after having had experience dealing with wild animals, dealing with the board would be easy for Noah, and so we were very hopeful that he would be the one. However, we found out that he had a drinking problem, and he came to the interview smelling like someone who lives in a zoo, and so the committee rejected him by a vote of 350 to 145—with five abstentions.

The next candidate was a man named Abraham. He, too, came with very good references. He had done very well in business, and had some military experience, as well. But some of the members of the committee were concerned about his age. Even though you are no longer allowed to ask a candidate his age, the rumors are that he was well up into his 70s when he changed careers and entered the rabbinate. Our committee was also concerned over the fact that he comes from Iraq. They were hoping to find a Galitsianer, and were willing to settle, if necessary, for a Litvak, but the members of the committee were very reluctant to hire an Iraqi and were not sure how he would fit in. There are some unconfirmed rumors, also, that he disagreed with his father over religious matters, that he had an affair with his wife's maid and that he tested his child beyond limits. The committee has decided to check these rumors out before inviting him here for a Shabbat. The decision to postpone inviting him was made by a vote of 300 to143, with seven abstentions.

The next candidate was a man named Jacob. This man evidently also came well recommended, but the committee was concerned over the fact that he had four wives, 12 sons and a daughter. The committee asked: Where, in the Delray area, will he be able to find housing for a family this big? And what kind of a salary will he demand with a family that size? There are some rumors about him, too—that he had some difficulty getting along with his brother and that he has a son who is a flashy dresser. The committee will check these rumors out carefully and let you know what happens. The vote to delay deciding whether to invite him or not was 300 to 142, with eight abstentions.

The next candidate was a man named Moses, who seemed very promising when we first read his resume. He has had lots of administrative experience and has demonstrated real leadership, even though he only entered the rabbinate as a second career at the age of 80. We had high hopes that he would be the one, but when we interviewed him over the telephone, it turned out that he has a speech defect, and so he would certainly not be able to give sermons here at Anshe Shalom. After all, our members are used to the kind of sermons that keep them up at night—because when they sleep during the day, they can't sleep at night. Not only that, but we heard a rumor that he is wanted by the police in Egypt in connection with the murder of an Egyptian taskmaster. And so the committee turned him down by a vote of 349 to 142, with nine abstentions. As you can see, we are getting closer to a consensus with every vote.

The latest candidate for the position of rabbi at Anshe Shalom is the Messiah. The committee was really impressed by his resume. He seems perfect, and we have heard that congregations all over the world are interested in him and waiting to talk to him, so we were really hoping that he would be the one for our synagogue. But we were turned off by the fact that he did not show up for the interview. Can you imagine if we had a committee meeting and had no idea when he was going to show up? One thing is certain: If we do hire him to be the rabbi of our synagogue, we will have to buy him a car. How would it look for the rabbi of Anshe Shalom to get around Atlantic Avenue by donkey? The committee voted to invite him for a Shabbat by a vote of 348 to 142, with 10 abstentions—but so far, we have not heard from him in response. We are waiting.

In the meantime, we ask the congregation to please be patient. As you can see, the committee votes are getting closer every time, and we feel confident that we will eventually find the perfect rabbi for our synagogue. It may take us some time, but we are determined to find a rabbi who will please every single member of our congregation—and the married ones, as well. We are looking for a great scholar who will never be caught studying on our time; one who will be both world-famous and modest; and one who will attract both older and younger members.

For the time being, we will have to make do with our present interim rabbi—even though he has many problems and many defects. His most serious defect is that he gives out kisses in public—during the reading of the Torah! We all know that many a rabbi has lost his job for giving out kisses without supervision, and we have asked him to please give out Tootsie Rolls instead, but so far he has not made this change. The search committee has notified the Rabbinical Assembly that this interim rabbi is causing embarrassment to our congregation by this kind of flagrantly immoral behavior, and they have promised never to send us an interim rabbi like him again.

For further information, come to the Purim service at Anshe Shalom on March 4, where all of these candidates and a great many others will be officiating simultaneously.

We look forward to seeing you there.

With best wishes for a happy Purim,

Rabbi Purim Dreamer,
Corresponding Secretary,
Search Committee,
Anshe Shalom Temple

## 20

# The Enormous Cultural, Political and Economic Influence of the Latke on the Modern World

### Purim

Since this is the week in which we will celebrate the somber and serious, the sober and grim, holiday of Purim, I have decided to give a sermon today about Hanukkah.

I urge you to listen carefully to every word of this sermon today, because I am going to solve three profound questions that have baffled experts for many years.

The first question is one that has puzzled cultural historians for many centuries. We know that, for most of human history, women have done most of the cooking. But who was the first male who found his way into a kitchen? And how did he get there? Who was the first male in history to cook a meal? And where, when and why did this event—which was surely a turning point in the history of civilization—take place? Listen to this sermon today, and you will learn the answer to this question—the question that no historian of human civilization has been able to discover, until now.

The second question which this sermon will answer is this: How did Donald Trump win the election and become the president of the United States? Not one of the experts on politics expected this to happen. Not one of the political experts took him seriously when he announced his candidacy. And yet this man, who had never run for any public office in his entire life—and who belonged to no political party—defeated 16 other candidates and won the nomination, and then he defeated a candidate whom all the experts thought was sure to win, and he became the president of the United States. All the experts agree that the reason he won was because of the slogan that he used in his campaign, which was "Make America Great Again," but no one knows where he got this slogan, what it means or why this slogan struck such a chord in the hearts of so many people all around the country. This slogan evidently touched the hearts of both whites and blacks; both immigrants and natives; both the educated and the non-educated. Experts believe that, more than anything else, it was this slogan that enabled Donald Trump to win the election. But what was it about his slogan that persuaded so many Americans, in so many states and from so many different social, economic and cultural backgrounds, to vote for him? Listen to this sermon and you will learn the answer to this question, which no political expert has been able to explain—until now.

The third question that this sermon will deal with is actually a two-part question, and one that has baffled all of the economists. Experts do not understand why Saudi Arabia, which is such a rich country and which has so much oil, is now going through a severe economic depression. Is it because there are now other sources of energy that are replacing oil? Or is it because the price of oil has gone down so dramatically? Or is there some other explanation? The experts simply do not know the reason, but if you listen to this sermon, you will find out why the economy of Saudi Arabia is in so much trouble today.

At the same time, economists are bewildered by another problem: What has happened to the Chinese economy? China is located many miles away from Saudi Arabia. It is on the other side of the world. And yet the Chinese economy is also in great trouble, just like the economy of Saudi Arabia is. So the economic experts are asking: What's the connection? How come Saudi Arabia—which is located on one continent—and China—which is located on another continent, thousands of miles away—are suffering from a severe economic crisis at the same time?

China is one of the mightiest countries in the world. It produces and sells many products to many countries all over the world. Unlike Saudi Arabia, China has an economy that is not dependent on just one product. Yet China, like Saudi Arabia, is undergoing a severe economic crisis. And nobody knows why.

But if you listen to the sermon today, you will learn the answer to this question, too.

The first part of this sermon came to me from a man named Irwin Keller, who revealed the explanation in an internet magazine called Tablet. The second and third parts of this sermon come out of my deep knowledge of political science and economics, for which I am world-famous. As I am sure you know, the only thing that I am more famous for than for my knowledge of culture, economics and politics is my modesty. I have more modesty in my little finger than most people have in their whole body. So please listen carefully to all three parts of this sermon, for taken together, they will explain three matters that have baffled all the other experts in the world.

Let me begin with a story that I believe explains the rise of masculinism, which is one of the great transformations in the history of civilization. This is the story:

> *Once there was a rebbe in Europe who was called the Krinker Rebbe. Do you know why he was called the Krinker Rebbe? He was called the Krinker Rebbe because he was the rebbe of a village called Krink. He had a wife who was called the Krinker Rebbitzen. Do you know why she was called the Krinker Rebbitzen? It was because she was married to the Krinker Rebbe.*
>
> *The rebbe and the rebbitzen of Krink lived in a small house that was located next door to the beit hamidrash. Every day, the Hassidim would come to the beit hamidrash to ask the rebbe for a blessing, to ask him to help them make a decision, to study Torah with him or just to be in his presence. The rebbe would answer their questions and teach them Torah, and the rebbitzen would sit on the other side of the door and listen to him teach.*
>
> *At night, after the Hassidim left, the rebbe would turn to his wife and ask, "Did I teach well today?" And she would say, "Yes, my dear, you taught very well today. But I have just one small question about what you said." Then she would ask him a question that threw a whole new light on what he had said. He would realize that he had made a mistake, and that he should have taught the Torah or resolved a legal dispute that day with a little bit more clarity, and with a little bit more elegance, than he had. So he would make a note of what she had said, and the next morning, he would begin*

*his class by announcing that he had changed his mind: this was the way he now understood the passage that he had taught the day before. And so he was very proud of her, and she was very proud of him, and all the people of Krink were very proud of them both.*

*Now, it was the custom in the village of Krink that on the sixth night of Hanukkah, the Hassidim would all come to the rebbe's house to wish him well. When the rebbe was finished teaching his people about the meaning of the holiday, the rebbitzen and some of the women in the neighborhood who helped her would come in, carrying trays and trays of latkes for their guests to eat, in honor of the holiday.*

*On all the other Hanukkahs of the years, the rebbitzen did not hesitate to ask the wives of the Hassidim to help her make the latkes. But this year, there was some kind of a virus going around, and so all the women in the neighborhood were sick. How could she ask them to help her make latkes when they were sick in bed? (By the way, do you know that the Hebrew word for sins is aveyros, and the Galitsianer way of pronouncing "aveyros" is "avayris"? The Galitsianer say that you never get sick from doing mitsvos; only from a virus. But that is a subject for another occasion.)*

*This year, the rebbitzen was stuck. What should she do? How could she make latkes for the annual Hanukkah party without the help of the women? How could she turn out 400 latkes all by herself?*

*The rebbitzen thought and thought and thought, and she figured out what she should do. Instead of making all the latkes on the sixth night of Hanukkah, as she usually did, she would start the job of making some on the first night of Hanukkah and make some more every night, until the sixth night of Hanukkah. So every day of Hanukkah, she ran the grater across the potatoes until her elbows ached. Then she chopped and chopped and chopped the onions, and she sprinkled matzah meal and beat eggs into the four pans that she had prepared. And then she stood at the stove, with four pans of oil sputtering, and dropped spoonsful of batter into the oil. She worked her way between the pans so that by the time she got back to the first pan, those latkes were brown on one side and ready to be flipped. By the time she got back to those latkes a second time, they were ready to be lifted from the skillet and put into the roasting pan.*

*It was hard work, especially since the air was full of onion and garlic—as was the rebbitzen's hair, and her apron, too. But she didn't mind. She felt as if God was standing right next to her while she worked, and she would pour out her heart to him as she made the latkes. She said to him, "Ribono shel oylom, may these latkes turn out well, and may my husband's Hassidim enjoy them, and may our people never go hungry, and may the whole world be at peace. Oomayn." And then she would sing a sweet and gentle niggun to herself as she worked.*

*By the fifth day of Hanukkah, she had made over 400 latkes—enough for the Hassidim to enjoy when they would come to her house, on the sixth night of Hanukkah. But she still had one problem to solve: Where should she store these latkes (since they did not have refrigerators or freezers in those days)?*

*She put on her coat and her gloves and her shawl, and she went next door to the beit hamidrash. She put the five big bowls of latkes in the cellar, because she knew that no one ever went down there and she figured that they would be safe there. She made five trips, one trip after another, and soon she had put all the latkes that she had made on the first five nights of Hanukkah into the cellar next door.*

*The next night—on the sixth night of Hanukkah, while the rebbe was teaching the Hassidim—she went back to the beit hamidrash to get the latkes.*

*And guess what? They had disappeared!*

*She looked, and she looked, and she looked—but the jars of latkes that she had put there were all gone!*

*She said to herself, "Where could they have gone? Who could have taken them?"*

*She had heard of serial killers, but she had never heard of serial latke takers, and so she did not know what to think. Then she thought of the one person who might have taken her latkes.*

*So she went upstairs and knocked on the door of Zalman, the shamash. When he came to the door, she said to him, "Reb Zalman, have you by any chance been in the cellar lately?"*

*Reb Zalman said, "Yes, rebbitzen, I have. It is funny that you should ask, because I almost never go down there, but we needed some more candles for the Hanukkah menorahs today and I remembered storing some candles away there last year, so I went down to look for them."*

*"And did you happen to see any jars of mine while you were down there?" asked the rebbitzen.*

*"Were those yours?" asked Reb Zalman. "As a matter of fact, I did see them. I don't know when you put them there, but did you know that they were full of latkes?"*

*"Yes, I know," said the rebbitzen.*

*Reb Zalman said, "They were cold, but they smelled good. I didn't know if it was kosher to eat last year's latkes or not."*

*"Last year's latkes?" said the rebbitzen.*

*"Yes," said Reb Zalman. "That is what I assumed they were, for who would put this year's latkes in the cellar? So I asked the rebbe, and he said it was better not to eat them if they were last year's latkes."*

*"He did?" said the rebbitzen.*

*"Yes, rebbitzen, that's what he said," said Zalman.*

*"And so what did you do with the latkes, Reb Zalman?" asked the rebbitzen.*

*"I fed them to the chickens," said Zalman. "I bet the chickens have never had such a good meal in their lives, and I bet that they will turn out extra-good eggs this year in appreciation."*

*The rebbitzen thought of many things that she could have said to Reb Zalman at this moment, but she gritted her teeth and said nothing, and she went back to her house.*

*When she got there, she saw the first of the Hassidim were already starting to arrive. She went into the kitchen and looked around. What should she do? She saw that she still had enough potatoes with which she could make more latkes. She saw that she still had enough onions. She saw that she still had enough oil. But she saw that she only had two hands. And so she wondered: How can I make 400 new latkes with just two hands?*

*And then she got an idea. She walked into the parlor, which was now crowded with men. Her husband was just lighting the candles.*

*"Oomayn," she said, as he finished the second blessing. The rebbe and his students turned to her, for they were not accustomed to hearing a woman's voice during the blessings. Reciting the blessings over the menorah was a man's job—everybody knew that—and usually, the rebbitzen of Krink waited in the kitchen until the candles were lit, as all good rebbitzens did.*

*The rebbe said to her, "Hartsele mein, is there something you want to say?"*

*"Yes, my darling, there is," she said. "I would like to make an announcement."*

*The room stirred as she cleared her throat.*

*"Let me tell you that this year, the sixth night of Hanukkah is going to be different from all the other sixth nights of Hanukkah in history. It is going to be very special. It will be remembered in history for two things: It will be remembered in history as the year that the latkes disappeared, and it will also be remembered in history as the year in which hidden treasures were revealed."*

*You can imagine the reaction that this announcement caused. The Hassidim all began talking at once. What could the rebbitzen mean? How could the latkes have disappeared? And what did she mean when she said that this was the year in which hidden treasures were going to be revealed?*

*The rebbe said, "Hartsele, kronele, what do you mean?"*

*The rebbitzen said, "If you will all follow me outside, I will show you what I mean."*

*And so the Hassidim put on their coats, their gloves and their scarves, and they followed the rebbitzen outside.*

*The rebbitzen pointed up to the heavens, and she said, "Gentlemen, what do you see?"*

*The Hassidim looked up at the sky, and they said, "We see the new moon of Tevet. It has come out tonight, just as it always does on the sixth night of Hanukkah."*

*The rebbitzen said, "Very good. Now tell me, do you see the whole moon of Tevet? "*

*The Hassidim answered, "Of course not. On the first night of Tevet, only a tiny sliver of the new moon can be seen. The rest is there, but it is not yet visible. It is hidden until the full moon comes out, on the 15th day of the month."*

*"Very good," said the rebbitzen. "You have seen only a tiny sliver of the moon tonight. The rest is there, but it is not visible. In the same way, I want you to know that you have many, many blessings that you do not usually see. You have clothes to*

*wear, you have beds to sleep in and you have food to eat. You have the Torah to study and learn from. You have ideas and you have a community of people to share your ideas with. You have skills that you don't even know you have. You have resources inside you that you have never been aware that you have. You have abilities inside you that you have never even thought of using. You have hidden treasures. You just have to notice that they are there.*

*Now, gentlemen, if you understand that, let us go inside."*

*The Hassidim filed into the house. And as they did, the rebbe took his wife's arm. She turned to him, and said, "Did I teach well tonight, my dear?" And he smiled, and said, "Yes, my darling. You taught very well. And I believe that you are the hidden treasure that I sometimes overlook, and now my Hassidim know that, too."*

*"That is very kind of you to say, my darling," said the rebbitzen, "but wait. There is still a little bit more hidden treasure that is waiting to be revealed."*

*The rebbitzen entered the house and clapped her hands to get the Hassidim's attention. She said, "Gentlemen, we are not quite finished yet. Follow me." And she led them into the kitchen. Most of the men had never been in a kitchen in their lives, but if the rebbitzen said that they should follow her into the kitchen—they followed her into the kitchen.*

*When they got there, the rebbitzen said, "And now, gentlemen, we are going to use your resources that have been kept in the dark until now. We are*

> *going to use the treasure that God has given you in order to solve the problem that we have tonight. Are you ready?"*
>
> *"Yes, rebbitzen, we're ready," they responded.*
>
> *"Good." The rebbitzen smiled. "Let's begin." And she reached for something that was lying on the table, and she held it up, and she said:*
>
> *"Gentlemen, let me introduce you to this object. This is a grater."*
>
> *And that is how it all began.*

Ever since that night, men have felt that they have just as much of a right to be in the kitchen as women do. And men have felt that they can be cooks and chefs, just as women can be. Men have felt that they have the right to vote, just as women do. And men have felt that they have the right to go to college, just as women do. And today, masculinism—the idea that men and women have equal rights—is taken for granted in our society. But it all began on that night in Krink, when the *rebbitzen* of Krink showed the men of Krink, on the sixth night of Hanukkah, that just as the moon is partly visible and partly hidden on Rosh Hodesh, so does every person—male or female—have a hidden treasure of talent and ability and potential located inside. Therefore, both women and men are allowed to make latkes.

The world has never been the same since, and we owe it all to the *rebbitzen* of Krink.

Now let me tell you the real story of how Donald Trump became the president of the United States: a story that has never been told before.

Donald Trump may not have much experience in governing until now, but he is a wise man. One of the proofs of his wisdom is that, when he does not know what to do, he is not afraid to ask other people for advice. And so, when he was thinking about running for president, he came to me and asked for my advice. I guess he figured that if I can be the interim rabbi of a congregation as sophisticated and as cultured as this one is, I must be a pretty smart person. And so he came to my office, and he said to me, "Rabbi, can you please tell me how can I get people to vote for me? People think that I am just a television star or a businessman. How can I persuade them to make me their president?"

I told him, "Mr. Trump, your whole program is based on the idea of making America prosperous again. Your goal is to change things so that America sells more overseas and buys less overseas, so as to improve the balance of trade. And therefore, this is my suggestion: You should try to persuade Americans to stop buying ready-made latkes in the supermarket, for most of these latkes come from Vietnam or Korea or some other such place overseas. You should start persuading Americans to make their own latkes at home. And for that, you need to have a slogan or a motto. And my suggestion is that the motto of your campaign should be this: ***"Make America Grate Again."*** G.R.A.T E. I said to him, "Trust me. If you use this slogan—if you put it up on every billboard in the country, if you put it on all your campaign buttons, if you exhibit it on placards and posters at every one of your campaign rallies; if you even put it on your hat, so that everyone who watches you on television sees it—I promise you that you will win the election." And he did. He listened to me, and he made "Make America Grate Again" his slogan, and that is how he won.

So this is the second example of how latkes have changed the world. Latkes brought about the rise of masculinism, and latkes brought about the election of Donald Trump.

The third example that I want to tell you about today is how latkes have changed the economies of both Saudi Arabia and China.

There was a time when American Jews bought oil from Saudi Arabia with which to make their latkes. But then assimilation took over in American-Jewish life. Now some

Jews no longer keep kosher; some Jews no longer observe the Jewish holidays; some Jews no longer observe Shabbat, or Rosh Hashana, or Yom Kippur, or even Hanukkah. I hate to tell you this, but some Jews no longer even make latkes. And so the economy of Saudi Arabia, which depends entirely on the sale of oil, has gone way, way down, and Saudi Arabia is now in a severe economic crisis … simply because of the assimilation that is taking place among the Jews of America.

You may think that I am exaggerating about the relationship between American-Jewish assimilation and the crisis in the economy of Saudi Arabia, but I am not. Let me prove it to you by citing my friend and colleague, Rabbi Jeffrey Salkin, who has done research on this topic. Rabbi Salkin found that there are approximately 5 or 6 million Jews in this country, depending on whom you count. Now, if all of these Jews celebrated Hanukkah, and if all these Jews made latkes—and if they all used my *bubbie*'s recipe, which calls for one-half of a cup of oil for every four to six servings of latkes—that would mean that the Jews of America would use at least ***500,000 cups of oil per night***! Now multiply that by eight nights of Hanukkah, and you would have ***4 million cups of oil*** being consumed during the holiday. And now you have some idea of what the assimilation of American Jewry is doing to the economy of Saudi Arabia.

The same thing is happening to the economy of China. How did Jews used to observe Christmas? By going to Chinese restaurants! Do you remember when Elana Kagan was nominated for the Supreme Court? She was being interviewed by the Judiciary Committee of the United States Senate, and for some reason—I don't know why—one of the senators asked her what she did on Christmas Eve.

She answered, very simply: "I do what all Jews do on Christmas Eve—I have dinner in a Chinese restaurant." And when she said that, everyone in the room laughed with approval, and she was confirmed.

That happened a few years ago. But I don't know if it would happen today, because Jews keep assimilating at a faster and faster rate. Some Jews no longer observe Jewish holidays, and some Jews no longer even observe the Christian holidays in the same way that they used to just a few years ago.

And do you know what that means? The Chinese restaurants these Jews used to go to on Christmas Eve were owned by immigrants who came here from China. When these restaurants flourished, their owners would send money back to their relatives who lived in China. And these relatives would then invest in the Chinese economy. But now that Jews have assimilated in large numbers, and now that Jews in large numbers no longer observe either Jewish holidays or non-Jewish holidays, the Chinese restaurants in this country are in big trouble. And so they are no longer able to send money back to their relatives in China. And that is why the Chinese economy is in such big trouble.

Therefore, it is clear that masculinism has come about because of the *rebbitzen* of Krink, who made men help her make latkes with which the Hassidim would celebrate Hanukkah in Krink; if it were not for her, the whole Western world would be very different today, and men would not have equal rights, as they do now.

And therefore, it is clear that Donald Trump only won the presidency because he listened to me, and made "Let's Make America Grate Again"—G—R—A—T—E—his slogan. And it is clear that the American balance of trade would now be in our favor, as it used to be, if we would stop buying ready-made latkes that come from Vietnam or Korea in the supermarket and, instead, we started making our latkes at home, the way we used to.

Therefore, it is clear that Saudi Arabia and China will only recover if the people in this congregation repent and reform, stop assimilating and return to the old and sacred ways of our people, which include keeping Shabbat, keeping Pesach and keeping all the other parts of the Jewish way of life—or, if they don't do that, then at least return to the ancient Jewish tradition that was followed by Justice Kagan and so many others, and go back to observing Christmas by eating in Chinese restaurants.

I hope that my sermon this morning has convinced you of the central role that the latke has played in the cultural, political and economic life of the Western world. I hope that it will inspire you to eat homemade latkes next year, and to keep all of the other practices, customs and commandments that make us a sacred people and a key force in the Western world.

I wish you all a *freilichen* Purim.

And to this, if you agree, will you say: Amen.

21

# How a Major Halachic Crisis Has Been Averted

## The Disassociated Press, Purim 5772

We are happy to report that a major *halachic* crisis has been averted in our community, thanks to the flexibility and the liberalism of the *beth din Tsedek* of Delray Beach.

The crisis occurred a few days before Purim, when a self-appointed member of the *Tsniut* Patrol was inspecting his neighbor's kitchen and discovered—may the Lord save and protect us—a container of Aunt Jemima's buckwheat located on the ***same shelf*** as a package of Uncle Ben's converted rice. In total disregard of the law that men and women should not be together in such close quarters, the crisis was compounded by the fact that the pantry in which Ms. Jemima and Mr. Ben were together had a closed door, so that who knows what kind of activities the two of them may have engaged in—without being married, or even engaged!

The crisis was re-compounded by the fact that Aunt Jemima's picture was on the cover of the buckwheat container—which made the container clearly forbidden for any pious person to look upon.

The people of Delray Beach were prepared to riot in protest against this desecration of all that is holy to our people. They were going to go on a house-by-house search of the entire city, to see if any other flagrant violations of the holy Torah could be found. And they were preparing to riot in the streets until such time as both products were taken off the market in every city in the entire county of Palm Beach. Fortunately, the *beth din Tsedek* of Delray Beach, which is noted for its flexibility and liberalism, acted quickly and worked out a compromise.

The first question that they had to deal with was whether Aunt Jemima and Uncle Ben were married. They decided that they could not be, since Aunt Jemima is an Ethiopian Jew—judging by her appearance—and we know that Ethiopian Jews are not really Jews. (Only Galitsianers and Litvaks are considered real Jews, and we are not completely sure about them.) And so the *beth din Tsedek* ruled that Aunt Jemima is not Jewish, and therefore the laws of the Torah do not apply to her. The fact that Aunt Jemima wears a *tichel* on her head is irrelevant, and it may in fact be part of her strategy to show off her *frumkeit*, which this *beth din* is too wise to be taken in by.

The second question was more complicated: Was Uncle Ben's converted rice kosher? This depends, of course, on who converted Uncle Ben. If he was converted by a Reform or Conservative *beth din*, *chas vishalom, chas vishalom, chas vishalom*, then obviously his conversion is not valid and he is not Jewish. This everyone in the world knows, because as it is written, "*Kulo olam lo pilegey*"—"the whole world is against divisiveness." But if the court that converted Uncle Ben's rice was a branch of the Chief Rabbinate—or some other such court that we do not recognize, but about which we only say two *chas vishaloms* instead of three, because we are flexible and liberal—the conversion is also not recognized by us. Therefore, we *paskin* that the conversion of Uncle Ben's rice is invalid, and therefore that the laws of the Torah do not apply to him.

Therefore we, the *beth din Tsedek* of Delray Beach, hereby decide that Aunt Jemima and Uncle Ben may be in the same pantry, especially since there are many other kosher products in the shelf that can serve as witnesses.

However, the *beth din Tsedek* of Delray Beach—which is known for its flexibility and its desire for compromise—sets forth two conditions:

First, that the two products should be housed on separate shelves and a minimum of four *amot* apart, and they should not be facing each other. We make this ruling because of *Marit Ayin*, which means: What would Mrs. Ayin think if she went by and saw these two inhabiting—or cohabiting—the same shelf? Since we always defer to Mrs. Ayin's point of view in *halachah*, we rule that the two products should be housed on different shelves.

The second condition we set forth is that the picture of Ms. Jemima must be removed from the container. Anyone who looks at this picture will see that she is a tantalizingly beautiful woman who would cause lascivious thoughts to enter the minds of young Torah students, *chas vishalom, chas vishalom, chas vishalom*, and therefore we rule that her picture must be airbrushed off the cover of this container.

By permitting Mr. Ben and Ms. Jemima to coexist in the same closet, and without requiring either one of them to come out of the closet—something that the *beth din Tsedek* of *Bet Shemesh* forbids for people, but insists upon for products that are not kosher—the *beth din Tsedek* of Delray Beach has once again demonstrated a flexibility and liberalism that has won the admiration of the entire world (except for those few Conservative, Reform and Modern Orthodox Jews—may their numbers decrease—who do not accept the rulings of the *beth din Tsedek* of Delray Beach).

The case of the *kashrut* of Mr. Clean is still being adjudicated. Everyone on the court agrees that Mr. Clean is *treyfe* and cannot be eaten. The only *halachic* question left to be decided is whether or not it can be used for cleaning purposes, even though it is forbidden as food.

We will provide the *beth din* of Delray Beach's decision on this question at Purim services, which will be held at Congregation Anshei Shalom next week. Please note that we are not announcing the day or the time that the Megillah will be read, because we are afraid that children may find out and come to the services, and that they may even tap their feet or wave their handkerchiefs when You-Know-Who's name is read, which would spoil the decorum of the services. Since Anshe Shalom is noted for its dignity and its decorum, we would not want this to happen. So please—please—***please***—do not tell your children that the Megillah will be read next Wednesday evening at 7 o'clock.

22

# Reflections on the Four Children

## Pesach

I want to do three things today, if I can.

First, I want to share with you a reflection on the passage about the four children that we read about in the *Haggadah.* I want to tell you why I have problems with this passage, and I want to tell you a story about how one father related to his child—a story that I believe we can all learn from. And I want to tell you about a passage we heard today that moves me very much every time I hear it.

Let me begin by saying that I know that most people refer to this passage as "the four sons," but that is a mistranslation. Just as *avot* means "ancestors," and not "fathers," so *arba banim* means "the four children," and not "the four sons."

Let me say one thing more about this passage, which I hope you will not be offended by: the passage that describes the four children is not my favorite part of the *Haggadah*

—not by a long shot. I am not comfortable with it because I do not believe that children should be labeled or categorized this way. If you tell one of your children that he is the smartest one, you will make him arrogant and conceited, and you will cause envy among your children. If you don't believe me, ask Father Jacob, who made that mistake and paid for it in pain. If you tell one of your children that he is bad, he will be bad: It will be a self-fulfilling prophecy. And the truth is that none of us are all-good, or all-bad. We are combinations of all of these qualities, and so are our children.

I learned this lesson from the artwork in the Conservative *Haggadah*. The illustrations in that *Haggadah* were done by an artist named Dan Reissinger, who used four colors in drawing the four children. Each color stands for a different characteristic: intelligence, wickedness, simplicity and inability to ask. Reissinger drew each of the four children in a combination of the four colors. In one drawing, one color is dominant; in another, a different color is dominant; but all four of the children have all four of the colors. This is his way of teaching us that we are all combinations. One may be smart in one subject but not smart in another. One may be bad in one area and good in another. One may be simple about some things and sophisticated about other things. One may not know how to ask about some things, but know how to ask about other things. All of us have all four of these qualities in our natures and none of us has only one of these four qualities. And that is a very important lesson for us to learn.

It is interesting to see how the different artists who have illustrated the *Haggadah* over the years have described the wicked child. There was a *Haggadah* that was done by J.D. Eisenstein back in the 1920s, and it had artwork by someone named Lola—whoever she was. That *Haggadah* pictured the wise son as a yeshiva student, and the wicked son as a prize fighter. Why? Because in the 1920s, in the world of the immigrant Jews, to be a prize fighter meant to separate oneself from one's family and from the Jewish way of life.

In contrast to that *Haggadah*, which glorifies the yeshiva student and criticizes the prize fighter, let me tell you about a *Haggadah* that does the very opposite. There were a number of *Haggadot* published by the secular *kibbutzim* back in the '30s and '40s, and in some of these, the wicked son was pictured as a yeshiva student. Why? Because the yeshiva student did not farm; the yeshiva student did not work; the yeshiva student did not fight; the yeshiva student did not involve himself in helping the illegal immigrants, and so he was pictured as the wicked child.

I have one *Haggadah* in which the four children are pictured as the four Marx brothers: Harpo, Chico, Groucho and Zippo. And I have one *Haggadah* in my collection that came out during the years of the struggle of Soviet Jewry. In this one, Khrushchev is pictured as the wicked child. I have one *Haggadah* that came out in the early years of the arrival of the Jews in America from eastern Europe, in which the wicked child is pictured smoking a cigarette that he has lit from the *yontif* candlesticks. Can you picture a more brazen act of defiance than that? In this picture, the father and mother are pictured trying to look away, trying not to see what the wicked son is doing to desecrate the holiday before their eyes. And in the *Haggadah* that David Moss did, the four children are pictured as playing cards. Can you guess why? Because the kind of children you get is a matter of chance. No one can predict, and no one can control—no matter what you do—how your children will turn out.

So there are many different *Haggadahs*, and they contain many different understandings of whom the four children represent. My favorite is the Gateways *Haggadah*, which came out recently. In this *Haggadah*, the one who does not know how to ask is the mentally challenged child, or the child with Down syndrome. He sits at the Seder—bewildered, confused, unable to ask and sometimes unable to deal with the noise around him. Of him, the *Haggadah* says *At pitach lo*—You must open him up: you must help him feel at home at the Seder, and you must explain to him what is going on, at his level. (By the way, do you know that there is an organization that tries to deal with the issues of these children and to make sure that they get a Jewish education? And do you know that this organization has a wonderful name? It is called "Pitach." Why is it called this? Likely because the *Haggadah* says *At pitach lo*—you should open him up—and that is what this organization was created to do).

The Gateways *Haggadah* has more than just translation or transliteration. It has braille in it, for those who cannot see. And it has pictures in it for every passage and every word in the *Haggadah*, so that those who cannot read can still understand the service.

How many are there who need such a book? If there is only one—and it is your child—then this book is well worth the effort that went into it. But we are now aware that the number of young Jewish people who are mentally challenged or who are handicapped is much higher than we thought. And so this is a very valuable *Haggadah*.

Now, let me tell you the story that I promised you.

But before I do, let me point out that this is a story that deals with questions that almost all of us have to deal with at some time in our lives. These are questions such as: What do you do if your child breaks your heart? What do you do if your child goes a different way than you have? What do you do if your child hurts you, shames you or disappoints you by the way in which he lives? And above all, what do you do on Seder night if he either does not come—or if you are not sure that you want him there?

I cannot look inside your mind or soul and say for sure, but I suspect that there are probably some people sitting here right now who have had—or perhaps still have—these questions. How does the old joke go? "Insanity is hereditary; you get it from your children."

And so I want to tell you a story about how one famous Jewish leader dealt with this question. The story that I am about to tell you is technically a Purim story, not a Pesach story, because it took place at a Purim *seudah*—at the festive meal you are traditionally supposed to have in order to celebrate the holiday of Purim. It is a Purim story, but I think it is a story that speaks to the hearts of many of us who—for whatever reason, the reason does not really matter—who are on the outs with one of our children or who have children who have chosen to live their lives differently than we do.

The story is about Rabbi Yitschak Izaac Halevi Herzog, who was the first chief rabbi of the State of Israel. Rabbi Herzog was a rabbi of the old school. He was a learned Torah scholar, and he did much after the war to help find and bring back Jewish children who had been given away by their parents for safekeeping and who had never been reclaimed again—either because their families died in the war, or because they were being raised in the homes of non-Jews who did not want to give them back.

You may not know the name "Rabbi Herzog," but you probably know the name of his distinguished son, Chaim Herzog. Chaim Herzog was the head of the Israeli Air Force during the Six-Day War. He was the Israeli Ambassador to the United Nations at a crucial time; and later on he was president of the State of Israel.

If you had a son who held all of these positions, you would probably be very proud of him. But Rabbi Herzog came from a different world than we do. He was proud of his son: he had *naches* from his achievements. But deep down in his heart, he wished that his son would have been a yeshiva student instead. Deep down he wished that his son would have continued in his footsteps and been an observant and pious Jew.

But what do you do when that does not happen?

Rabbi Sholom Gold, who says that he was present when this encounter took place, tells this story:

A young man went from America to Israel, in order to study the Torah there. While he was there, he and several other students from his yeshiva decided to take a train from

Tel Aviv to Jerusalem to see if they could get into the Purim *seudah* that was held every year at the home of Chief Rabbi Herzog. They somehow got in, and when the rabbi heard that one of them was an American Jew who had come all the way from America in order to study Torah in Israel, he put them in the seats of honor right next to him.

The boys looked around the room and saw that there were many celebrities there. There were cabinet ministers, poets and novelists; there were political leaders and spiritual leaders. There were distinguished members of the faculty of the Hebrew University there. And they felt very honored that they had not only been allowed to attend this *seudah*, but that they had been given seats of honor, right up front, right near the rabbi himself.

And then the door opened—and General Herzog, head of the Israeli Air Force, walked in. He was in full battle regalia, wearing what they used to call, in those days, an "Eisenhower jacket." His had half a dozen medals on it. And he came in accompanied by two bodyguards, as befit his position. He came in, quietly took a chair somewhere near the middle of the table, and sat down.

Chaim Herzog was a handsome, charismatic man. He was one of the most important and imposing men in the country. And so when he came in, a hush fell over the room. Then everyone turned to see what the father would say to the son whom he had not seen in a long time.

The father met the eyes of his son, who was sitting halfway across the long dinner table. He got up and walked over to him, and as he did, he said, "*Chaim'll*, my son, *Chaim'll*. How good of you to come!" He hugged his son and then he led him to the front of the table.

Chaim Herzog followed his father to the head of the table. When they stood there together, you could feel the warmth and the *derech eretz*—the respect that he had for his father, and the love that Rabbi Herzog had for his son.

And then Rabbi Herzog turned to Sholom Gold, who was sitting at the head of the table. He said to his son, "*Chaim'll*, do you see this boy? He came all the way from America to study Torah! Can you imagine that?"

Then the father said to his son, "Give this boy a *Sholom Aleichem*, will you, please?"

And Chaim Herzog, head of the Israeli Air Force, did as he was told. He reached across the table and said *Sholom Aleichem* to the boy who had come from America to study Torah.

Afterward, Sholom Gold said, he realized what was happening in that brief conversation between this father and son. The father had made his peace with the fact that his son had gone a different way. He was reconciled with the fact that his son had chosen to go into the armed forces, and that after that he would go into the diplomatic corps. But he was sending a message to his son. By introducing his son to Sholom Gold, and by telling him how impressed he was with a boy who had come all the way from America in order to study Torah in Israel, he was sending his son the message that he considered Torah to be the most important thing—more important than anything else. He was saying this and sending this message not with a rebuke, with chastisement, with an insult or with anger—but subtly, gently and tactfully.

That is how you should treat a son who decides to go in a different way than you do! You welcome him if he decides to come to the Seder! You welcome him, whether he comes on time or comes late. You welcome him, whether he comes alone or whether he brings with him someone you don't approve of. You welcome him because he is your child, and you love him—no matter what!

Isn't that a powerful story?

Most of us who are here today do not have the problem that Rabbi Herzog had. We do not have the problem of how do you deal with a son who does not want to live a life of Torah the way that we do. But some of us have problems that are a little bit like that problem. Someone here may have the problem of having built up a mighty business and now dealing with a son who wants to be an artist or a musician or a sculptor, and does not want to go into your business. Some of us are political conservatives who see the world one way, and may have children who are political radicals and see the world in a very different way. Some of us have broken relationships as a result of these conflicts. Some of us do not hear from and do not contact our children or our parents because they have chosen to live a different way than we do.

And what do you do if you have that problem?

I suggest to you today that, if this is your problem, then you should do what Rabbi Herzog did. I suggest to you that you welcome them to your Seder and that you thank God they are there, regardless of whatever separates you from each other. That is what most of the people of the first generation of Jews who came to America did, and that is what I urge you to do, this *yontif*.

I began by telling you about a verse in the *Haggadah* that I do not like: the one that labels children and categorizes them. Let me finish by telling you about a verse that I love.

It is the verse that comes at the end of the *haftorah* that we recited today. It is the prophet Malachi's vision of the way the world will be at the end of days. He says that when Elijah comes, "*viheyshiv lev avot el banim, vilev banim el avotam*"—that on that great day, God will restore the hearts of parents to their children—that, it seems to me, is not so hard to do—and God will restore the hearts of the children to their parents—and that is a real miracle when it happens.

May that day come soon, for all of us and for our children.

And to this, let us all say: Amen.

23

# What Should You Pack When You Go on a Trip?

## Seventh Day of Pesach

I have one thing I feel I have to say before I begin my sermon today.

My wife has made me promise that I will tell you that all of the critical things that I am going to say about her in this sermon are absolutely untrue—or, at least, are greatly exaggerated.

And I have now done so. So let me begin:

You should know that if my wife and I ever get divorced—*chas vishalom, chas vishalom, chas vishalom*, poo, poo, poo, *nisht far unts gidacht*, and God forbid, ***God forbid***, may it not happen—if we ever get divorced it will be over packing. That is the only time we ever fight.

Whenever we go on a trip, I always make the same complaint. As I put the 10th or 11th suitcase into the car, I say to my wife, "You know, my parents came to America with less luggage than we are taking for this weekend!"

By now, my wife is smart enough not to answer. She lets me grumble about how much we are taking with us. And then, when we get to the airport, she gets her revenge. When the security guard asks her, "Did anyone else help you pack these things?" she answers, "Are you kidding? I did it all myself. He didn't even lift a finger!"

My wife takes summer clothing with her and winter clothing with her, too, ***just in case*** the weather changes. She takes so many drugs with her that I am always afraid we are going to get arrested and accused of smuggling drugs.

For weeks before the trip, she lies awake at night, wrestling with these questions: Should I take a sweater, just in case it gets cold, and should I take a second sweater, in addition, ***just in case*** the air conditioning in the restaurant is set too high? Should I take sneakers, just in case my feet hurt? Should I take sandals, ***just in case*** we go for a walk on the beach? (Sometimes we take trips to places that are located hundreds of miles from the nearest beach, but you never can tell.)

Should I take a hat, just in case the sun is strong? And should I pack an umbrella, ***just in case*** it rains? (Even though it does not rain in the desert very often, you never can tell.) Should I take sunscreen to prevent sunburn? Should I take something else to cure sunburn, if I do get it, in spite of the sunscreen?

The key phrase in my wife's packing is "just in case." Like a Boy Scout, my wife tries to be prepared for any and every emergency that might occur—***just in case***. So, if we were to go to the Equator, we would probably take snowshoes with us, "just in case" it snowed. And if we were to go to the North Pole, we would probably take bathing suits with us, "just in case" it got hot. And that is why we travel for a weekend with ten or eleven suitcases packed to the gills. "Just in case" is the motto with which we travel.

This week it occurred to me that we are not the only ones who travel this way. In fact, now I know where my wife got this idea of taking things along "just in case." She got it from the Israelite women whom we read about in the Torah on the seventh day of Pesach.

We know that the Israelites left Egypt in a big hurry. The Torah says that they did not even wait for their bread to rise. When the call came to leave, they rushed out, taking only their luggage and their *matza* with them. I picture the Israelite women looking around for rope with which to tie their suitcases, and sitting on them to make sure that they closed, while their husbands yell at them, "C'mon already! If you don't finish packing already, they are going to leave without us. Hurry up, will you, please!"

And yet there is one line in today's Torah reading that surprised me when I read it this morning. The Torah says that God performed a great wonder: He caused the Red Sea to split, so that the Israelites could pass through in safety. But then, that God performed a second wonder: He caused the waters to come back together again, so that the Egyptians drowned in the sea. That part I knew already. That part I remembered from last year's Torah reading. But then comes a sentence that I had never really noticed before. The Torah says:

> *Vatikach Miriam, then Miriam, the prophetess, the sister of Aaron, took a timbrel in her hand, and all the women went out after her and they danced with timbrels. And Miriam chanted:*
>
> *"Ashira L'Adonay, ki ga-a ga-a,*
>
> *Sus virochvo yara bayam."*
>
> *"I will sing to the Lord, for he has triumphed gloriously;*
>
> *Horse and rider he has hurled into the sea.'"*

Do you see what is strange about this passage?

Read it again: "Then Miriam, the Prophetess, the sister of Aaron, took a timbrel in her hand, and all the women went out after her and they danced with timbrels."

Did you catch what is strange in this line? Not the word "timbrels." I imagine a timbrel is probably some kind of a tambourine. That is not the strange part of the story.

The strange part, which I had never thought about before, is this: Where did they get the timbrels from?

Surely there was no souvenir shop or music store anywhere near the Red Sea, where the women could stop and buy timbrels. Archeologists have searched the area on both sides of the Red Sea carefully, and they have not found a single music store or gift shop or tourist trap in the whole area.

So the only explanation that I can think of is that the Israelite women, on the night they left Egypt, must have chosen to pack timbrels and to take them along on the journey. Why did they do that? The answer is obvious. They did it ***just in case***.

I picture the scene this way: The Israelite women in Egypt spent their last night in slavery frantically going through their belongings, trying to decide what to take with them and what to leave behind. Should they take winter clothes? Probably not, because they were going to be traveling through the desert. But on the other hand, sometimes it gets cold at night in the desert, so maybe they should take along some winter clothing for themselves and for their husbands and children—just in case. And should they take jewelry? Probably not, because what use would jewelry be in the desert? But on the other hand, who knows? Perhaps Moses would want jewelry with which to make the breastplate for the *kohen gadol*, or for some of the furniture in the *mishkan*. Maybe they should take at least some jewelry, they decided, "just in case." And should they take stamps and stationary with them, so that they could write letters to their women friends in Egypt? Probably not, because once they left, they would very likely have little to do with these women. But on the other hand, they had lived in Egypt a long time and had formed deep friendships with some of these women. Maybe they should take some stamps and some stationary along with them—just in case.

And so it went. The Israelite women must have been up all night that last night in Egypt, trying to decide what to take and what to leave behind.

And then, guess what happened? As the women were going through their cupboards and their closets, they must have come across timbrels. This one found a timbrel in a closet; this one on a shelf; this one in a shopping bag that was lying on the floor in one of the back rooms. And each woman must have had the same thought: Who knows where we are going? Who knows what we will find there? We may find lots and lots of stores along the way—that could be. But what if something wonderful happens to us along the way? What if God does something for us that is so great, so wonderful, that we want to sing and dance to celebrate it? If that should happen, won't we need to have these timbrels with us? And besides, how much room does a timbrel take up in a suitcase? Not much, so let us take these timbrels along—just in case. And so that is what they did.

And their husbands, when they saw their wives packing these timbrels, must have "burched," just the way I do when I see how much my wife takes when we go on a trip. They must have said to their wives: "What on earth are you doing schlepping timbrels? Do you think you are going to a jamfest, or to a concert by the Grateful Dead? We are going on a trek through the wilderness, and we have no idea how long this trek will take. It may take weeks, it may take months—for all we know, it might take 40 years! And we are not going to have porters along to schlep this stuff for us. And do you know how much you have already packed? Do me a favor, will you, please, and leave these timbrels behind? For I ask you: What are the odds that we will need timbrels on this trip?"

That is what the husbands said to their wives on their last night in Egypt. And the wives? The wives, just like my wife does, ignored the complaints of their husbands. And they took timbrels, wrapped them up in newspaper, and stuffed them into their suitcases.

And guess what? When the Israelite women arrived at the far side of the Red Sea—when they saw the great favor that God did for Israel in splitting the waters so they could pass through, and when they saw the Egyptians drowning in the sea—they all unpacked their timbrels and broke out into song, and they all followed Miriam in a great dance.

And their husbands?

Do you know what their husbands said? Their husbands watched them dance, and listened to them play their timbrels, and they said to themselves, as husbands are wont to do: "I am sure glad that they listened to us and took along these timbrels like we told them to." And what the wives said when their husbands said that? That, I can't say in *shule*.

Why do I tell you this story today? Not, *chas vishalom, chas vishalom, chas vishalom*, in order to complain about my wife, God forbid, God forbid, ***God forbid***. I tell you this story today for a different reason.

The reason I tell you this story is because all of us go on journeys many times in our lives. We go on journeys not only in space, but in time, as well. Sometimes we go on journeys that we know are going to be difficult and even painful, and when we do, we should learn from the example of the Israelite women whom we read about today—to take symbols of joy with us, too, to have with us, "just in case."

All of us live lives that are a mixture of pain and pleasure, of suffering and joy. All of us live lives that have defeats and disappointments in them. But we need to take symbols that will remind us, even in the time of our defeats and our disappointments, that darkness will eventually give way to light, and that even if tears linger through the night, joy will come in the morning.

This is the point of this passage that we read from the Torah today: Pack timbrels with you when you go on a trip—just in case—because you can never know, in advance, when you will feel like dancing; when you will feel like celebrating; when you will feel like giving thanks—and so you need to take them with you, just in case.

The Israelite women were right when they ignored the kvetchings of their husbands and took their timbrels with them—just in case they would be needed. And my wife is right when she ignores my kvetching and takes raincoats and sunwear, sandals and high heels, galoshes and sunhats, umbrellas and sunscreen, whenever we go on a trip. She is right because you never can tell when you are going to need them. And so it is good to pack them and take them along—just in case.

And so this is my advice to you today—to you, and to myself:

All of us are on a journey, all the time, and none of us knows what lies ahead on the journey. We take galoshes and sunscreen and sweaters with us in order to have them on hand, in order to protect ourselves in case there are dangers on the road. And in the same way we ought to also pack timbrels with us, in order to express ourselves in case there are joys waiting for us on the road up ahead. We ought to take our timbrels—or whatever we have that expresses hope and faith in the future—with us whenever we go on a journey into the unknown, so that we can have them with us just in case we want to celebrate, and so that we can have them with us to give us confidence and faith that good things lie ahead.

May all of us, when we pack for the difficult journeys of our lives, pack our timbrels with us, as the women who left Egypt did. If things go well, we will be able to use them when we want to sing and dance. And if not? It is still good to have them along—just in case.

24

# Four Lessons from One Dollar Bill: A Story for Children (and for Adults, Too)

## *Yizkor,* Pesach

I am going to do something a little bit strange today. I know that some of you think that I do lots of things that are strange, but what I am going to do today is really a bit unusual, even for me. I am going to tell you a Hanukkah story—even though it is Pesach.

I want to tell you a story about Hanukkah gelt today. It is a very simple story, but I think that it teaches several important lessons, and I think that these are lessons that adults need to learn, as well as children. I think that the lessons that this story teaches are so important that I couldn't wait until Hanukkah to teach them to you. So let me do it now.

The story comes from Anat Ben-Ishai, who is director of the religious school at the Wilshire Boulevard Temple in Los Angeles.

Ms. Ben-Ishai says that when she was a little girl growing up in Israel, things were different than they are today. They didn't have computers. They didn't even have—I know this is hard to believe, but—they didn't even have color television. In fact, they didn't have black-and-white television, either. Nobody knew about cell phones or video games or email or trips overseas, if you can imagine that.

But they did have holidays, even back then. And these holidays were an opportunity for the family to get together to sing, to play and, of course, to eat.

On Hanukkah, when she was a child growing up in Israel, Anat Ben-Ishai remembers that there was Hanukkah gelt. Some families gave coins and others gave gifts, but the kids always got something in honor of Hanukkah.

Every year, when she was a child, the family would celebrate Hanukkah by going to visit her grandparents, who lived in a big, three-story house in Haifa.

On each floor of that house lived members of the family. All of her uncles and aunts and cousins lived in that big house. Only her own, immediate family lived far away, and only they came to visit just a few times a year. She remembers that whenever they came to visit, the children had a great time. They would run from one floor to the other, playing in each apartment. They would chase one another up and down the staircase, and they would go to their grandmother, Tova, to ask for snacks. When they left, their pockets would always be full of candy and other goodies that they had accumulated.

She says:

*Our zeidi did not pay as much attention to us as Bubbie Tova did. But twice a year he paid very close attention to us—on Pesach and on Hanukkah.*

*On Pesach, he made sure that we followed the Haggadah so that we would know the story of our people. And when we recited the Four Questions, he would beam with pride and pinch us on the cheek affectionately if we sang the questions well. And when we stole the afikomen, he always redeemed it with a generous gift.*

*And on Hanukah, especially on the first night, we all participated with him in the ceremony of the lighting of the candles. In the afternoon of the day before Hanukkah, we watched as Zeidi put on his suit, looking very official, and sat down at the table to make a list of all his grandchildren. He started with the firstborn, and he wrote down the name, and then he wrote the age of each one of his grandchildren. Then he would call Bubbie and ask her to check his list, to make sure that he had it right.*

*"Do I have everyone?" Zeidi would ask her. "Did I leave anyone out? Is the order correct and do I have all the ages right?"*

*"Yes, yes, Ephraim," she would say, after checking the list. "It is fine, there are no mistakes," she would reassure him, and then she would go back to the kitchen to peel potatoes for the latkes.*

*Zeidi then put the list inside his jacket pocket, put on his hat, took his walking stick in his hand and, with a straight and proper stride, walked out of the house.*

*"Ephraim, Ephraim!" my bubbie would call out after him. "You forgot the white bag!" She would then hand him a little bag made of white material, a bag that she had sewn for him and that he needed for this special annual walk. He would come back and take the bag.*

*"Zeidi, can we come, too?" we begged.*

*"No, no, you know you can't," he would answer. "I have a very serious matter to take care of. I will be back soon."*

*We all knew where Zeidi was going. He was going to the bank to get Hanukkah gelt for us. Soon we would see him coming back, walking slowly up the hill.*

*"Zeidi, can we see what's inside the white bag?" we would ask.*

*"No, no, go away. Go play. It's not Hanukkah time yet," he would say.*

*Eventually, the sun set. The room would fill up with family members, children and grandchildren, all dressed up for the holiday. The smells from the kitchen were so special. We all looked forward to the yummy latkes that Bubbie had been working on all day. Zeidi looked around the room, checking to make sure that all the children and grandchildren were present. He smiled with his big, blue eyes, and his silver hair shone. For a split second I thought it was Elijah the Prophet standing there, holding a candle in his hand.*

*The silver chanukiyah was placed on the windowsill. Zeidi lit the first candle, and with his strong, clear voice, he led us all in chanting the blessings. I loved it when we all sang together. We sounded like the best choir you could ever imagine when we sang the "Maoz Tsur"!*

*Then Zeidi sat down, reached into his pocket, and pulled out the white bag. He slowly but surely pulled the strings apart and opened the bag. From inside, he pulled out a package of notes: brand-new, crisp dollar bills. He placed them on the table on his right side, and then he put his hand into the bag again. This time he brought out a heap of shiny coins—a great, big heap. He placed these on the table on his left side.*

*"Are you ready? Are you all ready?" he asked, in his loud but so-sweet voice.*

*We were quiet. This was the moment we had been waiting for all day, all month, in fact, all year! It was the moment when we would get our Hanukkah gelt. My Zeidi had a system: he gave us Hanukkah gelt according to our ages. The older grandchildren got dollar bills, and the younger ones got coins. And you never knew if you were old or young in Zeidi's book until you got your gift. Every year, after the ceremony was over, all the big kids—meaning, the ones who had received bills—went out together to buy ice cream. (The ice cream in Haifa, I must tell you, was the best in the world in those days.) You can't image how eagerly I waited. How I wanted that ice cream! And how I wanted to be counted among the big kids! This year I was sure that I was old enough to get a bill, and that I would be able to go with the big kids. It would be the first time that I wouldn't have to stay home with the babies!*

*Zeidi began. He called my oldest cousin, Kalanit, and handed her several dollar bills. She kissed Zeidi and thanked him. Then he called my brother, Itamar, and handed him a few bills. My eyes were on the pile of bills. Were there going to be enough for me when my turn came? I sure hoped so. Zeidi continued, and it was finally my cousin, Miriam's, turn. My heart was pounding so fast that I was afraid it was going to leap up out of my body. I was so excited! There were three bills left on the table. If Zeidi gave Miriam two, he would still have one left for me! This year I was going to be able to go out and eat ice cream with the big kids—at last!*

*And then, much to my shock, I heard Zeidi call: "Uri."*

*What did he say? Did he say "Uri"? It wasn't Uri's turn to be called. It was mine!*

*Why was no one saying anything? Why was no one telling Zeidi he had made a mistake? Even my father was just standing there, not saying a word.*

*Uri came running up to Zeidi, a great, big, wide smile on his face. And as he ran by, I could see that he was avoiding looking at me. Big, salty tears filled my eyes and ran down my cheeks. Uri got the very last dollar bill.*

*I couldn't stand it any longer. There were only coins left on the table—no more bills. I ran into my bedroom, fell onto the bed and cried. I cried deep cries that came from the depths of my broken heart. My parents came in and tried to console me. My father even took a bundle of bills out of his wallet, pulled off three of them, and tried to give them to me. But I only cried louder and pushed them away. My saba came. He said, "I am so sorry that I didn't remember that you are three months older than Uri. Will you please forgive me?"*

*How can you not forgive your grandfather when he makes a mistake and asks you for forgiveness? I had to! But when he tried to hand me a dollar bill, I refused to take it.*

*Finally, the adults left me alone. They realized that I would eventually get over it.*

*After they left, Uri—who had been standing by the door the whole time—came into the room.*

*"I'm sorry," he whispered. "I should have said something, but I wanted to go out for ice cream with the the older kids so much. Please, please take it. It's yours." And when I shook my head, he put the bill down next to me, on the bed.*

*Uri stayed in the house all that evening. He didn't leave. The older kids tried to convince him; they tried to convince me; but we both refused, and so that year, they didn't go out for ice cream, either. Everyone stayed home.*

*When I got home from Haifa, I folded the bill that Uri had given me and placed it in the bottom of my jewelry box.*

*Time passed, and years later, in the fall of 1973, the phone rang in my home in Los Angeles. I answered, and immediately recognized Uri's voice. He was calling from Israel, where he was serving in the Yom Kippur war.*

> *"Shalom, cousin," he said, in his cheerful manner. "How are you? Do you still have that bill in your jewelry box?"*
>
> *"Sure, I do," I answered.*
>
> *"What do you say we take that bill and have some ice cream with it when I come back?" he said.*
>
> *"Ab-so-lu-te-ly!" I replied.*
>
> *But we never had the chance to enjoy that ice cream together, for Uri did not come back from the war. And every year since, on the first night of Hanukkah, I open my jewelry box, take out that faded, folded bill, and remember my cousin Uri.*

That's the story, in summary from Anat Ben-Ishai's column in the Wilshire Boulevard Temple Bulletin. Why do I tell it to you today? Why do I tell you a Hanukkah story on this, the last day of Pesach, the day when we have gathered together here to say *Yizkor*?

I do so because I believe that this story has at least four lessons to teach us, and that these are lessons that all of us need to learn—the grown-ups who are sitting here today as much as the children.

The first lesson is that parents, and even grandparents, make mistakes. When we are children, we think that our parents can do no wrong. We think that they are the strongest and the wisest people in the world. And one of the great turning points in the life of every person is when we come to understand that our parents, and our grandparents, too, are only human. That is the day when we grow up—the day on which we come to understand that they are only human.

Some of us can handle that realization and some of us can't. Some of us are so disappointed, so disillusioned, so upset, when we find out that our parents are not all-wise and all-powerful, that we turn on them with anger. Sometimes it takes many years before we are able to come to terms with the fact that our parents are only human. And so, this is one of the tasks of *Yizkor*. It is a time not only for asking forgiveness from our parents, but also for giving forgiveness ***to*** our parents. It is a time for realizing that, if they made mistakes in raising us, they did the best they could. And that they meant well. Therefore, we need to let go of the anger, the disappointment and the disillusionment that we may feel toward them. For if you are unable to do that, then you are not—and you will never be—a grown-up.

The second lesson in this story is that when your parents or your grandparents make mistakes, you should nevertheless show them respect. Notice how in the story, Anat's parents do not correct her *zeidi*. That is how great a respect parents used to show their parents, in the Jewish tradition. We have a word for it: "*derech eretz.*" Do you still know that word? If not, you should. "*Derech eretz*" is the word we use for the respect—for the reverence—that children are supposed to show their parents. For they are not just pals. They made us, they raised us, they taught us and they helped to form us. And therefore, this is why we Jews come to the synagogue four times a year in order to remember them and to show them respect. Not every culture or civilization has a tradition like *Yizkor*, but we do. For we believe in showing respect for parents—while they are alive, and even after they die. And that is the second lesson in this story.

The third lesson that comes out of this story is that, even if you are entitled to respect—even if you are entitled to reverence—that when you are wrong, you should say so, and you should ask forgiveness for your mistake. That is what the *zeidi* does in this story, and even though the little girl is too upset at the moment to forgive him, she remembers what he did for years afterward. She couldn't deal with it at the time, but years later, she remembers that her *zeidi* admitted he was wrong, that he apologized for what he had done that was wrong, and that he had asked her for forgiveness.

I must tell you that that is not a bad thing for a child to be able to remember. If you can't remember a parent or a grandparent who was perfect—and who among us can remember that?—the next best thing is to remember a parent or grandparent who realized when he or she was wrong and who apologized and asked for our forgiveness. And, if we were too upset to give them the forgiveness that they asked for when they were alive, let us at least give it to them now, shall we? Let this be the day on which we thank our parents and our grandparents for having acknowledged the mistakes that they made and let us grant them our forgiveness. Let us do it now, if we did not do it then.

And the fourth lesson in the story? The fourth lesson is perhaps the most important one of all. Remember how it ends? Years later, when she is living in Los Angeles, Anat gets a call from her cousin Uri, who is serving in the Yom Kippur War. And he says to her: "Cousin, do you still have that dollar that you saved back then, on that Hanukkah at *Zeidi*'s house, years ago?" And she says: "Sure, I do!" And they make a date to go out and spend it on ice cream when he gets back from the war. But guess what? He never got back from the war alive. And she was left with just her memories—and with the unspent dollar bill in her jewelry box. And every so often, she sees it—and when she does, she remembers her cousin Uri.

What's the lesson here? That if you have a good deed to do, or if you have a pleasure to enjoy—for God's sake, ***do it now***! Do it now, before it is too late, because nobody owns tomorrow. If there is nothing else that we learn from saying *Yizkor*, it is that we are all frail, fallible, mortal human beings. We look around the room and we see people here, people whom we know, and we know that some of them are here to mourn and to remember people who were old when they died; others are here to mourn and remember people who were terribly young when they died.

And so the lesson that all of us need to learn at *Yizkor* time—the lesson that we ***need*** to learn, not just up here in our heads, but down here, in our innermost being—is that life can be brief—terribly, terribly brief—and so, if there is a friend with whom we should be eating ice cream or a relative with whom we should be making up, now, now, ***now*** is the time to do it. Now, and not later; now, and not when we have time; now, and not "one of these days"!

And this brings me to Pesach. There is a wonderful pun in the Pesach story that I want to share with you—a pun that, I believe, contains much wisdom.

What is the difference between *matza* and bread? The only difference is time. If you pull the dough out of the oven in 18 minutes, it is *matza*; if you leave it in for longer, than that, it becomes *chametz*. And so, the sages of the midrash make a pun. They say, "*Matsa haba liyadcha at tachmitsena*"—if the opportunity of making *matza* comes to you, don't let it turn into *chametz* by waiting too long. And then they go on to say that what is true of *matza* is also true of *mitzvah*: "*mitzvah haba liyadcha al tachmitsena*"—if a *mitzvah* comes your way, don't let it turn sour by waiting too long. Do it promptly or it will spoil.

So maybe this Hanukkah story that I have told you and Pesach are connected, after all. They both teach the same lesson, which is that life is precious but precarious, and therefore, if you have the opportunity to tell someone or to show someone that you love them, do it on time—and don't delay.

Let me finish with one of my favorite poems. It is a poem that I think about many times during the year, and that I certainly think about at *Yizkor* time. It is called "*Things You Didn't Do*," and it says:

> *Remember the day I borrowed your brand-new car and dented it?*
>
> *I thought you would kill me—but you didn't.*

*And remember the time I dragged you out to the beach, and you said it would rain—and it did?*

*I thought you would say, "I told you so"—but you didn't.*

*And do you remember the time that I flirted with all the guys*

*To make you jealous,*

*And you were?*

*I thought you would leave me for good—but you didn't.*

*And do you remember the time I forgot to tell you that the dance was formal,*

*And you showed up in jeans?*

*I thought you would smack me—but you didn't.*

*Yes, there were lots of things you didn't do,*

*But you put up with me, and you loved me, and you protected me;*

*And there were so many things that I wanted to make up to you when you returned from the war—*

***But you didn't.***

That is what Anat Ben-Ishai has to remember and regret every time she opens her jewelry box and finds that folded, faded bill.

Let that not be what we have to remember and regret as we rise now to recite the *Yizkor* prayer. Amen.

25

# "But I Do It Anyway ..."

## Yom Hashoah

Dear friends,

I must confess that I do not know what to say today. I really don't. I don't know what to say because I was not there, and therefore I have no right to speak. When many of you were shivering with cold, I was safe and sound. While many of you were starving, I had plenty. And so I do not know what I can say to you today, and I do not know what right I have to speak.

I don't know what to say today because who can find words with which to express or describe or mourn what happened there? There are no words that do not sound glib and inadequate on this day. And so, I stand before you and say, in all seriousness and with no false humility, that I do not know what to say.

But I do have a word of Torah for you. I heard it from my friend, Rabbi Morton Leifman, and he says that he heard it from Rabbi Morris Shapiro. It is one of the most powerful statements that I have ever heard. I remember that I trembled when I heard Rabbi Leifman tell this story in the name of Rabbi Shapiro. So let me tell it to you today, in their names.

But first, you need to know who Rabbi Morris Shapiro was. He was a Galitsianer Jew who grew up in the world of eastern European piety. He studied in his youth in the Lublin Yeshiva, which was one of the great Torah institutions of Poland. And then came the war. His whole family was wiped out, but somehow—I don't know the details of how, but somehow—Morris Shapiro found shelter on the farm of a good and decent Polish family.

They hid him in the basement. And every night, when no one was around to see, they would lower two buckets down to him: one bucket contained food, and the other was for his physical needs. And the next night, they would raise the two buckets—fill one with food, empty the one that had excrement in it—and send the two buckets down to him again.

And that is the way Morris Shapiro lived for several years, until the war finally came to an end.

How do you keep your sanity, when you are cooped up like this?

Morris Shapiro kept his sanity by going over, in his mind, the material that he had studied back when he was in the yeshiva. He knew the material by heart, and so every day, all day, he would study the Talmud. He went through a number of the tractates of the Talmud this way, and this mental exercise was what kept him sane.

Sometimes Morris Shapiro would look out the window of the basement in which he lived. When he did, he could see one vine growing out there. That was all he could see from the narrow window in the cellar. But he stared at that single vine all day, day in and day out. He learned to appreciate the way it changed with the changing of the seasons. He learned to love this vine, because it was the only bit of nature that he could see during the time that he lived cooped up in that basement. And so he made a vow to God. He said that if he ever got out of there, he would plant a vine, like this one, in order to increase the beauty in God's world. And he made a vow that he would nurture and care for that vine.

Eventually, the war ended, and Morris Shapiro came out alive. He made his way to America, and he came to the seminary in search of a job. He met with Rabbi Wolfe Kelman, who was the placement director of the Rabbinical Assembly at that time. Rabbi Kelman was somehow drawn to this man, as he was to many European Jews who came to him for help, and so he enabled Shapiro to find a pulpit even though he knew very little English. Rabbi Kelman persuaded a congregation somewhere in Long Island to take him on, and promised the congregation that Shapiro would eventually learn English and that he would be a devoted and effective rabbi.

Sure enough, that is what he became. He served that congregation for many, many years, and because of his sincerity and his devotion, he was able to be a very good rabbi.

And Rabbi Shapiro kept the vow that he had made to God when he was cooped up in that basement. The first thing he did when he came to Long Island and moved into the parish house was plant a vineyard. He did that in gratitude to God for his survival.

Rabbi Shapiro remembered Rabbi Wolfe Kelman in gratitude, as well, and so every year before Pesach, he would come to the seminary and bring Rabbi Kelman a bottle of wine for the Seder—wine that he had made himself, from the grapes of the vine that he had planted. And when Rabbi Kelman died, Rabbi Shapiro transferred this annual custom to Rabbi Liefman, and brought him a bottle of wine for the Seder made from the grapes of his own vine.

This went on for many years until, eventually, Rabbi Shapiro retired from his congregation on Long Island. What does a rabbi do when he retires? Shapiro went to the seminary every single day and sat in the *beit midrash* and studied Torah. And after a while, students began coming over to him and asking him for help in understanding difficult passages that they were struggling with in the Talmud—and he would help them. After a while, the seminary leadership noticed what was going on, and so they appointed him as a tutor to students. And that is what he did until the day he died.

And now, the story:

After Rabbi Shapiro had been teaching in the Seminary Beit Midrash for a number of years, someone got the idea of inviting him to be the speaker at the annual Yom Hashoah service. After all, he had been there: He had lived through the *Shoah*. Surely it would be appropriate to invite him to speak. So they invited him one year, and he accepted.

Shapiro got up to speak, and this is what he said:

> *"You know, I am sure, that there is a special category in Jewish law called 'the Onen.' The law is that from the time a loved one dies until the time that he is buried, the mourner is excused from observing the commandments. He does not have to pray. He does not have to put on tallis or tefillin. He does not have to keep any of the commandments. All he has to do is busy himself with the arrangements for the burial of his loved one.*
>
> *I am sure that you all know this law. But you should know that I am an onen. I am, and I always will be, an onen—for the rest of my life. For I witnessed the death of all my family, but I was never able to bury them. I am, and I always will be, in that limbo state between their deaths and their burial.*

> *And therefore, legally speaking, I do not have to carry out any of the commandments. I do not have to daven. I do not have to put on tallis and tefillin. I do not have to keep any of the commandments.*
>
> *But I keep them anyway. I keep the mitzvahs, even though, legally, I do not have to. Why? I do so because I want to. I do so out of respect to my family's memory, for this is what they did all their lives and this is what they would want me to do. And I do so out of respect to God, who not only sent me to the house of that good and decent Polish family that saved my life, but who enabled me to stay sane all during the time that I hid in the cellar there—by enabling me to study the Talmud from memory every single day that I was there. And I do so in gratitude to God for having provided me with the view of that vine outside my cellar window, so that I could have one bit of beauty to look upon, during all the time when I lived in such dreadful darkness.*
>
> *I don't have to keep the mitzvahs anymore. I really don't. Any beth din would say that I am patur, because I am an onen, and always will be. But I keep the mitzvahs anyway, because I want to; because I love to; because I choose to."*

And with that, Rabbi Shapiro sat down.

I must tell you that, even though I was not there when he spoke that day, and even though I only heard the story secondhand, I trembled when I heard it. For this, it seems to me, is royal, noble Jewish heresy! This is *apikorses* of the highest and the holiest order, is it not?

Here was a man who felt entitled not to keep the commandments, after what he had been through. And who could have blamed him if he had not? Here was a man who felt that he was entitled to be angry at God after what he had been through, and who felt that he had the right to abandon his heritage and live without it. And who could have judged him if he had done that? And yet this was a man who chose to keep the commandments, and who chose to live by the Torah, even though he felt that he was no longer legally obliged to—because he wanted to, because he loved the Torah, and because he loved his God.

I have no right to speak to you today, for I was not there, and so how can I tell you, who were there, what to believe and what you should do? But Rabbi Morris Shapiro was there, and so I have told you what he said and what he did, for ***he*** has the right to speak to you today. And I ask you, and I ask myself, to listen to his words and to take them to heart, for I believe that his words are words of truth that contain much wisdom and guidance.

May the wisdom of Rabbi Morris Shapiro and the memory of all the *kidoshim utihorim*, of all the holy and the righteous ones whom we have come to remember on this day, guide us and teach us. May they help us understand how to observe Yom Hashoah, and how to live with decency and sanity even after all that has befallen us. Amen.

26

# How Can They Weep and Rejoice at the Same Time?

## Before Yom Ha'atzmaut

I want to teach you a law today that is almost impossible to observe. And I want to tell you about two great rabbis who gritted their teeth and observed this law when they had to. But first, let me ask you this question:

Do you know the difference between life in Israel and life in the diaspora?

I think that it is found in one strange quirk in the calendar.

Almost all of the holidays of the year are observed for one day in Israel and for two days in the rest of the Jewish world. However, there is one holiday in the calendar that is observed for two days in Israel and for one day in the diaspora.

Do you know what holiday that is?

It is Yom Ha'atzmaut.

We observe Israeli Independence Day (Yom Ha'atzmaut) in the diaspora. We hold parades, carnivals and special services; we recite Hallel. We do all these things because we understand that the establishment of the State of Israel was a blessing for us as well as for the people who live there. The fifth day of Iyar in the year 1948 was a turning point in Jewish history: From that day on, the Jewish people were no longer stateless. From that day, there has been one place on earth where all Jews can turn when they need help and know that they will be welcomed with open hands and open hearts.

Yom Ha'atzmaut is a *yontif* for us as well as for the Jews who live in Israel. But there is one difference between how it is observed there and how it is observed here.

In Israel, the holiday is observed for two days. There, they observe Yom Hazikaron first and then they observe Yom Ha'atzmaut. On the first day, everyone goes to the cemetery and visits the graves of those whom they love who have perished in one of the wars of Israel's existence. On this day, flags are flown at half-staff. On this day, the mood of the country is grim and somber and sad. And then, at sunset, the flags that have flown at half-staff all day are raised. Everyone breaks out in song and dance. And if you have ever been there, you have to wonder: How can people switch gears like this? How can they go from weeping over those whom they have lost to celebrating what they have gained—just like that?

If you look closely, you will see that some of the people dance with tears in their eyes.

And that is the difference between living in Israel and living in the diaspora. Here in the diaspora, we celebrate with joy and delight because we appreciate the importance of the state. But we celebrate for only one day, because we do not feel the pain and the cost of having a state in the same way that those in Israel do. We sing and dance on Yom Ha'atzmaut, but we do not grieve on Yom Hazikaron—at least, not as intensely and not as personally as they do in Israel.

And yet there are moments in our lives when we, too, experience the same kind of quirk in the calendar. What do you do if you have a loss, and your heart is broken—and then Shabbat or Pesach or Rosh Hashana comes along, and the law is that you must end your mourning, and celebrate instead? What do you do when the people around you think that it is Simchat Torah, and they are laughing and singing and drinking and dancing—but inside, your heart is heavy because just the day before you lost someone who meant the world to you?

There is a law that says that if you lose someone before a holiday, then the holiday cancels out the rest of your days of mourning; if you lose someone during a holiday, you are supposed to carry on with the holiday. You are supposed to sit at your Seder or sit in your sukkah or sit in your seat at the synagogue on Rosh Hashana, and then—after the holiday is over—***then*** you are supposed to sit *shivah*—a somewhat shortened *shivah*, but a *shivah* just the same.

How can you do that? Can you turn your emotions on and off, just like that? Can you postpone your tears until they are permitted? That seems to be asking more of us than we are capable of, does it not?

And yet, in my rabbinate—and I am sure that this has happened in the lives of many other rabbis, as well as members of my congregation—I have had to ask: What do you do when, on the morning of the wedding, the mother of the bride dies? Or what do you do if—as happened to my friend, Rabbi Shlomo Fox—the father of the bride passes away during the ceremony? Twice in my experience, the mother of the bride died a few hours before the wedding ceremony was to begin. And when that happened, the families were in shock. I was in shock. The families did not know what to do. I did not know what to do. And the guests at the wedding and the caterers of the wedding and the undertakers who had to make the funeral arrangements were in shock, too. But the advantage of belonging to an old and a wise people is that whatever can possibly happen in your life has happened before, and so you can look it up, and you can learn from the wisdom of the people who came before you. You can learn from the people who dealt with the same question—not under the pressure of a crisis, not under the stress and strain of an emergency and not at a time when you cannot think clearly because you are in shock—but from people who thought this question through in the calmness of the study hall.

And what is their answer? What do you do when a wedding and a funeral come together?

They say: You give full honor and dignity to them both. And so that is what we did on both of these occasions, in my experience, when the mother of the bride died just hours before the commencement of her daughter's wedding ceremony.

I can still remember the sight of the father of the bride, leading his daughter to the *chuppah* that night. His face was as white as a ghost. I am not sure whether he was leading his daughter or she was leading him, but he somehow made it down the aisle. For the rest of her life, this girl will have her wedding anniversary and her mother's *yahrtseit* inexorably connected in her memory, but she—and the family and I, and all the others who were there that night—somehow got through this event, because we had tradition to guide us and to tell us what to do at a time when, left to ourselves, we would not have known what to do.

Let me tell you about two giants of Jewish life in our time who were somehow—I don't know how, but who were somehow—able to observe this law that seems to be almost beyond the strength of human beings to observe.

The first was Rabbi Yehuda Amital, and the second was Rabbi Yekusiel Yehudah Halberstam. I learned their stories from two different sermons by Rabbi Haskel Lookstein of

New York, and I share them with you today in the hope that you will never need to know this law about the obligation to postpone mourning for the sake of joy, but in the hope that if you ever do, these two stories will be of some help to you.

Rabbi Amital came to Israel as a teenager. He arrived as an orphan. His entire family had been wiped out by the Nazis. The day he landed, they handed him a rifle, showed him how to use it, and sent him off to the Haganah. He fought in the 1948 War of Independence. When the war was over, he made his way to the Hebron Yeshiva, and there, he became a great rabbinic scholar. He founded the yeshiva in Gush Etzion, which was different from many of the other yeshivot of its time, because at Yeshivat Har Etzion, they believed that even the most observant Jews have a responsibility and an obligation to support the state and to protect the country. The yeshiva in Gush Etzion was one of the first in the country to institute a yeshivat hesder program, for which students enter the army but are given opportunities to study Torah while they are there. He helped to create a cadre of young people who were both soldiers and scholars.

In one of his books, Rabbi Amital describes his experiences during and after the Yom Kippur War. He says that there was one passage in Rashi's commentary on the first *sedra* of the Torah that had a profound effect on him. This commentary was on Chapter 6, verse 6 of the book of Bereshit: "*Bisha-at chaduta chaduta, ubisha-at aveyla aveyla*" ("When it is a time to mourn, you must mourn; when it is a time to rejoice, you must rejoice.")

This is, in summary, what Rabbi Amital writes:

> *Whenever I read these words of Rashi, I cannot help but remember the wedding of my eldest daughter, which took place in the yeshiva immediately after the Yom Kippur War. After all the pain resulting from that war—both the pain of the nation and the pain of our yeshiva, which lost*

*eight precious students—I found it very difficult to listen to the band. And I almost did not join in the dancing. But then I was approached by Justice Zvi Tal, whose son's wedding I had performed on Rosh Hodesh Elul, right before the war. His son went out to battle and never returned. Justice Tal quoted to me these words of Rashi: "In times of joy—you must rejoice; in times of grief—you must grieve." And he took me by the arm and led me into the dancing in honor of the bride, both of us with tears in our eyes.*

Rabbi Amital's lesson is one that we all need to learn and to store away in our memories, in case we should ever need to know it. The law tries to separate celebrations from grief, but sometimes, that simply cannot be done. Sometimes *simchas* come along in the midst of sorrows, and sometimes sorrows come along in the midst of *simchas*. And when they do, we have no choice but to try to honor both. We have to give ourselves the ability to mourn and to celebrate at the same time—difficult as that may be to do.

And that is what Israel tries to do when it observes Yom Hazikaron: when it lowers its flags to half-staff, when its people go to the cemeteries where their fallen children are buried and when they spend the day meditating on the awesome price that they have paid for their independence. And then, when the Day of Remembrance is over, this people raises its flags and wipes away its tears and begins to sing and dance and rejoice in gratitude for the existence of its state. If either day was observed without the other, it would be a terrible distortion, and so Israel observes both days—one right after the other. It goes from the pits of grief to the heights of joy—directly, without a pause, without missing a beat. And this is a lesson for all of us to remember and to learn from if and when our grief and our joy should ever coincide.

Now let me tell you the second story, the story of Rabbi Yekusiel Yehudah Halberstam—or, as he was better known, the Klausenberger Rebbe. During the *Shoah*, the Klausenberger Rebbe lost his parents, his siblings, his wife, and all of his 11 children.

"During the *Shoah*, he lost his parents, his wife, his siblings and all of his 11 children."

I just rattled off those facts, as if they were mere numbers, but can you comprehend what it must have been like to go through that many losses? Can you imagine losing your whole family like that? I can't imagine that I would ever recover from such blows.

I think that most of us would have lost our minds, or would have committed suicide, or would have become bitter and angry and full of a desire for revenge if anything like this had happened to us. Isn't that so?

On top of that, the *rebbe* was wounded during the war, and he lingered on the threshold between life and death for many months. While he was in the hospital, the *rebbe* made a vow. He said: "*Ribono shel olam*, if you enable me to survive, and if you enable me to reach the Holy Land, I promise you that I will devote all of my energies there—not only to rebuilding my Chassidic group, but also to the building of a hospital in Israel. And I swear to you that the hospital will be a place where every single man, woman or child who needs healing will receive the same dedicated medical care, regardless of his or her nationality or his or her creed."

Can you imagine a human being who had lost his entire family who had lost all reason to believe in the sanity of humanity—can you imagine a human being who had gone through what the Klausenberger Rebbe had gone through, making an oath like that—and keeping it, as well? The next time you are in Israel, go to Netanya, and visit the Laniado Hospital there, which Rabbi Halberstam created in fulfillment of that oath.

I cannot imagine that the Klausenberger Rebbe ever lived a single moment of his life after the *Shoah* without grief in his heart, after what he had gone through. I can't believe that he ever took a breath without thinking of those whom he had lost. And yet, somehow—don't ask me how, but somehow—he managed to live with his grief and with a desire to balance it with an act of goodness. Instead of devoting the rest of his life to vengeance, he chose to devote his life to caring for the sick and the vulnerable. And therefore, he built the Laniado Hospital.

That building is not just a model of first-class medical care. It is a monument to the capacity of a human being to somehow live with both suffering and joy crowded together in his heart at the same time. It is a model of how at least one human being has been able to endure *sinnat hinam*—senseless, purposeless hatred—and not only survive it, but respond to it with *ahavat hinam*—with equally unexplainable, wondrous love.

May all of us be spared from what Rabbi Avital and the Klausenberger Rebbe endured in their lifetimes. May all of us be spared from what the people of Israel have endured—from paying the price that they have paid so that they and we can have this precious state. And may all of us be spared from occasions in which joy and sorrow, happiness and grief, come together at one time in our calendars.

But if they ever do, may the stories of these two Torah giants—who not only lived but loved, who not only suffered but triumphed over their suffering, and turned it from a reason for hatred and grief into an occasion for love—may the example set by these two great spirits teach us and guide us and give us strength.

Amen.

27

# What Makes Israel So Special?

## Yom Ha'atzmaut

Dear friends,

You will probably think that I am joking when I say this, but I must tell you that I am always very nervous when I get up to give a sermon on Shabbat—and even more so when I get up to speak on *yontif.* I really am. Because whenever a rabbi rises to speak about the Torah on Shabbat morning, the words he speaks say more about him than they do about the Torah.

If you say trivial things about the Torah, it does not mean that the Torah is a trivial book; it only means that you are a trivial reader. If you only speak about the minor details in the Torah, and if you have nothing to say about the vision in the Torah, it only means that your mind lacks imagination and that your spirit is pedestrian.

And I think that this is especially true when Israel's birthday appears on the calendar.

What you say about Israel says more about you than it does about Israel. And so what should I say today, on the day when we celebrate Israel's birthday?

Should I say that Israel has a flourishing economy? That its gross national product is grosser than that of most of the other countries in the Middle East combined?

I could, but is that what my ancestors or yours would be impressed with if they were privileged to see Israel today? I don't think so.

Should I say that Israel is militarily strong? That it has planes and tanks and missiles and brave soldiers?

That is true, and we are thankful for that, but is that the most significant thing that we can say about Israel? Is that why our ancestors dreamed of someday having a state? So that we could have guns, uniforms, tanks, planes and soldiers? Or are these things only means—*necessary* means, *indispensable* means, but still, only means—to a higher and more important end?

Should we show, by the way we speak about it, that Israel is now 67 years old and, therefore, that we take it for granted and that are no longer thrilled and excited that it exists?

Should we show, by the way we talk about it on its birthday, that the wonder we once felt at having a Jewish state no longer fills our minds and souls? If so—if that is the way we talk about Israel on its birthday this year—then that only shows how empty our souls are and how barren our imaginations are.

I can remember how we danced in the streets on this day, 67 years ago, when Israel was born. And some of you can, too. I can still remember how we rushed to the synagogue in order to give thanks to God after the Six-Day War, and I can still remember how we prayed so fervently when we found out that Israel was being attacked on Yom Kippur some 40 years ago. And now? Now it is Israel's birthday *noch a mol*—again—and so we yawn as we settle back to hear what the rabbi will say this year? We wonder: Will what he says to us this year be any less trite, any less banal, any less obvious, than what he said on this occasion last year?

Believe me: What we say about Israel says more about us than it does about Israel.

Therefore, I am not going to say anything about Israel's economic achievements or its political problems or its military problems, today—and not just because I am not an economist, or a politician, or a military expert. I am not going to say anything about these things because these are not the questions that we should deal with on this special day.

Instead, I am going to talk about what makes Israel ***spiritually*** special, what makes Israel ***morally*** precious and what makes Israel ***truly*** holy. And I am going to do so by telling you three simple stories that have come out of Israel in recent years.

These three stories, for some reason that I can't begin to understand, did not make the headlines—but I believe that they have much to teach us on what Israel is really all about.

One story that I want to tell you today comes from the dedication of the Sara Davidson Towers of Hadassah Hospital on Mount Scopus, a couple of years ago. Another story comes out of Project Birthright, which I am sure most of you know about. And the third story comes from something that took place this week, at Har Nof, on the eastern side of Jerusalem.

Let me begin with the dedication ceremony that took place a few years ago, when the Sara Davidson Towers of Hadassah Hospital were officially dedicated. You remember, I am sure, that there was enormous publicity for this event. Press and media representatives from all over the world came to witness the cutting of the ribbon, the placing of the *mezuzot*, the presentation of the plaques and the ceremonies that took place that day. The architect spoke. The donor spoke. The mayor spoke. The head of Hadassah spoke. The representative of the Israeli government spoke. But there was one minor detail of that dedication that somehow did not make it into the news stories, and that is the detail that I want to tell you about today.

The people who were there that day were taken on a tour of the new facility. They were shown the new medical equipment that was state-of-the-art, and they were impressed. But they were also shown something that, I believe, was state-of-the-heart.

Do you know what it was?

It was the fact that, in every room of the Davidson Towers, there is a sofa bed, so that family members can stay with a patient overnight.

Have you ever been in a hospital overnight? If so, you know how lonely and scary it can be. If you have ever been alone in a hospital room overnight, you know what it is like to pull a cord, or to press a button, and then to wait and wait and wait until a nurse's aide finally comes, helps you off the bed, and takes you to the bathroom. And then, when you are finished, you pull the cord or press the button again—and you wait and wait and wait until the nurse's aide comes back, and takes you back to your bed.

That does not happen in the Davidson Towers, because every single private room in that hospital has a sofa bed in it. Your husband, your wife, your child or your friend can be with you through the night, to help you or to keep you company, if and when you need them.

I must tell you that when I heard that, I was impressed. It is nice that this hospital has the most up-to-date machinery in the Middle East. I don't minimize that—of course I don't. But I think it is also nice that they have a sofa bed in every room.

It is nice that there is a *mezuzah* on every door in the hospital. And it is nice that the kitchen of this hospital is strictly kosher. But I think that the fact that there is a couch in every room is part of what makes Hadassah a Jewish hospital, and that we ought to be very proud of the fact that these couches are there.

That is the first story that I want to tell you about Israel today.

The second story that I want to tell you today comes from Project Birthright.

Does everyone here know what Project Birthright is?

Project Birthright is a project that is co-sponsored by the Israeli government and the Jews of the world. It brings tens of thousands of Jewish young people to Israel for a 10-day tour. And it has had good results.

But I have a friend who is very cynical. He is a reporter, and so he has been trained to be suspicious of what people say and do. He does not believe that there is any such thing as a free lunch, and so he has always been suspicious of Project Birthright. He believed that it is just a propaganda device, and that its purpose is to brainwash young people. And so when he got a chance to go on Birthright, as a reporter, he jumped at the chance.

For the first five or six days of the trip, he stood on the sidelines and just took notes. And then, one night when they were in Jerusalem, he and one of the tour guides went out for a drink. In the course of the conversation, the tour guide—whose name was Yoav—relayed to him this story:

> *"I am a Likudnik. If it were up to me, I would not give back an inch of the territories. I would not give back an inch, not so much for religious reasons or for historical reasons, but for practical reasons. I say: 'Who are you going to give this land back to? And what are they going to do with it?' I say: 'Do you realize that from the West Bank, you can hit a plane landing at Ben Gurion Airport with ease?' And that is what I tell the kids on my bus, just as those who disagree with me tell the kids on their busses what they believe. And that is why the*

> *people who run Birthright make sure that the kids get to ride on different busses every day—so that they can hear different points of view."*

My friend did not know that, and he was impressed to learn it. He was impressed that Project Birthright is arranged so that the kids who go on it get to hear different points of view from their tour guides. But the next thing that Yoav told him that night in the bar really surprised him.

Yoav said that when Rabin was killed, he was really shaken. A Jew killed another Jew? ***How could that be?*** And he made himself a promise that day—a promise that if and when he ever got married, and if and when he ever had a child, he would name that child after Rabin, in response to what had happened. And that is what he did.

Sure enough, the next day, the guide called his son over from the back of the bus, and said to him: "Tell this man your name, and tell him who you are named after."

And the boy said: "My name is Yitschak, and I am named after Yitschak Rabin, *zichrono livracha*."

My friend is no longer cynical about Project Birthright. He no longer believes that it is just propaganda, and that it is just brainwashing. Now he feels that it is a place where people who live across all the lines that separate Israelis from one another work together, in harmony and mutual respect, in order to introduce Israel and to explain what Israel stands for to young people from all over the world.

Israel is a place where a Likudnik can name his child after Yitschak Rabin, and where tour guides can work together in harmony, across all the party lines that separate them—and that is one of the things that makes it special.

And now, my third story.

This is a story that was hardly noticed in Israel. It made the back pages in most of the newspapers, if it was recorded at all. But let me tell it to you, as I found it in Ha-aretz:

"This year, on Yom Hazikaron, a procession of Jews from Har Nof, dressed in traditional Charedi clothing, wearing *bekeshes* and *shtreimlach*, marched from their homes to a Druze cemetery located nearby."

What were they doing there?

They were there to pay honor to Zadar Saif, the Druze policeman who had been on duty at the Bet Aharon synagogue in November 2014, when terrorists came in during *Shachrit* and killed four rabbis who were *davening* there at the time, and wounded eight more. Zadar Saif was killed in that attack, but before he died, he managed to kill one of the attackers. And so thousands of Charedim came to his funeral, and many of them marched to his grave on Yom Hazikaron, to give honor to his memory. I am sure that there were many Druze in the cemetery that day who had never seen a Jew wearing a *bekishe* and a *shtreimel* before. I am sure that there were many Charedim who had never before set foot in a Druze cemetery. But this is what you do if you are a Jew, and someone gives his life to save you and to save your country.

These are the three stories that I want to tell you today: the story of the couches in the rooms of the Davidson Towers in Jerusalem; the story of the Likudnik, who named his child for Yitschak Rabin; and the story of the Charedim in Har nof, who went to a Druze cemetery. I think that these three stories, each in their own way, teach us why Israel is so special—and why Israel is so sacred to us and to all the Jewish people, wherever they may be.

And so I invite you to join me in saying: Glory be to Israel on its birthday. May we all take pride in both its spiritual and practical achievements. May we join our hearts on this, the week of Israel's birthday, and may we celebrate many, many more such milestones in its life. May God bless Israel with both strength and peace for many more years to come.

And let us be proud to be partners with Israel by loaning it money so that it can be safe and strong in this new year. Let us know that our grandparents would envy the privilege of loaning money to Israel. And let us thank God that we have the opportunity to do this *mitzvah* today, and let us do with it with a whole and happy heart.

Amen.

# 28

# The Real Reason Why We Eat Dairy on Shavuot

## Shavout

I got a call on Sunday from one of our members.

He said to me: "Rabbi, could you please give us some counseling?"

I said: "I will try. What is the problem?"

He said: "My wife and I have been having a very serious disagreement. If we are not able to resolve this matter, I don't know if our marriage is going to make it or not."

I said: "My goodness! What is this dispute about?"

He said: "My wife claims that her mother taught her that the reason we eat dairy on Shavout is because the Torah calls Israel the land of milk and honey. My mother taught me that the reason we eat dairy on Shavout is because the Israelites were not sure that they could handle all the details of *kashrut,* which they received at Sinai, and so they decided to start with dairy. And so, I want you to tell us: who is right—my mother or her mother?"

I realized at once that this was a very serious question, and I felt a great sense of responsibility. What if I gave the wrong answer? The survival of a marriage might be at stake! So I said to this man: "Let me do some research, and I will get back to you as soon as I can."

That night I flew to New York, which is where the Library of the Jewish Theological Seminary is located. The seminary library is the largest Jewish library in this country. It contains thousands of books and manuscripts, and so I figured that I would surely be able to find the answer there.

When the library opened at 9 o'clock the next morning, I was the first one in line. I read every single book and every single manuscript in the entire library, one by one, hoping to find the answer to this question. Some of the books had indexes, which made it easier to look for the answer; some of them did not. But I went through every single book and every single manuscript in the seminary library, one by one.

And do you know what I found?

I found that six or seven of the books and two or three of the manuscripts agreed with this man's mother, and six or seven of the books and two or three of the manuscripts agreed with his wife's mother. The rest of the books in the seminary library either did not deal with this question at all or offered other suggestions as to why we eat dairy on Shavout.

Do you know what it means when you have three, four or five different explanations for the same custom? It means that nobody knows for sure.

So do you know what I did? As soon as the seminary library closed, I took a cab to the airport, and I took a flight to Israel. When the plane landed, I took a taxi to Jerusalem. When I got to Jerusalem, I went straight to Hebrew

University's National Library of Israel, which is the largest Jewish library in Israel and contains many, many thousands of books and manuscripts.

When the Hebrew University library opened the next morning, I was the first person in line. I took a chair at one of the tables in the reading room, and I went through every single book and every single manuscript in the entire library.

And do you know what I found?

I found that a few of the books and a few of the manuscripts in the Hebrew University library agreed with this man's mother, and a few of the books and a few of the manuscripts in the Hebrew University library agreed with his wife's mother. Many of the books and manuscripts in the Hebrew University library did not deal with this question at all, or else they offered a ***different*** explanation for why we eat dairy on Shavout—an explanation that did not agree with either this man's mother's explanation ***or*** his wife's mother's explanation.

So do you know what I did?

I took a cab back to the airport, and I booked a flight to Rome. When I got to Rome, I took a cab to the Vatican Library.

I hope you are impressed with how devoted a rabbi I am, and with how hard I work when I feel that the marriage of one of our member families is in trouble. For the measly salary that you pay me here—which is in the low seven-figures—look at what I do when I am called upon for help by one of our families.

I believe that *shalom bayit*—preserving peace in the house—is one of the biggest *mitsvahs* in the Torah, and so I went to New York, and from there to Jerusalem, and from there to the Vatican, in efforts to help this family.

I was the first one in line when the Vatican Library opened in the morning, and I sat there and read every single book and every single manuscript that they had there. And sure enough, late at night—just when I was beginning to feel really tired, and just when I was on the brink of giving up—I found it!

I found a medieval manuscript that contained the real reason why we eat dairy on Shavout. I found it in a rare manuscript that came from medieval France.

And so I made a copy of this medieval manuscript, and I translated it from the medieval Latin in which it is written, into English, and I flew back home. As soon as I landed, I called this family from the airport and told them of my discovery.

The husband answered the phone, and do you know what he said? He said, "Thank you very much, but we are busy right now. We'll call you back." And he hung up.

Can you imagine? After all I did to find the answer to his question: after I flew to New York, and then to Jerusalem, and then to Rome—at my own expense—in order to search for the answer to his question—and he was no longer interested!

***Can you imagine?***

*Baalebatim!*

And so, this morning, I am going to tell you what I discovered.

You are going to be the first ones—the very first ones—to hear what this medieval manuscript says about why we eat diary on Shavuot. Since you are my friends, I want you to be the first ones to hear what I discovered. Tomorrow, I will call a press conference and tell the world, but I want you to be the first ones to hear the answer to the question that has baffled generations: Why do we eat diary on Shavuot?

Are you ready?

Listen carefully, and I will read to you the answer, exactly as it appears in the manuscript that I discovered in the Vatican library. This is what the manuscript says:

> *There was a rabbi named Rabbi Shlomo, who lived in the village of Troyes, in the 10th century. He*

*was a brilliant scholar. In fact, he was considered one of the most brilliant people in all of France. There was only one person in all of France who was considered wiser than he was, but I will tell who that person was later.*

*In those days, Troyes had only one synagogue, and it was fairly small. There were two sections in the synagogue: one for the men, and one for the women. They were separated from each other by a low curtain, called a mechitsah.*

*But over time, the Jewish population of Troyes increased, until there were not enough seats in the synagogue for everyone—especially during a holiday like Pesach, when everyone came to shule. And so, every year, the men would move the curtain over a little bit, so as to make more room on the men's side of the synagogue.*

*And then, one year, it reached the point where there was simply no room at all for the women in the synagogue. The men had to move the curtain* ***all the way over*** *in order to accommodate all the men who wanted to come to the services. And so the men came to Rabbi Shlomo and asked him what they should do. They did not want to build a bigger synagogue, because that would require a building fund and a lot of work. But if they didn't, then how would they accommodate all the people who wanted to come to shule on Passover?*

*Rabbi Shlomo said, "We have no choice. The men will simply have to take over the women's section, and the women will have to stay home. After all, women are not required to daven with a minyan. Let them daven at home."*

*All the men agreed that it was a good idea, though there was one drawback: Not one of the men had the courage to go home and tell his wife what they had decided.*

*And so, when the first morning of Passover arrived, the women came to the synagogue—and found that they had been locked out. So, pious as they were, they stood outside to offer their prayers. And when Rabbi Shlomo stood up inside, to address the men, the women on the outside turned to his wife, Rivka, and asked her to be their teacher.*

*Rivka was a very good teacher. As learned and as wise as Rabbi Shlomo was, his wife was even more so. And so the women were happy to listen to her words.*

*They all gathered around her, outside the synagogue, and she began to tell them the story of Pesach. She told them about how they were once slaves in Egypt; how the pharaoh would not let them go; how Moses took them out of Egypt and brought them to Mount Sinai; and about how, from that day, they were all free to worship God.*

*And when she said that, all the women looked at one another, and the same thought came to each one of them at the same time: If Pesach is the holiday of freedom, and if freedom means the right to serve God, then how come we are standing out here while the men are sitting in there?*

*The women were agitated, but Rivka calmed them down. She told them that a Jew is not supposed to get upset on a holiday. And she told them that, during the intermediate days of the holiday, they would get together and figure out what to do.*

*On the first day of the intermediate days of Pesach, Rivka and the other women went to see Rabbi Shlomo and the other men who ran the synagogue. The women told them that they wanted a bigger shule: one that would accommodate everyone who wanted to pray. And, in the meantime—until the new shule was built—they wanted their half of the sanctuary back.*

*The men did not agree. But they were very smart. They did not say "no." Instead, they said, "We will appoint a committee to study the matter." (That is the way that men have been managing to avoid dealing with difficult situations in the synagogue for many years: by appointing a committee to study the matter.) The men did so because they knew that to build a new synagogue was very expensive, and there was already a deficit in the budget. To build a new synagogue they would have to find an architect and raise money, and that would not be easy.*

*"But," the men said, "we will consider it. In fact, we will appoint a committee to study the idea, and maybe, maybe,* ***maybe*** *someday—one of these days, when the shule is running at a surplus—we will build a bigger sanctuary."*

*And in the meantime, they said, "Let the women be patient ... after all, men are required to pray with a minyan, and women are not. So if there is no room for women in the synagogue, and if they don't want to stand and pray outside, then let them pray at home."*

*Six weeks went by, between the end of Pesach and the beginning of Shavout, and the women saw no sign that the men were getting ready to build a new synagogue. There was no search for land, no fundraising campaign; there were no interviews with architects, and there was not even a meeting of the committee that had been appointed to study the matter. The women began to get impatient.*

*Finally, seven weeks after Pesach, Shavout came. Rabbi Shlomo got up in the morning and went to the synagogue, while Rivka, his wife, stayed home. He was glad she'd stopped arguing, and that she was staying home, so that she could have lunch ready when he returned.*

*But, much to Rabbi Shlomo's surprise, there was no lunch on the table when he came home from the synagogue. Rivka was sitting there, reading a book, and he smiled silently as he kissed her and wished her a good yontif. He waited for her to serve him lunch. He waited ... and waited ... and waited. A couple of times, he cleared his throat, and said, "Ahem!" But she went right on reading her book. Finally, he said, "I'm waiting ..." She lifted her eyes from the book, and said, "I know."*

*He waited a few more minutes, but Rivka went right on reading.*

*At this point, Rabbi Shlomo was very upset. He didn't know what was going on, but he figured he would go for a walk to clear his mind, and that by the time he got back, Rivka would have finished her book and would have lunch ready for him.*

*Shlomo went outside and went for a stroll. And lo and behold ... guess what? He saw all the other men of Troyes were out walking, too. He wondered what was going on. Could all the women have forgotten to make lunch? Could they all be reading? And if so, why?*

*As he turned the corner, he saw his old friend, Moshe, the shule president, walking down the street.*

*"Gut yontif, Moshe," he said. "Have you finished eating your lunch so early?"*

*"Oy," said Moshe. "Don't talk to me about lunch."*

*Rabbi Shlomo said, "Moshe, what's wrong?"*

*And Moshe said, "It's a new world. My wife, Rachel, refuses to make lunch. She says she's on strike."*

*Rabbi Shlomo stood there, shocked. Could it be? Could his wife, Rivka, also be on strike? Could it be that all the women of Troyes were on strike? Why? Could it be over the matter of the men taking over the women's section of the synagogue? Could that be the reason?*

*Without so much as a goodbye, Rabbi Shlomo turned away from Moshe and ran back home. When he got home, he waited to catch his breath, and then he casually walked into the house. Rivka was still reading her book, and there was still no lunch on the table.*

*"Rivka," he said gently, "wouldn't you like to put down your book and have something to eat?"*

*"No, thank you," she said. "I ate already."*

*"**You ate without me?**" he asked, shocked.*

*"You davened without me," she responded.*

*Rabbi Shlomo knew better than to argue. Besides, by this time, he was really hungry. So he looked into the cupboard to see what he could make. Shlomo had never made a meal in his life before, and he had no idea how to do it. So he found a loaf of bread, took a slab of cheese and put it on a slice of bread, and made himself a sandwich—because that was all that he knew how to make. And as he ate, he thought about what was happening.*

*Imagine having to eat dairy on a yontif! Who ever heard of such a thing?*

*And imagine the women of Troyes going on strike in order to get back their half of the sanctuary! Who ever heard of such a thing?*

*The men asked themselves: Where did these women get such a crazy idea? And what are these women going to think of next?*

*The day after Shavout, Rabbi Shlomo called a meeting of all the men. He proposed that they look for land, hire an architect, raise the money and build a bigger shule. And they should try to finish the project in time for Rosh Hashana!*

*In the meantime, he proposed, they should give the women back their half of the synagogue.*

*And for the first time in the history of Troyes—in fact, for the first time in the history of synagogue life anywhere—the motion passed unanimously! Without a single dissent! Every man in the room voted for it. This was something that had never happened before, in all the history of Troyes. And that has never happened again—not in our shule, and not in any other shule in the world. The motion to build a new shule, and the motion to give the women back their share of the shule until then, passed unanimously! Honest!*

*As soon as the meeting was over, all the men ran home as fast as they could in order to tell their wives about the vote. And each of the men claimed credit for the decision, because he wanted to impress his wife!*

*But deep in his heart, Rabbi Shlomo knew that the matter was not so simple. He had the feeling that this was only the tip of the iceberg, and that it was only the first of many steps still to come. Who knows what these women would want next. They may someday want literacy! Or the right to vote! Or the right to be on the synagogue board! Or maybe even the right to study Torah! Or maybe the right to be cantors! Or maybe—farfetched as it sounds—they might someday even want* ***the right to be rabbis****!*

*And Rabbi Shlomo wondered to himself: Will these things—if they come about—be good for the Jews? Will they be good for Judaism? Or not? Rabbi Shlomo did not know for sure, but he thought that they might be. And he felt that what had happened was important—so important, that it ought to be remembered.*

*And so he issued a decree that, from then on and in remembrance of this event, the people should eat dairy meals every year on Shavout: in honor of the new sanctuary, which got built very fast; in honor of the women, who went on strike; and in honor of the men, who didn't know very much about how to cook, and so had to eat dairy meals on that Shavout.*

And this is the ***real*** reason why we eat dairy meals on Shavout. At least, this is the explanation that I found while I was looking through the Vatican Library. I share it with you today so that you may be the first, the very first, to know the real reason why we eat dairy meals on this day.

And as soon as *yontif* is over, I am going to call a press conference and tell the world about this discovery, but I wanted you to be the first ones to hear about it—and that is why I have told it to you today.

So when you go home today and you meet your friends who go to other *shules*, tell them the real reason why we eat dairy on Shavout,—and tell them that your rabbi went all the way to New York, and then to Jerusalem, and then to the Vatican, to find the answer. Let them be jealous that they don't belong to this synagogue, and tell them that if they want to join, there is a short waiting list—a very short waiting list—but that you will use your influence to get them in.

There is one more thing I must say, before I finish:

The truth is that I did not go to the seminary library or to the Hebrew University library or to the Vatican, in order to solve this mystery of why we eat dairy on Shavout. And the truth is that I did not spend any of the synagogue's money making these trips. The truth is that I found it in a story that appeared in The Reconstructionist many, many years ago, and although I have embellished and developed it, it is not really mine. I called the Reconstructionist Rabbinical School library and begged them to help me find the name of the author, but so far, they have not been able to do so. And so I regret that I am not able to give proper credit to her, much as I would like to. If any of you know who it is, please let me know, so that I can.

But I still think it is a wonderful story, and I hope that not only the women but the men, too, agree.

And if you do, will you please join me in saying: Amen.

29

# How Do You Say Goodbye?

## Shavout *Yizkor* (or the graduation season)

This is the season when our children graduate from high school or from college. And so, I want to begin my sermon today by saying *mazel tov* to the parents and to the children who are celebrating this event. May you have much joy—now and always.

I don't mean to spoil your *simcha*, but I must say that if you think about it, graduation is a moment of mixed emotions, for parents and for children. For parents, it means that your children have achieved much, and this is a milestone in their lives and in yours in which you rejoice. But at the same time, it is a moment when you realize that they are now going to enter a new stage of their lives, and that they will be living further away from you, and so that joy is mixed with a bit of anxiety. They, too, have conflicting emotions as they graduate. On the one hand, they throw their caps into the air with joy, and they shout out: "Hurray! We made it!" But on the other hand, they realize that a precious period in their lives is coming to an end. They hug their classmates, knowing that this one will be going off to a college in the Midwest, and this one will be going off to a college in the Northeast, and that the likelihood is that they will never see each other again.

What should you say when you bid a classmate goodbye? A classmate whom you have studied with, played games with, dated with—and one whom you will probably never see again?

The kids write down each other's email addresses and cell phone numbers, and they promise that they will stay in touch—but they know, even as they make these promises, that they will probably not keep them. They know that they may stay in touch for a while, but eventually, they will drift apart. They know that they will each make new friends, and they will each have new experiences on their new campuses, and that sooner or later, the memories that unite them will begin to fade.

So what should you say when you bid farewell to a classmate, knowing that your lives are now going to go off in different directions, and that you may never meet again?

I have two suggestions for you.

One is a word that you all know, but that you have probably never stopped to think about the meaning of. And the other is a phrase that you have probably never heard of, but that I believe is worth using at such a moment.

The obvious word to say is "goodbye."

Does everyone here know the origin of this common word?

"Goodbye" is actually the contraction of a prayer. According to the Oxford Dictionary, it comes from the 16th century. It is a shortened form of the phrase, "God be with you."

I can understand why this prayer was said in the Middle Ages. If your friend was going to set sail on a boat, you hugged him and you said "God be with you," because you knew that traveling on the high seas was dangerous. Storms could topple the ship, sending it to the bottom of the sea; pirates could seize the ship, capture its passengers and sell them into slavery; contagious diseases could strike the passengers onboard the ship, and bring them to their deaths. And so, with good reason, when you stood on the dock and bid farewell to a friend who was about to set forth on a journey across the seas, you said, "God be with you."

And if your friend was going to travel over land, you worried, too. There could be robbers lurking on the roads, waiting to attack a passing caravan and rob its passengers. There were dangerous animals lurking in the forests that they would be travelling through. One could lose his way, and die of starvation. There were all kinds of dangers involved in travel in those days, and so, when you embraced your friend before he set forth on his journey, you said to him, "May God be with you."

Travel may be much safer today than it was in the Middle Ages, but we should still not take it for granted. The tradition is that when you come home after a journey overseas, or after an airplane flight, you are supposed to say the *Birkat Hagomel*, thanking God for having arrived safely.

I can still remember the days when you got off a plane after a journey and the first thing you did was find a phone booth and call your parents, so that they would know that you had arrived safely. We don't do that anymore—perhaps because there are no longer any phone booths at the airport—but maybe we should.

And we have all heard enough stories about cruises that became nightmares: when an engine broke down or when the power failed—and so we know that sailing is not always simple or safe. We remember the story, two years ago, of the luxury liner that crashed into a rock off the coast of Italy;

and the story, this year, of the luxury liner whose passengers had to endure horrible conditions, without food and without power, for days, until their ship was finally towed to land. And so, saying "May God be with you" when you see your friend off at the dock or at the airport or at the train station does not sound so naïve to me.

What's wrong, then, with saying "goodbye" when you bid farewell to a classmate, as you go off to one college and she goes off to another one?

Just one thing: Goodbye feels so final. It connotes the fact that you don't expect to ever see each other again. It connotes that your friendship is now over, and that you are both going off to meet new people and to have new experiences, and even if you should chance to meet again—at some class reunion or somewhere else—your relationship will never be what it once was.

"Goodbye" is a harsh word. It sounds not like the closing of a door, but like the locking of a door. And so I wish that there was a kinder word or phrase that we could use when we have to bid farewell to a friend.

A teacher by the name of Ben Greenberg reminded me that there is a term in the Jewish tradition that we ought to consider using, instead of "goodbye," at those moments when we must bid farewell to someone who was once an important part of our lives.

The phrase I have in mind is found on the last page of every single tractate of the Talmud. When you finish a tractate of the Talmud, you have what is called a *siyum*. A *siyum* is a celebration that marks the conclusion of a unit of the Talmud. It is not a small thing to finish a tractate. You have studied this volume for many weeks, and perhaps for months. You have studied it in companionship with a friend or as part of a group. You have studied it not only with a teacher and a study companion, but also with the help of the commentaries that are printed on both margins of the text, and in the back of the book, as well. You have lived with Rashi and the

Baaley Tosafot; with the Ramban and with the Rambam; with the Rishonim, as well as with the Achronim; and with the Tannaim and the Amoraim, who struggle with each other on every page of the Talmud.

And now the tractate is finished. You may be going on to another tractate. But how do you leave this one? How do you part from a volume that has been a part of your life for so many months? What should you say before you close this book and open another one?

At the back of every volume of the Talmud is a prayer to be said on such an occasion. The name of this prayer is significant. It is called a *hadran*, which means, "a promise to return." The key phrase in the prayer is "*hadran alach*"—"we will come back to you." We may be moving on to a new tractate, but we say, in this prayer, that we promise we will not forget you, and that we will come back to you, O tractate.

Ben Greenberg suggests that perhaps this prayer should be adapted slightly so that it could be said not only to a tractate, but also to a friend. If we could do that, we could say to our friend, *We may be parting now: we may each be going on to new places and new experiences—but we promise that we will come back to each other, if not physically, then at least in our memories. The things that we did together will not disappear, but will always remain a precious part of who we are and how we live. You are a part of me, and therefore, the memory of you will travel with me wherever I go; and I hope that I am now a part of you, too, and that the memory of what we did together will be with you wherever you go.*

Wouldn't that be a powerful way to say goodbye when we have to part with good friends who are now going off in different directions than we are?

I offer this prayer for your consideration, and I suggest that you share it with your teenagers to think about saying on the last day of camp or the last day of school or whenever they have to let go of friends with whom they have been so very close. I think that "*hadran alach*" is a kinder and gentler way to bid farewell than "goodbye" is. I think it is a better phrase because it points toward the future, and not just to the present and the past. Suggest it to your children, and see if they agree.

And now, let me say a word to the rest of us: to those of us who are not graduating at this season of the year.

In this age of tweeting and texting and smartphones and iPods and iPads, do we really have to lose contact with our friends when we separate? When our grandparents left the old country and came to America, they knew that they would never see their parents again. They knew that they would probably never speak to their parents ever again, either, for telephones were not common in their time.

I have a friend who lives in Israel who tells me that when she went on *aliyah*, back in the '70s, it was very, very difficult to keep in touch with her parents back in Brooklyn. She had to set a time when she would speak to them, and then she had to go to the drugstore and wait in line until the call came through. And then she had to tell them the news and describe the progress that the children were making as fast as she could, because in three minutes or so, the people behind her in line would get restless and they would tell her that it was their turn and that she had to get off.

But today it is not like that. Today we have more means of keeping in touch than ever before. Today you can speak to someone who lives on the other side of the world, and with Skype, you can even see them while you talk! What a blessing that is! And so, let me remind the graduates as well as the non-graduates that you ***can*** stay in touch with your friends from high school, or from anywhere else, even if you go in different directions. You can do that easier than any generation in history ever could. And for that, you should be grateful.

Don't take these wondrous inventions for granted, but appreciate them. Understand that thanks to these new inventions, you can live anywhere in the world and stay in touch with friends who live anywhere else in the world. Realize what a great *bracha* that is, and realize how fortunate you are to live in a time when this technology is available to make your lives better and to make your friendships stronger.

And for those who have come here today to say *Yizkor* for those whom we loved, let me say this: We can no longer call them up on the phone—would that we could! ***Would that we could***! But we can stay connected with them by means of memory. We can consult them when we do not know what to do. We can thank them when we have achievements that are based on theirs. We can bless them by continuing the values by which they lived. And if we do these things, then they are still a part of us and we are still a part of them.

So let us take comfort in the ease of communications in the world in which we live today, and let these instruments enable us to stay in touch with our friends, wherever they may be. Let us take comfort in the memories embedded within our souls that enable us to stay in touch with those we loved who are no longer here among us. And may their memories literally be a blessing—to us, and through us, until the end of time.

Amen.

30

# What Should We Do When The Neighborhood Changes?

## The Ninth of Av

Before I begin, let me say just one thing, which is that I revere and appreciate all the effort and all the sweat and all the donations that went into the construction of this building in which we meet. And let me say that I believe that this building and this neighborhood have a great present and a great future. Therefore, I hope that this sermon will not be misunderstood.

Yet I must tell you that I envy the building in which the Israelites worshipped as they made their way through the wilderness. I envy it because it was portable. When the cloud went up, they disassembled the *mishkan*, put it on wagons, and they journeyed. When the cloud rested, they encamped and put the *mishkan* together again.

Would that we could do that with the buildings we put up for the glory of God in our time, because sooner or later, the neighborhood changes: the Jews move out; and we are left with a mighty building that is no longer near our homes and that can no longer meets the needs of our people. And then what should we do?

I love the story that is told about Congregation Shaarey Zedeck, in Detroit. Shaarey Zedeck is over 130 years old, and in its history, it has moved three times. Each time, it has been sold to a black church. The story is told that one day, Rabbi Morris Adler pulled up to the synagogue—which was being built in Southfield—and he saw a black minister watching the construction. He said to the minister, "Excuse me, but what are you doing here?" And the minister answered, "I want to make sure that you do a good job."

I don't know if that story is true or not, but it is a bitter *gelechter* if it is. For what is true of Shaarey Zedeck is true of many other synagogues all over America that have been abandoned by their people and are now black churches.

And this is why Aitz Chayim, which is a synagogue in the suburbs of Chicago, has developed an innovative way of observing Tisha B'Av for our time. They believe that this should be a day for remembering not only the First and Second temples that were destroyed many centuries ago, but that it should be a day for remembering all of the other sacred Jewish buildings that have been destroyed ever since—including those that were once at the heart of our Jewish neighborhoods. And so what they do is they go back, each year, to one of the churches that was formerly a synagogue; or they go back to a building that was once a Jewish community center and is now a warehouse; or they go to a Jewish school that once flourished and is now abandoned; and they hold their Tisha B'Av services there.

They go to places where Jews once lived—places that have now become black churches but still have recognizable Hebrew words carved into the stone on the outside of the building, or stained glass windows with Hebrew lettering inside the building. They explain to the black minister, who now officiates there—and who wonders why there is a pool of water located in the basement—that this was once a *mikveh*. And for a brief hour or two, they bring what was once a Jewish center back to life again. And then they go back to the suburbs, and leave this once-Jewish building to its new owners.

That is the way of the world. Neighborhoods are born, and populations migrate. When a neighborhood changes, the institutions created to meet the needs of people within them change too. Synagogues are built when enough Jews move into a neighborhood, and synagogues close when enough Jews leave a neighborhood. There is very little that anyone can do to hold back this law of life. But the people of Aitz Hayim give these places at least one day a year to be remembered, and I think that that is a good thing to do.

Let me tell you the saddest poem about American Jewish life that I know. It is a poem called "*In the Temple*," and it was written in 1927. It was written by a Yiddish poet named Yehoash who came to America from Lithuania. Yehoash watched some of the great Jewish sanctuaries go up in the 1920s. He saw the Jews of Boston import marble from Italy, with which to build Temple Mishkan Tfillah in Roxbury; he saw the Jews of New York, Chicago and other cities doing the same thing. He saw the American Jewish communities investing a fortune in these buildings. These buildings were monuments to the power and the prosperity of American Jewry. But Yehoash had a sense that the prosperity that enabled the Jews of America to build these impressive edifices might not go on forever. And so he wrote this poem:

In the high temple
A bee buzzes.
In the high, quiet temple
A bee sings:
Buzz, buzz, buzz.
No saints with haloes round their heads exist in this building,
Just bees that buzz, buzz, buzz.
There are no marble pillars with blue and red veins inside anymore.
Just bees that buzz, buzz, buzz.
There are no plush seats inside anymore.
Just bees that buzz, buzz, buzz,
And then fly out through a window.
They fly out of the temple
Out of the temple—
That is now silent and still.

I must tell you that I shudder when I read this poem.

I shudder to think of this building, which once contained so many prayers that flew from there, up towards heaven, now sitting empty, alone and abandoned—with only the sound of the bees heard inside.

The truth is that this poem is not really completely accurate. Prayers are still heard inside some of these buildings. But they are not our prayers. They are not prayers in Hebrew. Now they are the prayers of their new owners. Now they are the prayers of the new people who live in these neighborhoods. The Jews are gone, and the buildings have been left behind.

And so, there is something that I want to ask of you today.

We never want this building to become quiet, with the exception of the buzzing of the bees; we never want this building to be empty and alone. We want this building to be full of noise forever. We want it to be full of the sound of little children learning Torah, and we want it to be full of the sound of brides and grooms dancing on the day of their greatest joy. We want this building to be full of the sound of Jews who have come together to discuss—and even to argue—about what to do to enhance Jewish life here and around the world. And so my question to you this morning is this: What can we do to ensure the future of this building, the future of our faith and the future of our community? What can we do in order to make sure that Yehoash's poem never comes true here? What can we do in order to make sure that this place never grows quiet and silent and empty of Jews?

I have two modest suggestions to make today, and I hope that you will consider them with an open mind and an open heart.

The first is that in order to preserve this place, we ought to leave this place—at least, some of the time. And the second is that in order to preserve this place, we ought to consider sharing this place.

Let me explain:

Does it make sense to have a sanctuary that is filled only three days a year, and empty the rest of the time? Does it make sense to have classrooms and committee rooms that are empty much of the year?

Why should we not go out to where our people are? And why should we not find ways of sharing this space with others who need it—but only part of the time—just as we do?

There are charter schools in this city that our children go to. Why not have some of our afternoon classes meet there, so that parents need not pick up their children and transport them here in the late afternoon, when many of them are still at work? If we move our classes to where our children are, perhaps they and their parents will come to us when we celebrate our holidays here, in this place.

And why should we not do what Congregation Rodfei Zedeck, on the south side of Chicago, did a number of years ago? When its neighborhood changed, Rodfei Zedeck's property was reconfigured and an arrangement was made whereby the local Jewish center uses part of it and others use part of it—so that the building is never empty and never quiet.

And why not think about someday doing what Congregation Kehillath Israel, in Boston, is now doing? Now that the neighborhood has changed, part of its building is being made into an independent living center, so that there will always be people living next door who are able to help maintain its *minyan*, attend classes and provide a dependable source of income, to ensure the synagogue's future.

And why should we not think of doing what Chabad learned to do years ago? Until recently, Chabad did not invest in buildings; instead, they made use of converted storerooms and houses. They went out and held classes and programs in the offices of their members. Lawyers and businessmen invited their colleagues and their clients to share lunch together, and to study Torah together in their offices. And it worked! The money and energy that others spent on buildings and on maintaining buildings, Chabad invested in people and programs—and that is one of the reasons for their success.

Please understand: I am ***not*** suggesting that we should not take pride in these buildings that we have inherited. Of course we should be grateful to those whose efforts gave us these buildings in which we pray today! I am only suggesting that the age of the cathedral synagogue—the age of the mighty edifice that towered over the neighborhood, giving a sense of awe, pride and status to the Jewish community; the age of the lofty building that was filled to capacity three days a year and that was empty the rest of the time—is not the kind of edifice that we need today, or that we will need in the future.

Instead, we need to learn how to share our building with partners who need it part-time, just as we do. We need to learn how to go out to where our people are, instead of sitting back and waiting for them to come to us.

For in the end, what counts is not how big or how impressive our building is, but how busy and noisy and full of life it is. What counts is if it is a place where God's Torah is taught and where God's people gather to sing, study, rejoice and to just be together: to live and to love together.

And, one more word: We need to remember that no one joins a building. People join a congregation. It makes no difference whether a building is big or small, beautiful or not. What draws Jews into Jewish life is whether or not they are welcomed and made to feel at home in the synagogue. What matters is whether they are shown to a seat, shown the page and shown that congregation members are truly glad to have them there.

This week, we will mark Tisha B'Av. This week, we will remember the two main times in our history when the Holy Temple was destroyed. Let us also remember, this week, how our people survived these two destructions. Let us remember that our people found new ways, and that they found new places, in which to worship God. Let us remember that our people created the synagogue and the house of study even before the Temple came down. Let us remember that our people learned to worship God through prayer and through the doing of good deeds even before the sacrificial system came to an end. And let us learn that we can do what they did—in our time, and in this place. Let us learn to build new houses of worship, and let us learn how to share the ones we have.

For if we do that, we can have faith that the blessings of the Lord will be upon the work of our hands.

Amen.

31

# The Marie Antoinette of the Talmud

## Tisha B'Av

This week we will observe Tisha B'Av, the day on which we commemorate the fall of the first and second Jewish commonwealths. And so it is about Tisha B'av that I want to speak to you today.

There is an interesting law about Tisha B'Av that I love. Tisha B'av is a sad day; it is a fast day. Therefore, you are not allowed to enjoy any pleasures on this day. You are not allowed to eat or to drink. You are not allowed to adorn yourself with perfume, or to make love on this day. This I understand. These are pleasures, and therefore you cannot have them on this day. But then the Code of Jewish Law goes on to say: You are not allowed to study Torah on this day. Why?

Because Torah study is one of the greatest delights that a human being can enjoy. It is a pleasure to study Torah, and therefore, you are not allowed to do it on Tisha B'Av.

I find that a fascinating restriction. Let no one ever tell you that the law is a burden, or that studying it is a chore and a bore. The law is a delight, and studying it is a joy. The proof of that is that you are not allowed to study Torah on a fast day.

So let me remind you of this restriction. I know that there are some who observe this law about not studying Torah not only on Tisha B'Av, but every day of the year. But, still, let me ask you to not study Torah on Tisha B'Av. Will you remember this restriction, please?

For those of you who really love to study, however, and who find it hard to go a whole day without studying any part of the Torah—especially on a day when you do not work and you do not watch television, and you do not play ball or play cards or have any other pleasures—let me tell you that there is a loophole in the law. The sages say that you are allowed to study the *agadot hahurban*, the stories about how and why the Temple was destroyed, most of which are found on Page 55A and B of the tractate of Gittin, in the Talmud. After all, if you study these stories, you will learn some lessons in how to live properly and morally, so that you do not commit the sins for which the Temple was destroyed.

Who knows any of the *agadot hahurban*?

In the *agadot hahurban*, there is the story of the party that went wrong. A man had a good friend named Kamtsa and a bitter enemy named Bar Kamtsa. The man had a party, and he intended to invite one and not the other, but somehow there was a snafu, and his enemy got the invitation that was intended for his friend. The enemy came to the party, thinking that he had been invited, and when he got there, the host went ballistic and threw him out. That is the incident, according to the sages, that led to the destruction of the Temple.

And then there is the story of Rabbi Yochanan ben Zackai, who managed to get out of Jerusalem during the siege and go to the Roman general, whom he persuaded to let him establish a school in the village of Yavneh. That school led to the continuation and advancement of the Jewish way of life after the fall of the Temple.

Perhaps we will study these stories during Tisha B'Av, if you come. But today, I want to study with you a lesser-known story—the story of a woman that is found in the *agadot hahurban*. Most of the stories we have in the Talmud are about men, but this is the story of a woman: a fascinating woman, a woman from whom I believe we have much to learn. Rebecca Linzer, who teaches Talmud in a marvelous educational institution for women in Israel taught me of this story, which I want to study with you today.

The name of the woman whom we are going to study today is Martha, the daughter of Boethius. Rebecca Linzer calls her the "Marie Antoinette of the Talmud," and I will explain why she calls her that in a few minutes, but first—listen to her story, as it is found in Gittin, Page 56A. The story is in three parts, and I think that if we read it carefully, it has three lessons to teach us for our own lives.

The story goes like this:

> *Martha, the daughter of Boethius, was one of the richest women in Jerusalem. She lived a life of luxury in a palatial home, and she had a great many servants. And then came the siege of Jerusalem.*
>
> *When the city was under siege, there was a great famine. Martha sent her servant out, and said, "Bring me some fine flour." I guess she wanted her cook to make some special delicacy, and so she wanted the best flour.*

*The servant went out and came back, saying that there was no fine flour to be had anywhere in the city; there was some white flour available, though. Martha sent him back to buy white flour, but by the time he got back to the marketplace, all the white flour was gone, too. The servant came back and told her that there was no white flour available, but that there was some dark flour. She told him to go and buy her some dark flour. But by the time he got back to the marketplace, there was no dark flour left; there was still some barley flour available, though. The servant came back and told Martha that there was no dark flour left, but that there was still some barley flour. She told him to go back and buy her some barley flour. The servant went back to the marketplace, but by the time he got there, there was no barley flour left, either.*

*Martha had already taken off her shoes, but by now she was so exasperated, and probably so hungry, that she decided to go to the marketplace herself. She said, "I will go out myself and see if I can find something to eat."*

*On the way to the marketplace, Martha got some dung stuck to her foot, and she died (perhaps in shock, for nothing like this had ever happened to her in her life). When Rabbi Yochanan ben Zackai heard what had happened to Martha, he applied to her a verse from the Book of Echa: "The tender and delicate woman who would not set the sole of her foot upon the ground has perished."*

There is a second version of the story, too. In the second version, Martha ate a fig left by Rabbi Zadok and became sick and died.

Who was Rabbi Zadok? Rabbi Zadok was a pious person who fasted daily, for 40 years, so that Jerusalem not be destroyed. He was so thin that when he ate anything, the food could be seen as it passed through his throat. When he wanted to restore himself, they would bring him a fig and he would suck the juice of it, and throw the rest of the fig away. This leftover part of the fig is what Martha, the daughter of Boethius, ate in her desperation; and it was this that killed her, according to the second version of the story.

And then there is a third version of this story. This version says that when Martha was about to die, she took all the gold and silver that she had with her—the gold and silver that she had taken with her with which she had intended to buy food—and she threw it away, saying, "What good is this gold and silver to me now?" When she did this, she fulfilled the verse that is found in the Book of Echa: "They shall cast their silver into the street."

What does this story mean?

Let us take the story apart, with the help of Rebecca Linzer, and see if we can understand what it means in its own historical context. Then let us also see if we can understand what it means to us today.

First, we need to know that Martha, the daughter of Boethius, was a very, very wealthy woman. She was the Mrs. Rockefeller of her time. She was the wife of Yehoshua ben Galma, the *kohen gadol*. In fact, according to the Talmud, she bought her husband the position of *kohen gadol* with her money.

And now we see this scene in which her servant goes running back and forth from her house, to the marketplace and back, reporting to her that all the luxuries she wants to buy are no longer available because the city is under siege and the people are starving. Each time he comes back and reports to her that something she wants is not available, she grudgingly agrees to accept the next best thing. Up until now, she has never eaten anything but fine flour in her life—but since there is none available, she is willing to eat white flour, etc. She has no understanding of what it means to live in a world in which there is no flour of any kind available. She has no idea what starvation or shortage means. She has no idea of what poor people go through, for she has never lacked for anything in her life. That is why Rebecca Linzer calls her the "Marie Antoinette of the Talmud." Martha simply cannot understand what it means when she hears that nothing at all is available, just as when Marie Antoinette was told that the people had no bread, she said: "Well, in that case, let them eat cake." Look at how many times the poor servant has to go back and forth, back and forth, back and forth, before Martha finally grasps the idea that there is no food of any kind available. She simply cannot comprehend the idea that the world outside is not available for purchase, because all her life, all she had to do was snap her fingers and tell her servants what she wanted, and they would bring it to her. The idea that the world outside has no food—not even for her—is simply too shocking and too bewildering for her to comprehend. And so, finally, she goes out to see the situation for herself. Up until this point, I imagine that she, herself, had never been shopping. Before, she just had to snap her fingers, and one of her servants would come running. But now, for the first time in her life, she is so hungry that she goes out to buy food herself.

According to the midrash, Martha is so eager, so desperate and so hungry that she goes out into the street without even waiting to put on her sandals. She goes out barefoot—perhaps for the first time in her life. And when her foot comes in contact with dung and dirt—something that she has never experienced in her rich and pampered life—she faints from the shock and the indignity, and she dies. Martha has never encountered the "real world"— the world of dirt and dung, the world in which all the rest of the people in her country live—and the shock and the disgrace of it causes her to faint. And she dies on the street, like any commoner.

The "*Midrash Echa Rabbati*" explains why Martha was so upset when she walked upon the streets without sandals. It says that when she wanted to go to the temple, her servants would lay out royal carpets from the entrance to her house to the temple, so that her feet would not have to touch the dirt on the streets. (It sounds a little bit like the red carpet that the movie stars walk on, when they arrive for the Oscars.) So, now, this woman who is used to walking on royal carpets has to walk, for perhaps the first time in her life, on streets—barefoot—and the shock and the shame is too much for her, and so she dies.

Now, what does the story of Rabbi Zadok and his figs mean?

Rabbi Zadok was a saint who devoted his life to praying, fasting and working to prevent the destruction of Jerusalem. That is why he only ate the juice of figs to keep him going, and nothing else. But what was this woman doing during these 40 years? She was living inside her house, utterly oblivious to what was going on outside. She was living a life of luxury, eating whatever delicacy she wanted, and ignoring the plight of the poor, the corruption of Jerusalem and the danger of its collapse. She was living a literally sheltered life, unaware and uninterested in what was going on outside. At the end, she realizes this, and she tries to do something to avoid the calamity. She decides that she will do what Zadok has done for these last 40 years: she will eat just the juice of a fig. But it is too late. By the time she understands how desperate the plight of the people is; by the time she is ready to take some action to save them; by the time she wants to copy the piety of Zadok—the die is cast. So she dies with the fig of Zadok in her hand. That is the meaning of the second version of the story of how Martha, the daughter of Boethius, died.

According to the third version of this story, when Martha realized that all her money could do her no good—when she realized that, no matter how much money she had, there was simply no white flour, no black flour, no fine flour, no barley flour, no anything for sale—she simply threw her money away. All her money was of no use when there was nothing it could buy. She was like the people in the Weimar Republic, between the two world wars in Germany, who used to go shopping with wheelbarrows of cash because their money devaluated so fast that it took a fortune to buy a loaf of bread. Martha throws her money away because it is no longer the basis of her status and the source of her power, as it has been until now. It was literally worth nothing, and so she threw it away.

And what do these three stories mean for us today?

Rebecca Linzer says that these stories are meant to teach us that we must be sensitive to the world around us, unlike Martha and unlike Marie Antoinette. We must not lock ourselves up in our fancy houses and in our gated communities, as they did, not knowing or caring about what goes on in the world outside. We must go out into the community—not as Martha did, when it was already too late, but before—and we must do whatever we can to help those who are struggling with poverty in our society. Martha waited until it was too late. We must act now, because, just as Abraham Lincoln said that a society cannot exist half-slave and half-free, so we must understand that a society cannot be secure when half its people are obscenely rich and the other half lives in body-breaking, spirit-breaking, miserable poverty.

Tisha B'Av is meant to be a time for contemplation. It is a time for thinking about why the two temples were destroyed and about whether our own society is also vulnerable. And so, let us take the story of Martha, the daughter of Boethius, seriously. Let us take it as a warning to ourselves about how we live and about the destruction that may loom for us if we don't change.

Let us not make the mistake that Martha made by going out and seeing what the world of the poor is like when it is too late. Let us not make the mistake that she did by trying to do what is right when it is too late. Let us not make the mistake that she made by living a life of luxury in our closed-in homes, oblivious to the problems of society around us, and then be surprised and bewildered when that world collapses.

The story of Martha, the daughter of Boethius, is almost 2,000 years old, but it speaks directly to us and to the way in which we live. Let us listen to her story and let us take it to heart now, now, ***now***—before it is too late.

Amen.

32

# What Should I Do with the Rest of My Life?

## Reflections on the 70th anniversary of my bar mitzvah

I must tell you that I am really very excited today.

I have been going around the house practicing my *haftorah* for weeks.

And I have been thinking, for months now, about what I should say today.

Unfortunately, I lost the speech that I gave at my first bar mitzvah. I have looked all over the house, and I can't find it, and so I had to write a new one for this occasion.

The subject of my sermon today is going to be: What should I do with the rest of my life?

And what advice should I give to you on what you should do with the rest of your life—when you get to be my age?

What should you do with your days when the mortgage is paid off and the children are on their own and the grandchildren are out of reach and you no longer need to work for a living? What should you do when you reach the stage when you can do whatever you want to do, and you don't know what to do? This is the question that I want to deal with today.

But before I begin, let me tell you that my childhood rabbi used to begin every single sermon that he gave the same way. He would say, "*Eder ich gey redden, gey ich zogen a pur verter*," which means, "Before I speak, I want to say a few things." And therefore, out of respect to his memory, I want to begin my sermon this morning the same way that he did.

Before I speak, I want to say "thank you" to a number of people:

First, I want to thank Rabbi Baum, for graciously giving up his sermon time in order to let me speak today. I don't know if you realize what a generous gift it is when a rabbi gives up his sermon time to another colleague. It means that he is going to have to walk around all week with an undelivered sermon inside, and that is not an easy thing to do. And so, I want to thank Rabbi Baum, and tell you that I am happy to call him my rabbi.

Second, I want to say "thank you" to this synagogue, which has taken me in and made me feel at home in my years of retirement from the pulpit. I think that this is a very special synagogue. It is warm and friendly, and it has a great many very good people in it. And therefore, I am proud to belong.

Third, I want to say "thank you" to those who have come from near and far to share in my *simcha* today. I want to say "thank you," first of all and most of all, to my children, Yosef and Vitina, and to my grandson, Nathan. They are very busy people and yet have taken the time to come and be with us today. I thank you for letting me have a place in your lives, and I am deeply honored that you have come to be with us today. And I want to thank my granddaughter, Naomi, who tried to get here but was prevented from doing so by the weather that closed the airport and caused her flight to be cancelled.

I want to say "thank you" to my nephew, Gerry, and my niece, Sue. And I want to say "thank you" to my friends, Phil and Selma Silverman, who have come all the way from California to be with us today.

I want to say "thank you" to those of you who are alumni of Beth Tikvah, and who have come back here today in order to share in my *simcha*. I want to say "thank you" to those of you who have come here today from Boynton, and from Wellington, and from Miami, in honor of my *simcha*.

And I want to say a special "thank you" to Sue for being here today. Sue has not been able to come to services for many years now, because she is not well, but she is here today because, thank God, she is feeling much better. There are two possible explanations for why she is feeling better. One is that she is on a new medical regimen, which is helping; the other is that we brought a woman into the house to help take care of her, and therefore, she feels threatened—and that is why she is getting better. Whichever it is, I am delighted that she is able to be here today.

And now, let me begin:

My sermon today is addressed to two groups within the congregation: It is addressed to those of you who are old, as I am, and it is addressed to those of you who may someday become old. And so if you are in either of these two categories, I urge you to listen to what I am going to say today.

People make all kinds of jokes about birthdays. But I think that underneath the humor, it is a very serious day when you reach a big number, like this one is. It is a time for looking back, and it is a time for looking forward. And it is a time for asking yourself some very serious questions.

One question that comes into your mind on a day like this is: How did I get to be this age?

After all, many people—who were better than I am, morally, and who took better care of themselves, physically, than I have—did not live as long as I have.

You and I know many good people who lived short lives, and we know many bad people who lived long lives. You and I know many people who watched their diets carefully, and who never smoked or drank, and yet died young; and you and I know many people who smoked, drank and overate, and yet lived to a ripe old age.

And so, you have to wonder: How come they died young? And how come I have lived so long?

The answer is: I don't know.

I don't know, but in my case, I have three guesses.

The first explanation I have for why I have reached this age is: exercise. I believe that the secret is that I never, never, never, never, ***never*** exercise.

I believe that exercise prolongs your life, but not by as much time as you waste exercising. And therefore, I have tried to live my life by the teachings of Robert Hutchins of the University of Chicago, who said, "Whenever I get the urge to exercise, I lie down until it goes away."

I believe that the second explanation for why I have lived so long is that all my life, I have adhered to a balanced diet. My idea of a balanced diet is pretzels in one hand, and candy in the other.

I have been faithful to that diet all my life.

The third explanation for why I have lived to reach this age is—and, I think that this explanation is as good as any other—really a *mazel zach*, a matter of luck.

I believe that how long you live is really a matter of good genes, good luck and the kindness of God, and so I claim no credit for this achievement.

I am not going to deal with the question of what I have accomplished in my life, and I am not going to deal with what I would do over again if I could—for these are personal questions, too personal to answer here, today. And I am not really the judge of what I accomplished in my life, anyway—God is.

I do not want to think about what I should have done differently in my life, because the past is the past and it cannot be redone. It gets you nowhere to think about all the "What if I had?"s, or the "What if I hadn't"s in your life.

That does you no good.

Instead, the question that I want to deal with today is this: What should I do with the rest of my life—however long or short it may be? And what advice should I give to you on what you should do with the rest of your life, if you should live to be my age?

In order to answer that question, I thought that I would go to some of the people who have reached this milestone before me, and ask them: How did you live out the last years of your life? And do you have any wisdom or any guidance, based on your experience, that you can share with me on what I should do with the remaining years of my life?

That is what I used to do whenever I had a problem and needed advice. But I found out that this is not an easy thing to do, because in this area, there are very few role models available who you can consult. The reason why there are so very few role models to consult is because, up until our generation, life expectancy was much shorter than it is today.

My father and one of my two brothers both died before they got to the age that I am now. Most of my teachers died long before they reached my age. And therefore, they are not available, and so I can't ask them my question.

But I did find some people who lived as long as I have so far, and so I went to them, and asked them: What can you teach me about how to live in old age?

And do you know what I found?

One of them gave me terrible advice. Really terrible advice.

A couple of them gave me fairly helpful advice.

And only two of them gave me really helpful advice.

Let me begin by telling you about the person who gave me really terrible advice.

There was a certain rabbi who lived in another state (I won't tell you his name, though, and if you guess who it was, I will deny it). But he was my classmate, and he was my age. Some years ago, this rabbi reached a milestone. It was not 83; it was 75. And when he reached this milestone, his wife decided to throw him a surprise party. She invited all of their friends, and she told them to come early. And then, when he arrived, she gave the signal; they doused the lights; and then, when he walked in, they all called out in one voice, "Happy birthday!"

And this rabbi was very angry.

He turned to his wife, and he said to her, in front of all of us: "How dare you do this? Who gave you the right to have this party without talking to me about it first?"

And he explained why. He said "I got this job that I now have by lying about my age. I told the interviewing committee that I was 70, not 75. And now, if they find out how old I really am, I may lose my job. And therefore, I am very angry at you for what you did!"

The rabbi sulked for the rest of the evening,

And that spoiled the party for his wife, and for all the rest of us who were there.

I think that I understand why he did that. He did it because we live in a culture that worships youth and fears the coming of old age. And so he felt that he had to lie about his age in order to get a job.

My friend is not the only one who has done that. We have a multi-million-dollar industry in America: face lifts, wrinkle removers and of cosmetics of all kinds, by which we try to deny the truth about how old we are.

My teacher, Dr. Heschel, used to say that in our culture, it is considered more rude and more intrusive to ask a person how old he is than it is to ask him how much money he has, or to ask him about the intimate details of his sex life.

I must tell you that, for one, brief moment, I was tempted not to have this *simcha*; I was afraid that people would treat me differently if they found out how old I was. But then I decided that I was going to have it anyway—because ***I don't want to live a lie***!

I grew up in a culture in which the older you were, the more respected you were. I grew up in a society in which the words of the Torah were taken seriously. The Torah says, *lifney seyva takum, vihadarta piney zaken*—"you shall stand up before the old, and you shall honor the aged." And therefore, this rabbi who lied about his age is not going to be my role model, because I don't want to live the way he did. I don't want to live in constant fear that someone will find out how old I am, and think less of me as a result.

That is a coward's way to live, and I don't want to live my life as a coward—hiding my identity, and hoping that I don't get caught. Therefore, I will not let this rabbi be my role model. No way!

The second person I turned to was a woman—I don't remember her name—who wrote a famous poem, called, "*When I Am an Old Woman I Shall Wear Purple*."

Do any of you know that poem? It is a lovely poem, and part of me likes it very much.

But I believe that it only teaches a half-truth. It says that when she grows old, she is going to wear purple if she wants to, and not worry about what people will say. She will do things that she would not have even considered before—such as taking the cellophane wrappers off the living room furniture and entertaining there.

Did any of you grow up in a house in which they kept cellophane wrappers on the living room furniture? And in which they only used the good dishes when company came to visit? I did.

And then, this poet goes on, saying that when she grows old, she is not going to deprive herself of things that she wants because she is saving for a rainy day. Instead, she will enjoy whatever she wants—whenever she wants to. And if it rains afterward? *Nu*—so it will rain afterwards. What will she care?

I like this poem, because it teaches an important truth, which is this: You should appreciate and enjoy every moment of your life, and not postpone pleasures until later, because there may not be a later.

And that is true.

But after I thought about it, I realized that this is only a half-truth. Now I realize that there is something missing in it. Do you know what's missing in this poem?

It only talks about not postponing the pleasures of life, but pleasure is not all that there is to life. There is more to life than enjoyment.

When you get old, you have to have a ***purpose*** in your life, and having fun is not enough of a purpose.

If all you have in your life is fun, you will soon find out that the best card games eventually get boring, and the best cruises eventually get wearisome, and the best tennis games eventually get tiresome. Your life will eventually become jaded, and boring, and empty, if all that you have in it is fun.

And therefore, with all due respect to this woman and to her wisdom, I don't think that she can be a good role model for us. Fun is not enough to fill your days, when you grow old.

So then I turned to Judith Viorst, and I asked her for advice.

Do you know who Judith Viorst is? She is a very talented poet and writer, and she has written a series of good books. One was about turning 50, one was about turning 60 and one was about turning 70. Now she has written a new one, called, "*Unexpectedly Eighty.*"

I thought: She's smart, and she's talented. I'll read her new book, and see what she can teach me about how I should live in my old age.

So I did. And do you know what I found out?

I hate to tell you this, but her book on becoming 80 is delightful and it is funny—but it did not give me any useful guidance on how to live in old age. None.

Listen to this poem, for example, called "*How Do I know That I'm Old?*":

> I remember running boards, Victrolas, and Frigidaires,
> And when the really rich were only millionaires,
> And I remember when it was still legal to start classes with school prayers.
> There was a lot of good in the days of yore,
> And they sure don't write songs like "*Stardust*" anymore.
> And the next verse is:
> I remember "*Our Girl Sunday*" on the radio,
> And watching television when the screen was mostly snow.
> And I remember staying out of swimming pools, because of polio.
> There were things both to cherish and deplore—
> But they sure don't write songs like "*Stardust*" anymore.

And she goes on that way for six more verses, contrasting the way it was in the good old days with the way it is today. And every verse ends with the same refrain: "They don't make songs like '*Stardust*' anymore."

Why am I uncomfortable with this kind of poetry, as clever as it is?

I am uncomfortable with this book because it is a glorification of the past at the expense of the present, and that is not a healthy way to live. The most boring people I know are those who live in the past, and who always want to talk about what life was like in the "good old days." We get bored listening to these people, because the past is past. And anyone who tries to live in the past ends up missing a lot of the pleasure that is available in the present.

Just as you can't drive a car by looking in the rear view mirror all the time, so you can't live in the present by focusing only on how good yesterday was. The truth is that, as my friend, Wolfe Kelman, used to say, "Even nostalgia is not what it used to be."

And this is why, with all due respect, I don't believe that Judith Viorst is a good role model in how to grow old—at least, not in my opinion.

So I wondered: Who should I turn to for advice and for guidance on how to be old?

By this time, I was really getting frustrated, and so I turned to two people whom I have turned to many times in my life when I needed advice and guidance. The first was my teacher, Dr. Heschel. Even though he, himself, did not live long enough to reach old age—he died at 65—he gave me some very good guidance nevertheless.

Heschel once gave a talk at the White House, at a conference on aging, and this is part of what he said:

> *"Old age should be regarded not as an age of stagnation, but as the age of opportunity for inner growth. The years of old age should be a time for attaining the high values that we failed to achieve before, the insights that we failed to acquire until now and the wisdom that we ignored when we were young, because we were so busy with less important things. The years of old age should be considered formative years: years that are rich in possibilities and as a time to unlearn the follies of a lifetime; a time to see through the self-deceptions we have lived by in our younger years, and to deepen our understanding and our wisdom.*

> *One ought to enter old age the way one enters the senior year at a university. We need senior universities, where the purpose of learning will be not to advance your career but to enrich your mind, and purify your soul. We need to create senior universities, where the purpose of learning will be learning for its own sake."*

There was a man sitting at that talk that day—I don't remember his name, but as he sat there, he said to me, "You know: he's right." And this man figured out that college dormitories are usually pretty empty during the summertime, and so they should be available cheap and faculty is available during the summertime, and so they should be available, too. And so this man created Elderhostel. And today, seniors can go to any college in America—and to many overseas, as well—and study for a week or two, not for a degree, and not for grades, but just for the sake of learning.

Dr. Heschel's talk that day led to that idea.

And then, Dr. Heschel went on to say something that I don't think has happened yet.

He said, "Judging by the programs that many senior citizens centers offer, we treat the old as if they were retarded—and not just retired."

He's right. Go into any one of these homes and look at the programs and daily schedules that are posted on the wall. They start with exercise, and then move on to movies, and then to card games, and then to dance classes and then back to card games.

Every senior citizen home that I know has a director of recreation on its staff, who is in charge of physical activities. Dr. Heschel said, "There is nothing wrong with that, but there ought to be a director of learning, who is in charge of educational and spiritual activities on the staff, as well. We insist on minimum standards of physical well-being at these places. We should also have minimum standards for intellectual well-being."

He is right. And that is why I am going to try to keep on reading and to keep on studying, for as long as God gives me the strength to do so. Because just as you have to use your muscles, or else they will atrophy, so you have to use your mind—or else ***it*** will atrophy.

I have made one slight change in my reading habits in recent years. I still read two or three books of Jewish interest every week, but now I try to read a book that has nothing to do with Jewish life, as well. Now I read books on history or psychology or on other subjects, as well: for no practical purpose, but just for the sake of learning.

But then, I asked myself: Is study really enough to fill your life in old age? And are there limits to how much you can study when you get old?

I think that there are.

And so I turned to other people who are living long lives, and I asked them what they could teach me about how to live in old age.

One of the people whom I turned to was I. F. Stone.

Do any of you know who I F Stone was?

I.F. Stone was a great journalist. He devoted his career to exposing scandals both in business and in government. Can you imagine how busy he would be, if he were alive today? Some of you may remember that he had his own newspaper. It was called the I. F. Stone Weekly. And he was a hero to many liberals, back in the '60s and '70s.

When I. F. Stone turned 80, he retired from journalism and closed down his newspaper. And he announced his next project.

He said he had hired a tutor, so that he could devote his life from that time on to learning Greek. Why? So that he could study Plato, Aristotle and Socrates, in the original. He announced that he was going to do that because you can't really understand these philosophers in translation; it is not the same. He said: "I want to be able to study them in the original, and so I am going to spend the rest of my life learning Greek."

So I wondered: Should I make him my role model? This man who began studying Greek at the age of 80?

At first, I was tempted; but then I thought it over, and I decided not to—for a very simple reason. I admire him for trying to learn a whole new language in his 80s, but I don't think that I can do it. And if I tried, I think that I would just be setting myself up for failure, because it is just not realistic.

And therefore, with all due respect to I. F. Stone, I am not going to learn Greek, or Arabic or Chinese, or any other language—not at my age. And I am not going to go back to school to learn how to be a nuclear physicist, or a brain surgeon or a mathematician, either.

I may open up a driving school. That's possible. Other schools teach defensive driving. I could teach ***offensive*** driving. That I could do. But I am not going to try to learn a new language, or learn a new profession, or take on a task that is beyond my ability to accomplish, because if you try to learn something that is beyond your ability to learn, you are only setting yourself up for disappointment—and that is not something that I want to do. Let's face it: I am just too old to learn a new language or a new skill anymore. That is a fact—like it or not.

So whom can I turn to to be a role model to me, in how to live in my old age? If not Judith Viorst, and if not I.F. Stone, and if not the woman who wrote "When I Am an Old Woman I Shall Wear Purple"—if not these people, then who can I turn to who can guide me in how to live the rest of my life?

The answer is obvious, and therefore it took me a long time to figure it out.

The answer is *Moshe rabbeynu*—Moses our teacher—because Moses was 80 years old when God told him to make a mid-life career change. God told him to give up the shepherding business that he was engaged in, and to go into the business of leading the Jewish people. Moses was 80 when God told him to go down to Egypt and tell old Pharaoh to "Let my people go."

I went back to that scene in the Bible, where God tries to persuade Moses to become the leader of the Jewish people, and I noticed something that was so ***obvious*** in that passage that I had never noticed it—at least, not until now.

In this passage, Moses uses all kinds of arguments to get out of his assignment. He says, "I have a speech impediment." He says, "I stutter." He says, "The Israelites will not listen to me." "And," he says, "even if they do, the Egyptians will not listen to me." He tries, in every which way he can, to get out of it.

But there is one argument that he never uses. Did you notice? He never says that he is too old. That excuse just does not occur to him. Evidently, he felt that if the task was important enough, age was irrelevant. And so, regardless of the fact that he was 80, Moses ended up taking the job.

And I think that you will agree that, once he took the job, he did it very well.

Then, look at what happens at the end of the story. Forty years later, God says to Moses: "OK, it is enough. It is time for you to retire. I need a younger man to bring the people of Israel into the land."

If you were Moses, what would you have said?

I think I would have said: "OK." I think I would have taken social security, and moved to Florida. Wouldn't you? But Moses does not do that. He fights as hard as he can to keep on working—if not as the leader, then as an assistant. And if not as an assistant, then in any capacity that he can.

Moses, at the age of 120, fights as hard as he can to keep his job—or, if not that, then to have some other job.

I would like Moses to be my role model. And I hope that you will make him yours, too. Because what we can learn from him is that when you reach old age, you need a job. It need not be a job that pays a salary, but you need to have a job—an important job, and a job that makes a difference, or else your life will be dull and empty and pointless.

So, what am I going to do with the rest of my life?

Thanks to Moses, I think that I have figured it out. If God lets me live longer, and if God gives me strength of mind and strength of body, do you know what I want to do?

I want to keep on doing just what I have been doing until now.

Which means: If anyone asks me to speak at their congregation, I will accept. On one condition: My bottom figure for speaking engagements is free. I will not go below that. I have some pride.

Second, I will continue to spend much of my day, as I do now, writing sermons and teaching rabbis how to write sermons. With God's help, I want to continue doing that, because I believe in this task, and I believe that I fill an important need and a sacred need by doing it.

Third, I spend much of my time doing reading and reviewing books for the local Jewish newspaper, and for other Jewish newspapers around the country and overseas. With God's help, I want to continue doing that, because I believe that when a person invests his soul in writing a book, it should not just disappear and be ignored. It should not be like throwing a pebble into the water that sinks to the bottom, and is never seen again. A book deserves a response. And people who want to know what the Jewish scholars, poets and novelists are thinking deserve to hear about and from them, and so I want to call these writers to the attention of readers.

I can't learn a whole new trade, as I. F. Stone did, even if I wanted to. Let us face it. I am too old for that. But I think that I can do these three things that I have been doing until now for the rest of my life, if God will help me. After all, I have a lot of experience in doing these things, and who knows?

Maybe I can even learn to do them better in the future than I have in the past, if I really put my mind to it.

And so this is my goal: to do what I have been doing all these years until now, and maybe even a little better in the future than I have done them until now, if I can.

I think that this is a do-able goal—not like learning Greek, or nuclear physics or brain surgery at my age.

And so, this is what I want to do with the rest of my life.

And this is my advice to you, as you grow older:

Have a job. It doesn't have to be a job that pays money. But it has to be a job that you believe is important. It has to be a job that you believe in. For if it is, your days will be full and your life will be blessed.

Let me finish by telling you about one more role model, from whom I have learned a lot.

And this time, if you guess who it is—I will admit it.

I have a very special friend, who is getting up in years. I won't tell you how old she is. It is up to her to tell or not tell her age.

My friend is not doing so well, physically. She walks with a cane or a walker. She has real balance problems, and she sometimes falls. She has back pains, and stomach pains, and all kinds of other aches and pains. And she does not get out as much as she used to any more.

But she has a job and that keeps her going.

In fact, she has a number of jobs.

She has at least five.

First of all, she takes care of her husband—and that, believe me, is a full-time job.

She once said to me, "I'm tired, and I'm sick. I think that I am ready for assisted living."

And I said to her, "I'm healthy, and I'm happy. I am not ready for assisted living."

And she said to me, "Are you kidding? You've been in assisted living ever since you married me."

And there is great truth to that.

This woman, whose name I have not told you, also gives much love to her children and her grandchild. She supports them emotionally, and sometimes even financially. That is her second job, and that takes a lot of time and energy to do. Believe me, it does.

And then she belongs to a book club, a book club that means a lot to her. She tries to go to every session of the book club that she can. She does not always read the book, though, because nowadays—as you may have noticed—they make the print in books much smaller than they used to.

In this book club, she has an office. She is the treasurer of the book club. The women donate a couple of dollars to *tsedaka* at every session. And it is her job to collect the *tsedaka* money, and then to send it in to the charity that they choose each year. That is her third job, and she takes that responsibility very seriously. If they should ever audit her books, I am sure that they will find that they are in perfect order.

Her fourth job is to cheer for her football team, every Sunday. Usually, she cheers for the underdog, because she feels that they need all the help they can get.

And her fifth job is that she has a whole bunch of people in her life whose birthdays she keeps track of, and to whom she sends birthday cards every year. Some of the people whom she sends birthday cards to probably get no cards from anyone else, except her. But that is her job, and she does it very well. It gives her a sense of purpose, and a sense of purpose is a vital thing to have—at any age.

And therefore, this is my wish—for you, for me, and for all those whom we love.

On this, the day of my second bar mitzvah, I ask this:

May God help each of us find our task in life, and may God help us to do it well. For if we have a job to do—paid or unpaid—and if it is an important one, then our days will be full of meaning and our lives will be full of purpose, for as long as we live,

And to this, let us all say: Amen.

33

# Gone with the Wind

## Reflections on the Hurricane That Passed Us By

What a week this has been! I don't know about you, but for the last few days, I have been on an emotional roller coaster. I sat glued to the television set, day after day and hour after hour, and I listened anxiously to every bit of news and every single rumor that came to us from the reporters and meteorologists. First, they told us that the storm would land near Miami. Then, they said that it would land somewhere in Broward County. And then they said that it would turn east, and go out into the ocean, and then they said that it would turn west, and go inland. I got a call from Temple Anshe Shalom in Delray Beach, in which they said that not only would there be no *minyan* there on Thursday or Friday, but that they were cancelling services there—for the first time in their history—on Shabbat, as well. And then, late on Thursday night, the storm finally came—and on Friday morning, it left. Now, *baruch hashem*, it seems to be over—at least, for those of us who live in this part of Florida.

Therefore, I think that we came to services this morning with mixed feelings in our hearts. On the one hand, we felt relief that our homes and our lives have been spared, and that Hurricane Matthew missed us; on the other hand, we felt pain and empathy in our hearts for all the people in Haiti, in the Bahamas and in Cuba, and for all the people who live north of us, where the hurricane struck with great cruelty. We feel for the more than 850 people who have died in Haiti alone, and we feel for all the people—both south and north of us—whose homes have been destroyed, whose trees have come crashing down onto their streets, and who have suffered so much devastation.

The truth is that most of us here in Boca came out fairly well. Some of us lost power for a few hours. Some of us have an awful lot of debris to clear away. Some of us lost some food, which spoiled when the electricity for our freezers went off for a while. But most of us escaped with relatively little damage—certainly when compared with what the people who live south and north of us received.

There, the water broke through people's windows, came into their homes and smashed and spoiled their furniture. It destroyed their most precious possessions and it broke their hearts. We have come into our synagogue here in Boca, this morning, feeling relaxed and relieved. They will come into their synagogues—if and when they can get to them—feeling exhausted, weary and sick at heart.

I imagine that when the people who live in these areas are able to go to services—if and when that time arrives—that they will be asking themselves three questions. The first one will be: How could this have happened to us—so quickly and so cruelly? How could our lives have been turned around overnight? How could we have gone from being so high to being cast down so low, in such a short time?

And I imagine that they will be asking themselves a second question. When they look around, and see the mud and the muck and the debris that fill their homes; when they look around, and see the paintings they brought back from their big trip to Europe that are now waterlogged; when they see the pictures of their grandchildren's bar and bat mitzvahs; when they see the pictures of their children's weddings; when they see the samovar that their grandparents brought over from Europe, now lying on the floor in pieces; and when they see the knick knacks and the *tsotchkes* that they have treasured all these years, now lying on the ground, they must be asking themselves a second question, which will be: How can we put a price on these treasures? And how can any insurance policy begin to cover the sentimental worth that these things have to us?

How can these precious objects now all be gone with the wind?

And the third question that must be in the hearts of the people in Jacksonville, in Juno Beach, in Savannah, Atlanta and in many other cities north and south of us—the question that they are probably not ready to think about yet, but that they soon will be asking—is this: What do we do now?

And I imagine that they must be asking themselves something else: Is there any wisdom, or any guidance, within our Jewish tradition that can help us to get through this dark and dismal moment in our lives?

So, these are the questions that I want to deal with this morning: What do you do when your life changes overnight, and you go from being on the heights to being in the depths of despair? What do you do when the things that you value the most break into pieces overnight, and you are left feeling bereft, bewildered and confused? And what do you do when the storm passes, and you look at your broken business and your shattered house, and you wonder: Now what should I do?

What would I say? What would you say if you were the rabbi of one of these *shules*, and the people who suffered from these hurricanes came in, bedraggled and bewildered, and asked you these questions?

The first thing that I think that I would say if I could speak to these people north and south of us, who have been hit so badly by this storm, is that you are not alone in your distress. You should know that calamities and catastrophes come upon all of us at some time in our lives, and that they often come upon us with very little advance warning, just as this one did to you.

Let me give you just three random examples of this law of life.

The first is a man who lived in the White House in the early 1990s. His name was George Herbert Walker Bush. Do you remember him?

In September of 1992, George Herbert Walker Bush was one of the most popular men in America. The war that he led over Iraq had gone wonderfully. He drove Iraq out of Kuwait in less than three weeks, and with very few American casualties, and so he was a hero to us all. The economy was booming. The market was high. As a result, his approval rating was over 73 percent in September of 1992. And then, some unknown governor of Arkansas whom nobody had ever heard of before, a man named Clinton, came out of nowhere and defeated Bush in the election in November.

I can picture him sitting in the White House the morning after the election, saying to himself: How could this have happened? How could my life have turned around so fast? How could I have gone from being one of the most popular president in all of American history to losing the election? How could I have gone from a 71 percent approval rating to a 42 percent approval rating in such a short time?

He must have felt like a hurricane had hit him. And in a very real sense, it had.

And he is not the only one to whom something like this has happened.

I think of three brothers who live in Toronto. You may have heard of them: the Reichman brothers. If ever there was a family with a fitting name, it was this family, because "Reich-man," in Yiddish, means "rich man"—and these three brothers were rich beyond anyone's wildest imagination. They were billionaires. They owned the Park Avenue Atrium in New York. They owned the Arco Tower in Dallas. They owned the Exchange Square in Boston. And they owned dozens of other companies in Cape Town and in London, in Buenos Aires and in Rio, in Paris and in Berlin, and in many, many other places all around the world.

And one year later?

One year later, the Reichmans have filed for bankruptcy.

Their company is called Olympia and York. And so the initials of their company, on the big board, are O.Y. But today, O.Y. no longer stands for Olympia and York. Today, it stands for oy.

I am sure that the Reichmans are in *shule* today, because they go to *shule* every day of their lives. But I am sure that they must be thinking to themselves, as they *daven*: How did this happen? How did our lives change so much—and so fast?

I am sure that the Reichmans must feel, today, as if a real hurricane has hit them … and in a very real sense, it has.

Let me give you just one last example of someone whose life was turned around in a short time. Do you remember the Soviet astronaut who held the record for being up in outer space for the longest time? I don't remember his name, but at the time, he was world-famous. He was up in space for 318 days, and at the time, that was the world record for the most time ever spent by any human being in outer space.

The story is told that, while he was up there, the Soviet Union collapsed.

And so, when he came down, this was the conversation that went on at the dinner table that night in his house:

He must have said to his wife: "Darling, it is so good to be back home again in Leningrad."

And she must have said to him: "Darling, we no longer call it Leningrad. Now it is called St. Petersburg."

And he must have said to her: "***Really***? How can that be? Wasn't Lenin the father of Communism?"

And she must have said to him: "Darling, there is no more Communism."

And he must have said: "***Really***? How could Gorbochev have let this happen?"

And she must have said: "Darling, there is no more Gorbochev."

And he must have said: "***Do you mean to tell me that Yeltsin is now in charge of the Soviet Union?"***

And she must have said: "Darling, there ***is*** no more Soviet Union."

And he must have said: "I think that I am having a Maalox moment."

And she must have said: "I am sorry, but we don't have any Maalox in the house. And I called the drugstore, and they say that they are completely out of it, too."

And he must have said: "*Nu*. I guess there are some things that never change."

I feel for that astronaut, really I do, because he went up from one world and came down into another, and he must have felt as if he had been hit by a hurricane when he learned how many things had changed on earth while he was up the stratosphere. And in a very real sense, he had.

And so, if your life has been turned around by this hurricane, you may take comfort from the fact that the same thing that has happened to you happened to George Bush, Gorbochov, the Reichman brothers, and to lots of other people. Perhaps there is some comfort in knowing that.

And I am sure that there are many other people whom you and I know who can tell you that they have been hit this year—by a medical hurricane, or by a business hurricane, or by a family hurricane, and one that came upon them with no advance notice and no warning.

I have a friend in St. Louis who felt fine in every way, but his wife made him go for a checkup, because he always beat her at tennis—and that day he lost, and he lost badly, and he had not let her win on purpose. She had also noticed some other changes that seemed to be going on in him that he himself did not notice, and so she suspected that something was up, and she insisted that he go to the doctor's and take a test.

Let me ask the men in the room: What do you do when your wife insists that you do something?

You do what she tells you to do. Right?

And so, just to humor her, he went to the doctor, and just to humor her, he took a cardiogram or an MRI or an X-ray or whatever it is that they give you these days—and an hour later, he was in the hospital being prepped for heart surgery.

They took my friend straight from the doctor's office to the hospital, and they got him ready for surgery. One minute he had a pocket calendar in his pocket with a list of all the important meetings that he had to go to that week; the next minute, all those meetings were forgotten. One minute he had a pocket calendar in his pocket that told him where he was supposed to be every hour; the next minute, he was wearing one of those stupid gowns that they give you in the hospital that allows you no dignity, and that has no room for your pocket calendar or anything else. When you go, in just a few moments, from the world in which your meetings are so important to a world in which they are no longer important at all, that is kind of a hurricane of a sort, isn't it?

And when your business is going well, and one key customer changes his mind and decides to buy from someone else—all of a sudden, with no notice—and all of a sudden, your profit and loss statement only has losses on it—that, too, must feel like a hurricane, does it not? And I am sure that there are some people who are sitting here right now who have had that experience during this last year.

And so, the lesson that I think that all of us need to learn from Hurricane Matthew is that the possessions that we value the most are not the only things that can be gone with the wind; indeed, even our lives are not in our control.

Our lives are not in our control: that is why we recite the *Unitane Tokef* on these days. That is why we recite the words, "*mi yichyeh umi yamut*"—who will live and who will die, in order that we may realize—in order that we may realize, and not forget—that our lives are not in our control. In order that we may realize—realize, and not forget—that even our permanent possessions are not as permanent as we think they are.

How do we come to terms with this truth—the truth that our lives and our possessions are not in our control?

Let me offer you several suggestions.

The first lesson I learned from what happened in our house in the hours of Wednesday and Thursday, before the hurricane arrived. Did this happen in your house, too? I think that the newscasters probably made it sound worse than it actually was, and so all day Wednesday and all day Thursday, we kept getting phone calls. They came from all over the country. The phone kept ringing off the hook, with people calling to tell us that they were worried about us, and asking us if we were safe, and wanting to know whether we were going to evacuate or not.

And then, when the storm was over, we got calls from people all over the country, expressing their relief that we were safe.

Did you get calls like that, too?

If so, did you notice who they came from?

Did you notice that they did not come from your customers, or from your clients, or from your competitors? They did not come from your business associates or from your casual acquaintances. They came from your siblings, and from your nieces and nephews, and from your very closest friends.

And what I learned from that— what I hope that I will remember, and not forget, and what I hope that you learned from that, as well—is that the people who care about us the most are not the people whom we buy things from, and they are not the people we sell things to. They are the people whom we are bound up with in bonds of family and in bonds of friendship.

And if that is true, then I have to ask you: Why do we spend so much of our time and energy worrying about our businesses, and why do we not spend more of our time and energy on those whom we love and who love us? When the chips are down, and when we are in trouble, these are the people who will come through for us. I learned—or relearned, this week—that ***family comes first***, and I hope that you did, too. I hope that you learned this lesson from the people who called you on Wednesday and Thursday, too, and I hope that you will remember this lesson from now on.

And now, I want to tell you the three lessons that I learned this week about how we should feel toward our property, and then I will let you go. One lesson is about how we should feel toward our property while we still have it. One lesson is about how we should feel toward our property when we lose it. And the third is a lesson in what we should do and how we should live after a disaster strikes.

One of these lessons I learned from something that happened to my blue blazer. One of these lessons I learned from Elizabeth Taylor, *aleha hashalom*. And one of these lessons I learned from something that happened on the opposite end of this country.

First, let me tell you the story of my blue blazer.

When we got married, my wife bought me a blue blazer as a gift. I don't know how much it cost, but I suspect that she probably spent a lot of money on it. It was a beautiful jacket, and it had gold buttons along the sides, and it fit me just right.

A few months later, the synagogue that I served had its annual donor dinner. I was tempted to wear my blue blazer for this event. I took it out of the closet, and I started to put it on, but then I said to myself: No, this affair is not really important enough to justify wearing this blue blazer. I am going to save it for a more special event than this. I am going to save it for some really, really special event. And so I took my blue blazer off, and I put it back into the closet, and I put on something else.

Six months later, the synagogue had another affair. This time it was a testimonial dinner in honor of the synagogue president, who was going out of office. This president was a very fine man, and we had worked well together, and so I thought that perhaps I should wear my blue blazer for this occasion. But then I thought it over, and I decided that while this was a special event, it was not special enough to justify wearing my blue blazer. And so I put it back in my closet, and saved it for a more auspicious occasion. I decided that I would save my blue blazer for some event in the future that was really, really special.

That went on for years. Finally, ***finally***, there came an occasion that I thought was special enough to justify wearing my blue blazer for. A few months ago, the Jewish Theological Seminary had its annual donor dinner at Bnai Torah. And the Seminary is a cause that is very close to my heart. This year, they were honoring two wonderful people whom I have tremendous respect and admiration for, Harold and Beatriz Jacobson. And so I decided that out of respect for the seminary, and out of respect for the Jacobsons, this would be the right time to wear my blue blazer.

And so I took it out of the closet. And do you know what happened?

Can you guess?

My blue blazer no longer fit.

I couldn't even button it. I don't know how to explain it. One of two things must have happened: either it shrunk, or else I gained weight. But either way, I could not button it. And so, even though it had beautiful gold buttons on both sides, I had to put it away and wear something else for the seminary dinner.

And so, let me tell you that the lesson of Hurricane Matthew is that if you have a jacket like that; or if you have a dress like that, that you have been saving for a special occasion; or if you have a cruise that you have dreaming of taking someday; or if you have thinking of taking your grandchildren on a trip one of these days; and if you have been postponing wearing this blazer or wearing this dress or going on this trip until the time is right, let the first lesson of Hurricane Matthew be this: Wear it now! Use it now! Enjoy it now! "*Chap arein*!" "Seize the day, because tomorrow it may not be here, and because tomorrow ***you*** may not be here. Tomorrow, a hurricane may come into your life and take it away. So use it now. For nobody owns tomorrow."

The second lesson that I would have you learn from Hurricane Matthew comes from Elizabeth Taylor, *zichrona livracha*.

Some years ago, thieves broke into Elizabeth Taylor's home and stole her jewelry—some of which was very expensive. And I remember that the reporters asked her, "Did you cry for your jewelry when you found out that it was gone?"

I still remember her answer. Elizabeth Taylor said to the reporters, "I don't cry for things that won't cry for me."

It is as simple, and as basic, as that.

***Things are only things.***

***And money is only money.***

That is what the governor kept saying when he told us to evacuate our homes if necessary, because things can be replaced—lives can't.

And that is what Elizabeth Taylor was teaching us that day when she lost her jewelry: ***Things are only things!*** And if they won't cry for you when you are gone, then you should not cry for them when they are gone.

The last lesson that I would have you learn about what to do after a hurricane that I want to teach you today comes from the Pacific Northwest.

The Pacific Northwest is about as far as you can get from Florida. We are on the southeast tip of the United States; they are on the northwest tip. And yet I want to bring you a lesson that comes from there, because it is a lesson in what you should do after life knocks you down. So if that has happened to you this week, or if you fear that that it could happen to you sometime in this new year, then listen to this story:

I have a friend who lives in the state of Washington. That is where Mount Saint Helens is located. Mount Saint Helens is the place where a volcano erupted some years ago: tons of lava spewed out of Mount Saint Helens, and it choked the lake and the land around it. It poisoned the vegetation on all sides. It filled the area with mud and muck and mess. The experts said that nothing would ever grow there again.

And then, do you know what happened?

My friend visited that area this week, and he told me that the lake is still polluted, the roads are still full of dust and debris and you have to drive carefully, because there are still fallen trees on the roads. But he told me that, if you look very closely, you can see that things are beginning to grow again. If you look carefully, you can see that, little by little, grass is beginning to emerge from between the crevices. He told me that if you look at this area closely you will see that life is beginning to return from death. Hope and vegetation are beginning to emerge out of destruction. Somehow, some way, from somewhere—I don't know how to explain it, but you can see it—Mount Saint Helens is beginning to come back to life again.

And therefore, my prayer for the people who live north and south of us, for the people of Haiti and Nassau and

Cuba, for the people of Fort Pierce and Jacksonville and all the other places where homes have been smashed and businesses have been destroyed, is this: If that can happen in the Northwest, then perhaps it can happen here, too. Perhaps in the hovels of Haiti, and perhaps in the havoc that is Fort Pierce, and perhaps elsewhere as well—if they are determined enough, and if we are generous enough to help them, who knows? Perhaps life can start over again here, just as it has there!

Let the last word as we enter the new year come from the cartoonist, Ziggy.

Ziggy is my favorite cartoonist. I have a dream of someday doing a new edition of the Machzor with cartoons by Ziggy as the commentary. Who knows? Perhaps one of these days I will do it. But, in the meantime, here is my favorite Ziggy cartoon phrase:

"If I had to do it all over again—then I would do it all over again."

The new year has begun in a scary way for many of us, and for the state in which we live.

But this is my wish—for you, for me, for all those whom we love, and for the people of Haiti, and the people of the Bahamas and Cuba and Fort Pierce, and for the people in this synagogue who have been hit by all kinds of hurricanes—medical hurricanes, or business hurricanes, or family hurricanes, in this year that has just come to an end. To all of you, I says: If we should have to do it all over again in this new year, may we have the courage and the resilience and the spirit that it requires, and to do it all over again.

Let us begin this new year with courage in our hearts,
And may God be with us on our journey.
Amen.

34

# The Lessons You Have Taught Me

## Farewell Shabbat–*Anshei Shalom*

Before I begin, let me just say that I hope that you believe everything that was said about me today and that I hope that I don't, because if I do, I will be really unfit to live with.

I am sure that you have heard this before, but do you know the difference between a eulogy and a testimonial? At a eulogy, there is nobody who believes everything that is being said. At a testimonial, there is one person who does.

Let me just say three brief thank-yous.

First, thank you to my classmate, Rabbi Hering, for your kind words and your generous praise.

Second, thank you to the officers and the board of this congregation, for this lovely gift which I will treasure.

And third, thank you to all of you for this wonderful year that we have spent together, which I will treasure even more.

There is a passage in the Talmud that all the rabbis who are here today know very well, but which I must say that I never really understood until this year.

The Talmud quotes Rabbi Yehuda Hanasi, who said, "*Harbey lomadti mimoray, yoter meychaveyray, viyoter mikum meytalmiday*"—"I have learned much from my teachers, more from my companions, and most from my students."

When I learned that passage, I said to myself: What sense does that make? We who went to the seminary had the greatest scholars in the world as our teachers. We had Saul Lieberman, who was the world's greatest expert on Greek in Jewish Palestine, as our Talmud teacher. We had H.L. Ginsberg, who was the world's greatest expert on Ugaritic, as our Bible teacher. We had Heschel and Kaplan, who were the masters of modern Jewish thought. We had Max Arzt, who was on the committee that translated the Bible from Hebrew into English. ***And the people in our synagogues were going to teach us?*** I must tell you that when I graduated, that idea seemed really far-fetched to me.

But now, I know better. My teachers may have been masters at how to translate the Torah from Hebrew into English, but the people in this congregation have taught me a number of lessons in how to translate the Torah into life. And that is why I have loved every minute of my stay here. And that is why I will take away from here many important lessons in how to live that I have learned from you.

Let me tell you just four of the lessons that you have taught me.

The first lesson you have taught me is that with willpower and determination, a human being can transcend his or her body.

I learned that lesson from the number of people in this room who come to *shule* every single Shabbat, even though they can no longer walk very well. I watch them come in here, and some of them arrive every week at the very beginning of the service. They come in slowly, one step at a time, and then

I watch them park their walkers here in the front of the *shule*, and find their way to their seats. I watch the caretakers who bring them in and then sit outside and wait for the service to end.

I must tell you that, to me, this "parking lot" of walkers down here is a holy place, because it represents the courage and the determination with which these people come to *shule* every week. I have a rule that I try to keep, which is never to pass a person who is coming in with the help of a walker. It is just not right to do. To brush by somebody who can't walk as fast as you can is committing the sin that the sages call *Lo'eg Larash,* which means, "embarrassing someone who can't do what you can do." It is not right to embarrass a person by passing him by. I confess that I sometimes violate this rule, because there is one person here who walks so slowly that I am afraid that if I walk behind him, by the time I get inside, the services will be nearly over, but as a rule I try to walk with or behind anyone who comes in here with a walker, and not just pass them by.

But let me say that one of the lessons that these people have taught me, and one of the reasons why I have so much respect for this congregation, is that those who climb up onto the *bimah* every week for an *aliyah,* or in order to show people how and when to open the ark— those who come in here every single week with the help of caretakers or walkers or canes—***these people are my heroes.*** For they have taught me that the spirit can be stronger than the body. God bless each one of you for teaching me this lesson.

The second lesson that you have taught me is kindness and compassion. I remember how many of you went to Rabbi Gerald Weiss's funeral, and I remember how many of you came here for the *shloshim* service that we held in his memory. As many people from this *shule* came to his funeral as came from the synagogue that he served for 10 years! And I asked one of you whom I saw there at the funeral, "Why did you come today?" He said to me: "Because I was not sure that anyone else would be here, and so I came just in case nobody else did."

That is the kind of kindness and compassion that you have taught me many times during this last year … and for this, I am grateful.

And let me mention one more act of kindness that I am grateful for. On occasion—I won't say how many times, but on occasion—on very rare occasions—I have spoken a little bit too long. And when I did, there was tremendous pressure on Cantor Sapir to finish on time, for he batted last. And yet … he has not murdered me. At least—not yet. If he did, no jury would convict him, and so for this act of kindness, I am very grateful to Cantor Sapir.

The third thing that you have taught me is that to be Jewish means to care—not only for yourself, and not only for your family, and not only for your local community. To be Jewish means to care about the welfare of the whole Jewish people, wherever they may be. You taught me that a few months ago, when things were bad in Israel—when people were being run over by terrorists who had cars or trucks, and when people were being knifed at bus stops—and two people in this congregation, Jerome and Barbara Cohen, responded to those acts of violence by sending an ambulance to Israel. Do you remember that day when we went outside and dedicated that ambulance? I do. It was one of the best days that we have ever had in this *shule*, and I came away from that experience feeling so proud to be a small part of this great congregation.

And there is another lesson that you have taught me.

And that is that to be Jewish means to revere books and to understand that education, like youth, is too good a thing to be wasted on young people. You taught me that studying books is at the heart of our existence. You taught me that lesson twice this year.

The first time was when the army of ISIS conquered the city of Aleppo, in Syria. Do you remember that day? Aleppo is one of the oldest cities in the world, and it is a city that contained priceless records that go back for centuries. It is a city that contained priceless manuscripts. And do you remember what ISIS did? The first thing that the terrorists did when they took over that city was to break into that library and burn the books and destroy the manuscripts that were there.

And do you remember what we did that day?

I came to *shule* that day feeling disgusted and sick at heart because of what I had heard on the news. I remembered what the poet, Heine, had said a century and more ago: people that start out burning books will end up burning people. I arrived here in a very sad mood.

And do you know what I found when I got here? There were a hundred people or more, standing outside in the parking lot, preparing to dance a new *Sefer Torah* into the ark. And when I saw that, I realized that this was our answer to ISIS. If they burn books, we will dedicate books. If they desecrate books, we will honor books. If they profane books, we will sanctify books. And so I came away with joy in my heart. I thank you for what you did that day.

There was one more day when you made me very proud. That was the day when Rabbi Harold Kushner came to town, and Mr. and Mrs. Jack Bushinsky honored us by donating the new *Etz Chaim* edition of the Torah. Rabbi Kushner said to me that day, "I have never seen such a crowd in *shule* as you have here. Are they really all members? Or did you hire actors just to impress me?"

That was the day when you taught me what respect for Jewish learning means, and I am very grateful to you for that.

And there is one more thing that I must say about the role of education in this place. I have been in *shules* that are richer than this one is. I have been in *shules* whose buildings are bigger and fancier than this one's is. But I have never before been in a synagogue that has a class, or a program or an activity going on ***every single day of the week.*** That does not happen anywhere else that I know of. And so, for teaching me that this is possible—which I would never have believed until I came here, and saw it with my own eyes— I thank you and I thank Larry Feinberg, who have made it happen.

And so, for teaching me these four lessons:

No. 1: That the strength of the spirit can triumph over the weakness of the body;

No. 2: That kindness and compassion are the way for Jews to live;

No. 3: That to be Jewish means to care about all Jews… wherever they may be,

And No. 4: That at a time when people overseas are burning books, it is our task to dedicate books and to study them;

For teaching me these four lessons, and many more, I will always be grateful to you, and I thank you very much.

I wish you well. I envy your new rabbi the joy that will be his, and I wish him well.

And may God bless you and him with much happiness for many, many years to come.

Amen.

35

# How Should You Live in Old Age?

## Reflections on My Bar Mitzvah Anniversary

Thank you very much, Rabbi Adler, for giving me the privilege of speaking here once again. I am truly honored.

I am going to do something different this morning from what I usually do when I speak here.

In all the previous times that I have spoken here, I have tried to be as entertaining and funny as possible. But this year, I am going to be serious. This year I am going to talk *tachlis*.

The reason why I am going to be serious today is because this is the 75th anniversary of my bar mitzvah … and that is a serious number.

When you reach this number, it is not a time for fooling around or for telling jokes. When you reach this number, it means that you are rounding the home stretch of your life—or, as my parents would have said, "*mer halten shoin bai neilah,*" which means, "we are now beginning the last service of the Yom Kippur day."

Today is a serious day in my life, and therefore, I want to speak to you as honestly and as openly as I can about the question which is now the ***central question of my life***—and, which I suspect, is the central question in the lives of many of you who are sitting here today. The question is this: What should you do and how should you live when you reach the twilight years of your life?

What should you do when you reach the stage when your phone and your doorbell hardly ever ring anymore, and when you are alone with your thoughts all day and all night?

What should you do when your calendar or pocket diary that used to be ***so full*** of dates is almost blank? Do you remember back to when your calendar and your pocket diary were full of dates for committee meetings, and for business lunches, and for social events? The only appointments that we have on our calendars now are for visits to the doctor.

What should you do when you stare at the clock on the wall, and it hardly seems to have moved from the last time that you looked at it?

And what should you do when you stare at the television set, and all that ever seems to be showing on it are the same reruns—over and over and over again?

Above all, what should you do ***when you have nothing to do***?

That is the question that I want to talk to you about. And if you are my age, or if you hope to someday become my age, then I ask you to listen and to think about what I am going to say to you today, because the question that faces me today may be the question that faces you tomorrow.

There are probably a great many possible answers to the question of how you should live when you grow old.

I am going to offer you just two answers today.

The first is: Avoid depression. And the second is: Have a job.

I urge you to avoid depression like the plague. Because that is what it is—it is a plague. I urge you to fight depression with all your strength, because if you give in to it, it will suck the joy out of your bones and cast a dark shadow over your life.

The second word of advice that I want to give you today is this: When you get old, ***have a job***! It doesn't matter if it is a job that pays you a salary or not; I urge you to have a job. If you don't, your life will be empty, boring and meaningless, and that is no way in which to live.

In order to talk to you about how to fight depression, I want to introduce you to two people.

The first person whom I want to introduce to you today is a person whom I am sure that everyone here knows very well. The reason we all know him well is because we spend six or seven weeks every year, in October and in November, studying his life. The reason that I want to study his life today is because at one point in his life, he fell victim to depression, and it nearly ruined him—and therefore, I believe that he can be a role model to us in how ***not to live*** when we grow old.

The second person whom I want to study with you today is a man whom many of you probably remember from the time when you were young. The reason why I want to talk about him today is because this man used to sing a song that I believe we should remember, and that I believe we should hold on to in our old age.

The name of the man whom I want to introduce you to first is Yaakov Avinu—Jacob, our father.

There is a scene in the Bible that is very strange.

In chapter 47 of the book of Bereshit, Yosef brings his father, Jacob, to the palace, and he introduces him to the pharaoh, the king of Egypt. And the pharaoh asks Jacob what seems to be a very simple question. He says to him: "Tell me, how old are you?"

And listen to Jacob's answer. He says, "The years of my sojourn upon this earth have been only 130." And then he says, "The years of my life has been very few and very painful."

I ask you: ***What kind of an answer is that?***

The years of my life have been ***only*** 130? What do you mean: ***only***?

I don't know about you, but if I were given 130 years of life, I don't think that I would complain, and I don't think that I would say "***only***." Would you?

And how could Jacob say that the years of his life had been few and painful?

***Was that really true?***

There is no question that Jacob had some tough days in his life. He was caught between a mother who loved him and a father who loved his brother more. And that cannot be pleasant for any child to have to live with.

It is true that he had to run away from home because of the hatred that his brother felt toward him, and that he had to live in the house of Laban for 20 years—and Laban was not very nice to him, to put it mildly.

It is true that he lived for years with the mistaken belief that his beloved son, Yosef, was dead … which is surely a terrible thing for any father to have to endure.

But on the other hand, he had some very good moments in his life, too, didn't he?

Jacob had two women who loved him: Rachel and Leah.

I know some single people, and I know some married people, who would be very, ***very*** happy if they only had ***one*** person who loved them. And Jacob had ***two*** women who loved him. And yet he says that his days on this earth were few and painful! How can that be?

Jacob had 12 sons and one daughter. I know some people who would be very happy if they just had ***one*** child. I know some people who march from one fertility clinic to another, and who go from one adoption agency to another, in the desperate hope of somehow, some way, ***someday*** having a child … to no avail. And Jacob had 13 children, yet he complains and says that his days were few and painful. How could he say that?

Jacob was a rich man. When he met his brother, Esau, on his way back home from the land of Laban, he gave him 500 animals as a gift—and the Torah says that he had many more animals left over after he gave his brother that gift, and yet he complains, and says that his days on this earth were very few and very painful. How could he say that? If you or I were as rich as Jacob was, would we complain and say that our days were few and painful? I don't think so.

It is true that Jacob lived for years with the mistaken belief that his beloved child was dead, but then he discovers that his child is still alive—and not only is he still alive, but he is ***the prime minister of Egypt***! If you found out that your son was the vice president of the United States, wouldn't you have *naches*? Wouldn't you be happy?

And yet, here is Jacob—sitting in the palace, sitting next to the man who is one of the most powerful people on the planet, and when the pharaoh asks him how old he is, all he can say is: Don't ask. A life like mine I wouldn't wish on my worst enemy. My life has been short, and my life has been painful, from its beginning until this day.

I ask you: Why does Jacob talk this way?

Why, on what should have been one of the happiest days of his life, does he complain, and lament and say that his life has been only bad?

My guess is—and I admit that I can't prove it, and that it is only a guess—but my guess is that Jacob was suffering from severe depression on that day, and that is why he spoke in such a dark and morbid way.

I believe that what you can learn from this biblical passage is that depression has the power to spoil, and to strain, and to warp and to blight your life to the point where you cannot see your blessings, and you can only wallow in your misery.

Depression can make you feel that all of your achievements are only trifles that do not really matter, and that all of your tasks are mountains that you cannot begin to climb.

And therefore, the resolution that I want to make for myself on this, the anniversary of my bar mitzvah—and the lesson that I want to offer you, for your consideration, today—is this: That we should strive, to the extent we can—and, I know, that is not an easy thing to do—***believe me***, I know—that we should try our best to focus on the positive aspects of our lives, and we should not brood over the disappointments that we have experienced in our lives. My suggestion is that we should try to put emphasis on the victories that we have achieved, and that we should not obsess over the defeats that we have had. Because if we forget about all the triumphs that we have had in our lives, and if we focus only on the defeats that we have had in our lives, we will do great harm to our physical and emotional well-being. It will deprive us of whatever joy life has in store for us. And it will shorten, and spoil and warp our lives, just as it shortened, and spoiled and warped the life of Jacob, our father. And so, my advice to you today is to ***not*** do what Jacob did. Do not despair, and do not let depression consume you, for if you do, it will ruin your life.

And now, let me tell you about another man—a man who gave us a song that I believe has the power to teach us a wiser and a better way in which to live.

How many of you in this room are old enough to remember Bing Crosby?

Bing Crosby was one of the most popular singers in the country when I was a teenager. And there was one song that he used to sing that I bet that you still remember.

It was written back in 1944, which was a very difficult year for the people of America. In 1944, our soldiers were fighting overseas. They were fighting on two fronts at the same time. They were fighting against Germany and Italy in Europe, and they were fighting against Japan in Asia. No one knew for sure how, or when, the war would end, and so people were understandably tense and apprehensive and depressed. And therefore, Bing Crosby sang this song wherever he went, in order to give the American people a measure of hope. And I believe that this song contains a truth that we still need to hear and to learn to live by today.

I won't sing the lyrics, out of courtesy to the cantor, but I bet that if I did, many of you could join in. And I bet that if I asked you to sing this song with me, many of you would not only sing it, but that you would snap your fingers and tap your feet in time with the words!

Let me see if I am right:

The song says:

You've got to accentuate the positive,
Eliminate the negative,
Latch on to the affirmative,
Don't mess with Mister In-between.

And then it goes on to say:

You've got to spread joy up to the maximum,
Bring gloom down to the minimum,
Have faith or pandemonium
is liable to walk upon the scene.

And then it says:

To illustrate his last remark,
Jonah in the whale, Noah in the ark,
What did they do
Just when everything looked so dark?

Man, they said, We better ac—cen—tuate the positive,
E—lim—inate the negative,
Latch on to the affirmative,
and don't mess with Mister In-between.

I think that these lyrics are very wise. They really are.

And so, let me say to every one of you who is here today, who is feeling depressed: Know that you can master it, and do not let it master you.

I ask you to accentuate the positive, for that is the way to live, especially in old age.

And now let me turn to the second point that I want to make today, which is this: When you get to be up in years, you have to have a job. If you do, it will give you a sense of dignity and a sense of purpose. If you don't, your days will drag on and on, and you will have no desire and no reason to live.

I want to tell you about some of the people from whom you can learn this lesson. One of lived in Providence, Rhode Island; some are in this room right now. And one of them is a woman whom I know who lives in Boca.

The first person I want to tell you about who understood this truth was Rabbi William Braude, of Providence, Rhode Island.

Rabbi Braude was the rabbi of Temple Beth El in Providence. On the day that he turned 65, he retired from that position. He retired in order to take on a new project. He wanted to translate Bialik's "*Sefer Agada*" from Hebrew into English. He wanted to take on this project because he believed that Reform Jews needed to make a connection with Rabbinic Judaism, or else they would not be authentic Jews.

If any of you know "*Sefer Agada*", you know that it is a very big book. It is over 600 pages long. And many of the words in this book are difficult to translate. But Braude wanted to take on this project. He worked on it day and night, for many years. He worked on it as if he was in a race against time, and I guess that he was, because he was already 65 when he started on it and he knew that it would take him years to finish. But he was determined to do it.

At one point, he had a heart attack—and they rushed him to the hospital. He worked on this project while he was in the hospital. And then they moved him to a rehab facility, and he worked on this project the entire time that he was in the rehab facility.

And then they brought him home again, and he worked on this project from the day that he came home. And then, the big day finally arrived. One day, he arrived at the last page of the book. He made the last correction to his manuscript. And do you know what he did then?

He put down his pen, took off his glasses, and he said to his wife, "Darling, I'm finished!"

And he died.

I believe that that is the way to go: to have a job to do that occupies your mind and heart, and then to finish it—and then let go. That is the way to die!

I was talking to a good friend of mine the other day. We were sitting in the dentist's office, and she said to me, "If I have my choice, I would like to die in my sleep, with no muss, no fuss and no pain. If it were up to me, that is the way I would like to go."

And I said to her, "You may be right, but if I have my choice, I think that I would rather go at my desk, while working on a project that I cared about."

I would not want to go in the middle of a sermon—because that would create a fuss, and spoil the dignity of the service—but I would like to go while at my desk, finishing up a project that meant a lot to me. I think that that is the way I would like to go. And that is the way that I recommend to you.

And now, let me cite just one last example, and I will let you go. There is one woman I know who can't be here today, because she is not in very good health.

This is a woman who used to be full of spirit and energy.

This woman used to be the treasurer of her book club, and she did that job very well. This woman was a devoted mother who raised four children by herself, and she did that job very, very well, too. This woman worked at one time at the Goodyear Store in Hollywood, and I have no doubt that if she had stayed in that job instead of marrying me, she would have become the national head of Goodyear's by now.

But now, she has to wear hearing aids—because otherwise, she can't hear very well. And now, she has to use a walker—because otherwise, she can't walk very well. And now, she has to take sleeping pills—because otherwise, she can't sleep very well. And now, she has to spend most of her days in her recliner. And therefore, no one would blame this woman if she was depressed as a result. She told me yesterday that she has 20 different creaks in her body, plus the five that she picked up this week! With that many different illnesses, I think that she could qualify for the Senior Olympics.

And yet she has turned that recliner in which she sits into the nerve center of the house. She has a number of buttons that are located right next to her recliner. One of those buttons controls the television set. Another of those buttons controls the temperature in the room. One of those buttons controls the lights in the room. And one of those buttons—controls me.

And with all of her handicaps, this woman still has a number of important jobs to do—and she does each one of them with great devotion.

She has to make sure that I drink enough water every day, because if I were left to myself, I would probably not do so. She has to make sure that I don't nosh on too many pretzels or too much candy or too much chocolate before dinner, because left to myself, I would. And in addition to these small jobs, she has one big job.

Her main job is to make sure that, before I go out to teach on Wednesday mornings, or before I go out to *shule* on Shabbat morning, she has to check me out. She has to make sure that my shoes match my socks. And she has to make sure that my tie matches my shirt. She has to make sure that my hair is combed properly, or else she will not let me leave the house. If it were up to me, I would not care whether my socks matched each other—much less that they matched my shoes—but she cares. And so she makes it her job to make sure that they do.

And if they don't? Then she makes me go back and change my socks, or change my shirt or change my tie, and she does not let me leave the house until I look right.

May God bless her for doing these things … and may she continue to do these jobs as conscientiously and as lovingly as she does, for many, many more years to come.

And so, this is the lesson that I would have you learn from her, and from Rabbi Braude:

***Have a job!***

Have a job, and do it well: for if you do, your life will be a blessing.

That means that if no one ever calls you—***then call them***. And if no one ever writes you, ***then write them***! And if no one ever pays attention to you—then ***pay attention to them***! And do so for your sake, as well as theirs.

Do it because it is a great *mitzvah* to pay attention to those who are neglected in this world: and do it because it will bring joy and light and purpose to your life, as well as to theirs.

Have a job, whatever it is, and it will bring you dignity, purpose, joy and blessings.

This is my wish for you, for me, and for all those whom we love.

Have a job, whatever it is: whether it is helping to make a *minyan*, or teaching your grandchildren how to read, or making sure that your husband looks right when he leaves the house. But have a job, for if you do, it will enrich your life as well as the lives of others.

And one last word, if I may:

If you get to be my age and you still have people who are willing to let you talk, as you have done for me today, be grateful to each and every one of these people.

And when they have *simchas*, promise that you will reciprocate for the patience and the kindness that they have shown you today by listening to them.

And to this, let us all say: Amen.

36

# Reflections on a Birthday

First, I would like to thank Rabbi Adler for giving up his sermon time today and inviting me to give the sermon in his place. I don't know if you realize what a very generous thing it is when a rabbi gives up his sermon time for another rabbi.

Do you know the definition of a rabbi? A rabbi is a person who will walk 10 miles in order to give a sermon, but who won't walk across the street to hear one. And so, this is a real act of friendship on his part, and I am very grateful.

Today is a very special day in my life. I won't tell you how old I am, but I will give you a hint. Today is the 74th anniversary of my bar mitzvah.

I said this to one of my friends this week, who is—how shall I say it politely—who is mathematically challenged, and she said, "Can you give me another hint as to how old you are?"

And I said that to another one of my friends, who is very kind, and she said, "You were probably so precious that you were bar mitzvah at the age of 6 or 7."

The truth is that I am not the only one: we are all ambivalent about getting a year older. On the one hand, we all want to live long; on the other hand, we don't want to get old. You can see this ambivalence that we all feel reflected in the birthday cards that we send and receive.

I got one this week that said, "A friend is a person who remembers the ***day*** you were born, and forgets the year." And I got another one that said, "The three scariest things in the world are: an appointment with the IRS; an appointment for an MRI; and the arrival of another birthday." (By the way, they took an MRI of my brain recently, and they found nothing there.)

But the truth is that birthdays should not be scary. They should be joyous. They should be opportunities for thanksgiving, by which I mean that they should be opportunities for both thanks and for giving.

And so I want to do three very simple things today, in honor of my birthday. Then I want to tell you a couple of my favorite stories, and I will let you go.

First, I want to count out some of the ways in which the world has changed since I was born; second, I want to count out some of the ways in which the world has ***not*** changed, since I was born; and third, I want to share with you one word of the Torah that constitutes my goal for the coming year.

First, let me count out some of the ways in which things have changed in just the last 25 years.

Twenty-five years ago, we all wanted to have long hair; today, most of us would be satisfied if we just had hair.

Twenty-five years ago, we were all into acid; today, we are all into antacid.

Twenty-five years ago, we all wanted to go out to a new, hip joint; today, we are all afraid that we may soon need a new hip joint.

Twenty-five years ago, we all yearned to look like Marlon Brando; today, unfortunately, most of us ***do*** look like Marlon Brando.

Those are just a few of the ways in which things have changed in just the last 25 years.

Now, let me tell you some of the ways in which the world has changed since I was born.

When I was young, closets were for putting things into; now, they are for coming out of.

When I was young, timesharing meant sharing time; it had nothing to do with condominiums. In fact, when I was young, nobody had anything to do with condominiums, because they hadn't been thought of yet.

When I was young, a chip was a piece of wood, and hardware was hardware, and software had not been invented yet.

When I was young, "made in Japan" meant "cheap."

When I was young "grass" was mowed, not smoked.

When I was young, pot was something that you cooked in; not something that you inhaled.

When I was young, "aides" were kids who helped out in the school office, or who volunteered in the hospital; not the name of a disease.

When I was young—hard as it may be for our children to believe today—television had not been invented yet. And, more important, neither had the Salk vaccine, penicillin, organ transplants, bypass surgery, sonograms, petri dishes or surrogate parenting.

When I was young, there were no frozen foods, except those foods that we put into the icebox. When I was young, milk and ice were delivered to the house every day—by the milkman and the iceman. Do any of you still remember the milkman and the iceman?

When I was young, there was no Xerox, no radar, no contact lenses, no credit cards, no computers, no boomboxes, no dual-career families, no mutual funds, no bi-coastal marriages, no VCRs and no DVDs.

When I was young, there were no CDs—not in the bank, and not in the record store.

When I was young, there were no professional caterers in the synagogue. The only person who was expected to be able to cater to the entire congregation back then was the rabbi.

When I was young—I know this is hard to believe, but—when I was young, people got married first and ***then*** they lived together, strange as that may seem today.

When I was young, when we spoke about "the pill," we meant Aspirin.

When I was young, we had no ballpoint pens. We had the kind of pens that were called "fountain pens." How many of you remember fountain pens? And we had inkwells on our desks in school. Does anyone know what the purpose of those inkwells was?

Who remembers?

It was to put ink into the pigtails of the girl who sat in front of you.

As you can see from this brief list, the world is very different today than it was when we were young. And it continues to change at an ever-accelerating rate of speed.

Proof? Most of the scientists in the history of the world are alive today.

And most of the medical knowledge that has been acquired in the history of the world has been acquired within our lifetime.

My parents were born in 1894, which is not ***that*** long ago. And yet, they were born before the invention of the telephone, or the automobile, or the airplane, and before the discovery of electricity. Think of that: My parents started out in life before the invention of the automobile, and they ended up living long enough to see a man land on the moon! In one lifetime, they went from living before the invention of the telephone to living in the age of the computer. So, as you can see from these few examples, the world is changing—frequently and rapidly.

I went into Radio Shack the other day, and I said to the salesman, "I would like to buy some cassettes." And the salesman, who was probably around 18 or 19, said to me, "Excuse me, sir, what is a cassette?"

We live in a fast-changing world, in which the time between when a new invention comes in—and you simply have to have it—and the time when this new invention goes out—and you no longer need it—has become shorter and shorter.

And so we are all like passengers on a subway that is hurtling down the tracks, at many miles per second, and we clutch onto the straps above our heads for support as the train goes faster and faster and faster.

This is the first point that I want to make today: that the world has changed, and that the world continues to change—rapidly. And therefore, if we want to live in this world, we have to recognize these changes and we have to be able to respond to them.

The second point that I want to make today is that despite all of these changes, and despite all of these new these inventions, there are still some things in this world that have ***not*** changed and that ***will not*** change ever.

Hi-fi phonograph records may be out of date, but high fidelity in marriage still means the same thing that it always meant.

The rise of foundations and endowments and the new tax laws have made charitable giving more sophisticated and more complex than it used to be. But *tsedakah* is still the same indispensable *mitzvah* that it always was.

New prayers and new music have added much to our services. But a broken heart and a yearning soul are still what count the most in prayer.

And people may now be able to fly to Europe in five or six hours, whereas years ago it took them much longer, but the real question still remains:

***Where are you going?***

And why?

And, ***what are you going to do with yourself when you get there?***

For you may be able to fly faster now than ever before, but you still take ***yourself*** with you, wherever you go, just as you did before.

And so a lot has changed within our lifetimes, but a lot still remains the same—and always will.

Let me name a few of the things that have not changed, and that I believe will not change.

God hasn't changed. The mitzvahs haven't changed. The need to control our *yester hara* hasn't changed. The struggle to overcome the temptations of greed, lust and envy are just as strong today as they ever were. And the importance of living a good and moral life is just as great today as it ever was.

The moon still means the same thing to lovers as it always did, even though some people have now walked upon it.

And sunrise and sunset, love and hope, good and evil, faith and responsibility still mean the same as they always did, even though so many other things have changed. These things still mean the same thing that they always did, and I think that they always will.

And we need to realize and remember that. Because it is easy to get carried away and to be so dazzled by the speed at which things change that we forget the things that will never change. But it is the things that will never change that are, ultimately, the most important. The PalmPilots, the cell phones and all the other gadgets that we are so fascinated with today will be obsolete tomorrow. But the values that we hold on to today will still be here, as long as human life continues.

Let me give you just one example of how some things never change.

This is the first generation in human history in which parents have moved away from their children. Up until now, we have seen children move away from their parents: that is the way of the world. Parents are supposed to push the young birds out of the nest. But now, for the first time in human history, parents move away from their children. People use to work until they died; now they retire, and move to Florida. And so, if they want to see them, the children have to go to Florida in order to visit their parents.

Somebody said to me recently that in Florida, you give 5 dollars to charity, in gratitude, when your grandchildren come to visit. And you give 10 dollars to charity, in gratitude, when they leave.

And yet, think for a moment: What exactly ***is*** the season during which the snowbirds and the snowflakes come to Florida?

They come from the day after Thanksgiving until the week before Pesach. Why?

Because Thanksgiving and Pesach are the two great family holidays in the calendar. And ***family still counts***. That hasn't changed. And I pray that it never will.

And now, let me tell you my resolution for the new year of my life that now begins. I don't know if I will really live this way or not. Like you, I have made many resolutions that I meant to keep and didn't, so I don't know for sure if I will live this way or not. But this is the way that I ***hope*** I will live in this new year of my life that now begins. My resolution for the new year comes from one word in the Torah.

It is a word that fascinates me. The Torah says that the Israelites hear the Ten Commandments at Mount Sinai, and then Moses goes up the mountain to bring back the two tablets of stone. While he is away, the people violate the Torah by building a golden calf. When Moses comes down, and sees what they have done, he is so angry that he smashes the tablets. He feels that if they don't want to live by the law, then they don't deserve to have the law. So he takes the tablets and he breaks them into pieces, before their eyes.

Then comes the line that fascinates me. The Torah says: "When the people saw Moses smash the tablets, *vayitablu*, they mourned: they grieved for the tablets that they had lost."

To the best of my knowledge, this is the only time in the Torah where the word "*aveyl*," which means "to mourn," is used for an object. Usually, the word "*aveyl*," or "*aveylut*," is used when you lose a person. But here, the people mourn over the loss of the tablets.

Think of it: One day, they violate what is written on the tablets; the next day, they mourn and they cry when the tablets are broken.

When they had them, they didn't appreciate them; when they lost them, they mourned.

They grieved and they wept and they mourned, as deeply as they would have if they had lost a person.

When I read that passage, I realized: Aren't we all like those Israelites?

When we have something—whether it is our health, our wealth, our spouse, our job, whatever— we take it for granted. We think that we deserve it; we think that we are entitled to it; we think that we will have it forever. And then, when we lose it, *vayitablu*—then we mourn for it, and we realize how precious it was.

My wish for this new year of my life is simply this: May I not be so stupid. May I not take my blessings for granted now, and them mourn for them afterward. Instead, may I appreciate what I have while I have it—and not just later. May I realize what a special wife I have now—now, and not later. And may she appreciate what a wonderful, handsome, talented and modest husband that she has now—now, and not later. And may we both appreciate all the many, many blessings that we both have now—now, and not just afterward.

I remember reading some years ago that the "*Mona Lisa*" was once stolen, and then, after a few years, it was recovered and put back in its place again. And I read that during that period when it was missing, ***more people came to the Louvre***

***to stare at the place where it once was than came to see it when it was there***!

My wish is that I may not be so foolish.

My wish is not that I acquire more things during this coming year, because, *baruch HaShem*, I already have more things than I know what to do with.

We bought a big house because I didn't want to have to choose between my books and my wife: I wanted a house that would be big enough for both. And do you know what? In a short time, we have filled this big house up to capacity, and almost beyond its capacity. So I know that I have enough—and more than enough—things, more things than I can possibly use.

When I realized that my birthday was coming, I wanted to register at Bonwit Teller & Co., or at Bloomingdale's or Brooks Brothers, but my wife said: "That's not nice. *Past nisht*." And so what we did instead is we told people that if they wanted to give gifts in honor of my birthday, they could give donations to the synagogue, or to any charity of their choice.

The reason we did that was because, *baruch HaShem*, we have enough things—more things than we know what to do with. And so, instead of wishing for more things, my wish for the new year is this: May I be wise enough, and may I be smart enough, to appreciate what I have ***while I have it***.

This is my wish, today—for me, for you and for all those whom we love: May we be wise enough to appreciate what we have while we have it, and not just afterward. May we know what we have while we have it, and not just mourn over its loss, afterwards, like the Israelites did.

I remember a story that I once heard from Rabbi Lehrman of Miami. He said that when he was a child, a certain famous Chassidic rebbe came to America, and his mother took him to the rebbe to get a blessing from him. Hundreds of people came, and they lined up for the rebbe's blessing. And so they had to stand outside, in line, in the hot sun, for hours. Finally, they got to the head of the line.

The rebbe said to his mother: "How is your *gezunt*?"

She said: "*Baruch HaShem*, thank God, our health is fine."

The rebbe said: "How is your *parnosseh*?"

And his mother said: "*Baruch HaShem*, thank God, our livelihood is fine."

The rebbe said: "And how are your children?"

And his mother said: "*Baruch HaShem*. Thank God, our kids are fine."

The rebbe said: "If your health is good, and your *parnossah* is good, and your children are good, then what *brocho* do you want from me?"

And his mother said: "*Zol noh nisht farshtert veren*. May it just not be spoiled. May it never get worse than it is right now."

That's the way I feel today.

My health, *baruch HaShem*, is good. My children are, *baruch HaShem*, good. My grandchildren are, *baruch HaShem*, wonderful. It should only never be any worse than it is today. This is my prayer to God. All I ask is this: May it never be any worse than it is today. And may I realize how good it is while it is good, and not just later.

One last word: I spoke to my friend, Rabbi Irwin Witty, some years ago. I mentioned that I was going to have a *simcha*, and he said to me: "You know, the Hassidim have a two- part *brocho*. They say: May you celebrate many *simchas*, ***and*** may you celebrate your *simchas* ***bisimcha,*** which means, "May you celebrate your happy occasions in happiness."

Do you understand what that means?

Not everyone is able to celebrate their happy occasions in happiness.

I have seen fathers come to a child's wedding haggard and unshaven, because they were still in mourning.

I have seen weddings pushed up and held early, or held at a hospital bedside, because a parent is terminally ill.

And I have seen people who had *simchas*, but who were unable to enjoy their *simchas* because so-and-so didn't come; or because so-and-so ***did*** come; or because so-and-so didn't give a big enough present; or because they sat me at this table, instead of at that table; or because one detail, out of the millions of details that go into a *simcha*—the flowers, the orchestra, the caterer, the rabbi, the *chazen* or the dress, or something else—didn't go exactly right. A thousand details of the *simcha* ***did*** go right, but they focus on the one thing that went wrong—and they make that a reason to be unhappy.

And so my wish for you, for me and for all those whom we love, is this: During the coming year, may we celebrate many *simchas* in each other's lives, as we do today, and may we celebrate them *bisimcha*. May we celebrate them with joy, and with gratitude, and may we not let whatever detail isn't just right spoil the joy of the things that do go right.

This is my wish for the new year: for you, for me and for all those whom we love.

Amen.

37

# What Does It Mean to Be a Rabbi?

I want to speak to you today as honestly and as openly as I can about the question that every rabbi thinks about many times in the silence of the night, but that very few rabbis ever talk about in public. I want to talk to you about the question that is the central spiritual question of my life.

The question is: What does it mean to be a rabbi?

The reason why I want to talk to you about this subject today is because I believe that this is a question that not only rabbis but congregations, as well, need to think about at some time in their lives, because—whether you know it or not, whether you realize it or not—congregations influence rabbis at least as much as rabbis influence congregations. You may not realize this, but congregations train and educate rabbis at ***least*** as much as seminaries do. What is central to you inevitably becomes central to us. And therefore, if one part of the congregation measures its rabbi by how good he or she is at public relations; and if another part of the congregation measures its rabbi by how good a scholar he or she is; and if another part of the congregation judges its rabbi on how good he or she is at fundraising, they can literally tear him or her apart with their conflicting and their contradictory conceptions of what it means to be a rabbi.

Do you know the story of the chameleon? They put him on a red background—and he turned red. They put him on a blue background—and he turned blue. They put him on a scotch plaid—and he went *meshugah*.

I have seen that happen to some of our best rabbis, and therefore I believe that it is important that, at some time in its history, a congregation thinks through what it really wants from its rabbi. At some stage in its life—perhaps when it is engaged in the task of choosing a new rabbi—a congregation ought to consider what it believes is central and what it believes is peripheral; what it considers to be primary and what it considers to be secondary, in the task of its rabbi. And therefore, this is the question that I want to talk to you about this morning. And I ask you to hear me well:

When I started out, my first position was in the placement department of the Rabbinical Assembly. One of the questions that I would ask to those who came to us looking for a rabbi was: "What kind of a rabbi are you looking for?" And I can still remember some of the answers that I received.

One search committee said to me: "We are looking for is a rabbi who is young, and who has many years of experience." Another search committee said to me: "We are looking for a rabbi who will be a national Jewish leader, and who will also be available in the synagogue office all the time." One search committee said to me: "We are looking for a rabbi whose name will be known throughout the Jewish world, and we are looking for a rabbi who will know our names as well." Yet another search committee came to me with that complaint that—honest, I did not make this up—that they had hired a graduate of the Seminary, and so assumed that he was fully trained. And they said: "We found out that he is still studying."

And this is my favorite job description: A friend of mine who was the chairman of the search committee of a certain congregation in the Midwest once called me and asked for my help in finding the right rabbi for his congregation. I asked him: "What kind of a rabbi are you looking for?" And he said to me, in all seriousness: "We are looking for a strong rabbi—who will take orders." For some reason, we were not able to find a rabbi that could meet the requirements of this congregation.

In order to be a successful rabbi in our time, I think that a rabbi has to have a great many different skills and talents. He or she must be, at one and the same time, an administrator and an arbitrator. He or she has to be, at one and the same time, a bar and a bat mitzvah teacher and a benedictor. He or she has to be a counselor and a charismatic leader; a devout meditator and a dynamic speaker; an editor and an educator; a fund raiser and a friend to every family in the congregation; a go-getter and a greeter; a High Holy Day services conductor and a *halachic* authority; an interfaith advocate and an intellectual; a judge of disputes and a *kashrut* inspector; a literature expert and a liaison to other groups; a motivator and a negotiator; an organizer and a public relations expert; a ritual director and a supervisor of services; a unifier and a quick witted thinker; an efficient executive and a sacred exemplar; a qualified officiant at Jewish divorces and a skilled Torah reader; a competent youth advisor and a willing substitute for every member of the staff; a wonderful after-dinner speaker and a Zionist spokesman; and, if there is no one else available—a Xeroxer, as well. And I am sure that there are many other tasks and talents that a rabbi has to have that I have left out.

But over and above all of these talents, it seems to me that there are two qualities that a rabbi must have in order to succeed in our time. If he or she has these two qualities, then I believe that he or she can learn all the other tricks of the trade—but if he or she does not have these two qualities, then all the other skills and talents that he or she may have will not help him or her succeed.

The first quality that a rabbi has to have in our time—which is a very difficult quality to have, believe me—is a deep, and a real and and a serious faith in God. The second quality that a rabbi has to have in our time—which I believe may be an even more difficult quality to have than the first—is a real, and a deep and a serious faith in people.

It is very easy for a rabbi to delude him- or herself and to believe that he or she is more than merely human. You raise your hands—like this—and the whole congregation rises. You lower your hands—like this—and all the people in the congregation take their seats. You make a *motsi*, and everyone in the room is permitted to begin the meal. You recite the benediction, and everyone in the room is permitted to leave. You know more about Jewish literature and Jewish liturgy and Jewish law than anyone else in the congregation, and so it is easy to begin to believe your own press releases. You are the one that people turn to for guidance and instruction at all of the turning points in their lives, and so it is easy for you to begin to believe that you are all-wise and all-knowing. It is easy for rabbis to become impressed with their own wisdom. It is easy for rabbis, if they are not careful, to become vain and arrogant and unfit to live with.

Imagine what happens to the soul of a rabbi who is able to give a powerful and persuasive sermon on the importance of humility. How can you not be proud of yourself for having delivered an eloquent sermon on such an important spiritual subject? And yet, if you walk back from the pulpit with a smile of triumph on your face or with a sense of smugness in your heart at having spoken so well about the need for modesty, does that not undo everything that you have said?

I know many rabbis who have been successful in their work and who have been spiritually destroyed by their success. You ask them a question, and they give you a quote from their last press release. You bow your head for their blessing, and as you do, you see them glancing at their wristwatch, thinking about the next appointment on their schedule. When you see that happen, you know that you are in the presence of a rabbi who may be learned and eloquent and talented, but who is a spiritual failure.

The truth is that the struggle to overcome pride is a challenge that every spiritual leader in every generation has had to face—with no exceptions. How do you succeed and survive success?

The story is told that when it came time for the Baal Shem to die, his disciples gathered around his bedside, and they asked him: "Rebbe, who shall we choose to take your place?" And he said to them: "I cannot tell you whom to choose, but I can tell you whom ***not*** to choose. If anyone applies for the position, ask him if he knows the way to permanently overcome the temptation to pride—and if he says that he knows, he is not the one."

For the struggle to overcome pride is a never-ending struggle. Sometimes it is two steps forward and one step back, and sometimes it is one step forward and two steps back. And so the Baal Shem was warning his people, then, and he was warning us, today, to beware of the one who claims to know how to conquer pride permanently. For whoever says that he knows is not one who is fit to lead our people.

We are not the first generation in Jewish history to face this problem: the Hassidic *rebeyim* faced an even bigger challenge than we do. The Hassidic *rebeyim* were worshipped by their people. People struggled to grab hold of a piece of bread that the *rebeyim* had blessed, and hung on to their every word. People rose when they entered the room and stood when they left. And so, the Hassidic *rebeyim* had to struggle all of their lives against the temptation to think of themselves as more than human.

Let me tell you two stories about Hassidic rabbis who faced this problem—this problem of how to succeed and not be destroyed by your success. These are stories about rabbis who understood that there are two central teachings in

Judaism: One is that there is a God in the world—and the other is that it is not you.

There was once a famous Hassidic *rebbe* named Naftali of Ropshitz. He was revered and worshipped by his disciples. They followed him around and they learned from everything that he said and did. They treated him with more reverence and with more admiration than we treat movie stars or football players today.

And of him it is told that he was once sitting in his house while the hassidim were gathered around him, telling his praise. One hassid said: "Our rabbi is the greatest scholar of Talmud in the whole world!" Another hassid countered the first by saying: "Our rabbi is the greatest scholar of Zohar in the world!" A third hassid said: "Our rabbi is the most righteous person in the whole world!" And so it went, on and on and on, with the hassidim taking turns praising their rabbi for his many good qualities. And Rebbe Naftali of Ropshitz sat there, saying not a word, hoping that the hassidim really believed what they were saying—and hoping even more that he would ***not*** believe what they were saying. Finally, he could stand it no more, and so he got up and left the house and went for a walk, leaving his hassidim behind.

The *rebbe* walked up and down the streets of the village of Ropshitz in the dark, and he happened to come across a night watchman. The *rebbe* stopped to shmooz with the night watchman for a few minutes. In the course of their conversation, the *rebbe* asked the night watchman a question:

Tell me, "who do you work for?"

The night watchman told him, and then, not realizing who he was talking to, the night watchman asked the famous Rabbi Naftali of Ropshitz: "And who do you work for?"

The *rebbe* thought for a few minutes, and then he said: "Tell me, would you be willing to come and work for me?"

"I would consider it," said the night watchman, "but first, tell me: what would my duties be?"

The *rebbe* said: "To ask me that question three times a day."

If Rabbi Naftali of Ropshitz, who lived in a small village in eastern Europe two centuries ago, felt that he needed someone to ask him that question—"Who do you work for? Who do you ***really*** work for?"—then how much more do we—who work for the UJA and the JNF and the ZOA, and the RA and the CRC and at least half a dozen other organizations; we, who work for our synagogue, and for our egos, and for our bankbooks and for our families—how much more do we need someone who will ask us that question at least three times a day: "Who do you work for? Who do you ***really*** work for?"

This is the question that every rabbi has to answer in the privacy of his or her own heart many times during his career.

"Who do you work for? Who do you ***really*** work for?"

And this is why a rabbi—if he or she is to succeed, and if he or she is not to be spoiled by his or her success—has to have a deep and a real and a serious faith in God.

Now let me tell you a second Hassidic story that deals with the same question:

There was once a great Hassidic *rebbe* named Rabbi Avraham Yehoshua Heschel of Apt. He was the ancestor of my teacher, Abraham Joshua Heschel, of blessed memory, whom many of you may have heard of. Whenever Rabbi Avraham would give a sermon, someone would inevitably come up afterwards and say to him: "I enjoyed your sermon very much today. And I want you to know that I thought that your talk was very clever!"

Whenever someone said that to him the *rebbe* would wince, because he did not intend for his sermons to be enjoyable. He did not mean for them to be entertaining. He meant for them to be life-changing. And he did not believe that he was being original, or that he was being clever, when he spoke. He believed that he was only transmitting the Torah that he had received.

And so, once, when someone said these words to him, he responded by telling this story:

*Once there was a mayor of a small village in eastern Europe. It was the great dream of this mayor that he might someday see the czar of Russia. But he knew that this was an impossible dream: for how could he, who was the mayor of a small, insignificant village that was far off the beaten track, ever get to see the czar of Russia in person?*

*And then one day the czar came into the mayor's office—incognito. He was dressed as a plain, ordinary peasant. He was wearing old and tattered worker's clothes, and on his head he wore a plain peasant's cap. When the czar revealed who he really was, the mayor was overwhelmed with emotion. He fell on his knees before the czar, and kissed his boots, and said to him: "Please let me organize a parade in your honor, your majesty. Let me give you a tour of this village. Let me arrange for a brass band to go before you and tell the people that you are here!" But the czar declined. He said, "Wherever I go, people behave differently because I am there. I want to see life as it really is, and not how it is when it is on display. I want to see how people live in the real world, and not when they are putting on a show in order to impress me. And so, please take me on a tour of your village, but let no one know who I am."*

*The mayor begged and pleaded with the czar, but to no avail. When they came out, the mayor pleaded with the czar to sit in the seat of honor in the mayor's carriage, but the czar refused. Instead, the czar insisted that the mayor sit in the seat of honor and he sat at his feet.*

*And so that is the way that they went up and down the streets of the village and as was custom in that village whenever the mayor passed by, everyone stopped what they were doing and everyone stood at attention—and everyone saluted the mayor.*

And imagine how the mayor felt when everyone stopped whatever they were doing, and stood at attention and saluted him—***and no one noticed the czar***.

That is the way that Rabbi Heschel of Apt said that he felt when people told him that they enjoyed his sermon or that he was very clever—and no one noticed the czar.

And as he said that, the rabbi lifted his hand and pointed to the One Above.

That is the secret of how to succeed as a rabbi—and to survive your success.

We can learn this truth from the first rabbi of the Jewish people: from *Moshe Rabbeynu*—from Moses, our teacher. If you look, you will see that Moses is never referred to in the Torah as "Lord Moses" or as "King Moses" or as "Sir Moses." The only term that the Torah uses to describe Moses is "eved"—which means "servant." And it says that, at the moment of their greatest triumph—at the moment when they went through the Red Sea and saw their enemies perish in its waters, "*Vaya-aminu Ba-Adonay - uvimoshe avdo*"—that the people trusted in God and in Moses, His servant. What that passage really means is that the people trusted in God ***because*** of Moses. It means is that they trusted in God because Moses considered himself to be only a servant of God. For Moses, the message was more important than the messenger. And that is the way it must be for every rabbi who wants to succeed—and not be destroyed by his or her success.

The second quality that every rabbi must have—a quality that is just as difficult to possess, and perhaps even more difficult to possess—is a deep and a real and a serious faith in people. For if you do not believe that people can learn, you cannot teach. If you do not believe that people can listen, you cannot preach. If you do not have faith in the ability of people to grow, and to change—then you cannot be their leader.

It is not easy for a rabbi to have faith in people in our time. So many of them are illiterate and indifferent. The synagogue is filled one week with people who have come because they have been invited to a bar mitzvah or a bat mitzvah or an *aufruf*, and then they leave and are replaced by another group the next week who have come for a *simcha*. There are very few people who come every week: very few who come out of a real religious commitment. And so it is almost impossible not to be discouraged and not to give up faith in the Jewish future. We rabbis sometimes feel as if we are "the last of the Mohicans"—that we are the last generation that will know and that will care about the heritage. We sometimes have the feeling that it will all end with us. And it is understandable that we feel this way.

But if you study Jewish history, you will learn that it is not necessarily so. You will learn that many times before in Jewish history, the spiritual situation of the Jewish people has been even worse than it is today, and that many times before a small but devoted corps of teachers has transformed the situation.

The Talmud says that when Rav came to Babylonia, he found a Jewish community that knew little and that cared less. He could have turned around and gone back to Israel, but he didn't. Instead, he stayed and he taught. And as a result, Babylon eventually became the spiritual center of the Jewish people. The Talmud that was created there became even more important than the Talmud that was created in Jerusalem—only because Rav stayed. Thanks to him and to the small, dedicated group that worked with him, Babylon helped create the Judaism that we know today.

Historians tell us that when Moshe of Coucy came to France, there was nothing there. It is said that he had to go from door to door giving out *mezuzahs*, because no one had one. Would you have blamed him if he had turned around and gone back to where he came from? And yet he did not do that. Instead, he stayed and built a school. And that school became the foundation of Ashkenazic Jewry. And out of that school came Rashi, who made it possible for the people of that time and of our time to acquire knowledge of both the written and the oral Torah.

When the Baal Shem Tov began, eastern Europe was a spiritual wilderness. There was the learned aristocracy, whose Torah was erudite but dry, and there were the masses, most of whom were illiterate. The Baal Shem chose five disciples, and he taught them. These five disciples then went out and formed five communities, and these five communities became mighty spiritual centers, and within a few decades, Hassidism had captured the hearts of half the Jews of eastern Europe.

Therefore, no matter how difficult and frustrating the work of a rabbi may seem; no matter how little his or her people may know or care—a rabbi must never lose faith that his people's souls can be touched, and that their minds can be taught, and that they can change and grow. For if he does, he can no longer be their leader.

Again, we can learn what it means to be a rabbi from the first rabbi. The Torah says that when God told Moses that he would not lead the people into the Promised Land, his first reaction was not to picket and not to protest. Later on, he did do that, but his first reaction when he was told this decree was to express concern for his people. What will happen to them? And so Moses asks God: "Who will take my place?" And he prays that God will choose a leader for the people of Israel "*asher yeytse lifnehem v'asher yavo lifneyhem*"—who will go out before them, and who will bring them in.

The Kotsker Rebbe who knew very well what it meant to deal with difficult and insensitive followers from his own personal experience, who knew what it meant to try to form a spiritually sensitive community out of stubborn and recalcitrant people, who knew what it meant to be angry and be impatient and who knew what it meant to lash out at his people, just as Moses did, explains this passage this way. He says that Moses prayed: "May God choose a leader for this people"— *asher yeytse lifnehem—ver vedt osgein far zei*, which means, "who will pour himself out for them," who will give everything that he has for them.

The Kotzker was right. The people believed in Moses—because he believed in them. They believed in Moses because no matter how many times they disappointed him, and no matter how many times they rebelled against him, he believed that they could become more than they were. He does not say "You are holy"—for that would not be true. He says to them: "You can ***become*** holy—that is your goal, and that is your purpose." And that is why they listened to him.

This is what it means to be a Jewish leader. And therefore, this is my prayer for you today: May God help this great congregation to find a leader who is worthy of this place. And may God help whoever is chosen to be the kind of leader that you need: one who believes in God more than in his or ego. And one who believes in you.

And when you find this rabbi, may you join your hands and your hearts with his or with hers. And may you work together in friendship and in harmony.

And may there come true in this time and in this place the promise that is found in the prophets: "*Vinatati lachm ro-im kilibi, viyiru etchem da-at viheskel*"—I will give you pastors after my own heart, and they will nurture you with wisdom and understanding.*

May this come to be.

Amen.

---

* With thanks to the blessed memory of Rabbi Samuel Dresner, who taught me these Hassidic stories—and much more.

38

# How Should We Live In a World That We Cannot Control?

## Shabbat Shuvah
## Reflections on Hurricane Irma And What It Taught Me

My sermon this morning is going to be different from the kind of sermon that I usually give here.

Usually, I tell as many jokes in my sermon as I can, because I want to be liked—and so I try to be as entertaining as I can be.

But this year my mood is different, and I suspect that yours is different too, because all of us have gone through a tremendous trauma in these last two weeks, and so we are in no mood for jokes.

And therefore, I am going to be very serious today.

I am going to be serious today for two reasons. One is that this is Shabbat Shuvah, and Shabbat Shuvah is meant to be a serious day. Shabbat Shuvah is meant to be a day for thinking about what we are doing with our lives, and not a day for talking about superficial things.

But I am going to be serious today for another reason. I am going to be serious today because of what we have all gone through in the last two weeks. I think that I can say—without any exaggeration—that we have all gone through a near-death experience. Because, if the storm had not turned away from Boca at the very last minute—we might have been hurt, and some of us might have died! And I don't think that any of us have fully recovered from that experience yet.

I walked around this room on *yontif*, and I heard one person say to another: "Where were you?" (You didn't have to explain what you meant when you asked that question: Where were you? Everyone knew what you were referring to.)

And the other person said: "I was stuck in my house—without power—for five days." And then that person said to the first one: "And where were you?" And that man said: "I got out of Boca in order to be safe, and I drove all the way to Naples, and I got hit by the storm there."

And I couldn't tell which of these two men was more upset.

Let me give you just one example of black humor that I heard this week.

I saw a friend of mine here in *shule* last Shabbat, and I said to him: "How did you do during the storm?" And he said: "Not bad. I only lost one limb."

When I heard him say that, I was shocked.

And I said: "***You lost a limb?*** That's terrible!"

And he said to me: "Oh no, I didn't lose a limb from my body … I just lost a limb from one of the trees in my backyard."

That is black humor.

I heard that kind of exchange from a great many people in this room, on *yontif*. And so I believe that I am not the only one here today who has not yet fully recovered from the storm. And I am probably not the only person in this room here today who is suffering from post-traumatic stress disorder.

I am sure that there are many people in this room right now whose experiences were much worse than mine was, but let me tell you my story. I was lucky. *Baruch Hashem*: We had a generator, and our son had stocked up on food … and so we were in pretty good shape. We were in better shape than many of you were. But still—all the windows in our house were boarded up, and so I felt like I was living in a dark cave for five days. And that was no fun.

And then I had a very strange experience. On the fifth day I left the house, and went to Publix. And when I walked in, the store was almost completely dark. There were only a few lights on here and there. I guess they were trying to save power. But it felt very strange to be in Publix, and to see it almost completely dark. Have you ever seen Publix in nearly total darkness before? I haven't.

I walked into Publix, and there were only two or three customers in the whole store. And that, too, felt strange. I had never seen Publix so empty before. It felt like a deserted village. There was something that felt ghostly about seeing Public in almost total darkness, and about seeing it almost empty of customers.

I walked into Publix and I saw that there were no carts and no baskets anywhere. Do you know how many carts are usually available at the entrance to the store? There wasn't a single cart or a single basket to be seen in Publix that day. I don't know why. I guess that they had put them away for safe-keeping so that they would not roll away and hurt someone. Or perhaps there was some other explanation. But whatever the reason, it felt very strange that there were no carts and that there were no baskets.

I walked into Publix, and there were some sections that were completely empty. And I had never seen that before.

There were some sections that looked as if they had been ravaged. And there were some other sections that were completely full. I noticed, for example, that the section where they sold vegan foods and gluten-free foods was full, and I was not sure why. Did it mean that it had been restocked, or did it mean that no one wanted to buy these products? I don't know, but either way, it felt strange to see some shelves completely full and some shelves completely empty.

And as I walked in, I saw a sign at the cashier's that said they were only accepting cash. I guess that the banks had lost power and so they could no longer take credit cards.

And so, standing in Publix in semi-darkness, with only a few other customers around, and with no wagons and no baskets available, and with some sections empty and some sections full—it felt very strange.

I found myself drawn to the section where the cereals are kept, and I found myself buying three big boxes of cereal, even though I knew that our son had already bought enough cereal to last us for a few weeks.

Why did I do that? I don't know. Perhaps I was thinking: What if this situation lasts for more than a few weeks? Or perhaps I was thinking that I wanted to show that I was part of the family and that I could make a contribution to our welfare too. I don't know why I did it, but I found myself buying three big boxes of cereal. There were no shopping carts, and so I had to carry these three big boxes of cereal under my arm, but that is what I did.

And then, I found myself drawn to the section of the store where the candy and the pretzels and the chocolates are for sale. And I found myself taking four big bags of pretzels. I was already carrying a book. Those who know me know that I would no more go anywhere without a book in my hand than I would go somewhere without my clothes on. And so, I had to make my way to the cashier carrying a book, and three big cartons of cereal, and four big bags of pretzels. And on the way, I dropped one of these bags of pretzels or one of these boxes of cereal several times, and I had to bend down and pick them up each time.

And now, when I look back over this experience, I think I know why I bought those pretzels. The week before I had gone to the doctor's, and he had said to me: "I'm telling you that you have to cut out sugar, and you have to cut out salt, and you have to lose some weight, because if you don't, you are going to end up a few years from now with diabetes."

And that is why I bought those pretzels. I bought them, because something inside me was saying: ***I could die today, and if so, what do I need to worry about something that might happen to me in a few years?*** Something inside me said: ***I'll show that doctor that threatened me***, and I think that is the reason why I bought those pretzels.

And if it is—then that is an example of a post traumatic stress disorder symptom.

I am sure that many of you have much worse stories to tell about what you experienced during the storm than I do. And I am sure that many of you are sitting here today feeling dislocated—and bewildered—and ill at ease—either because you have not gotten back into your house yet, or because you ***have*** gotten back in, but when you walked in—you found yourself knee-deep in water, or you found that the food in your refrigerator had spoiled, or you found that some of your most precious belongings were soaked and spoiled beyond repair. And so I think that many of you have come to *shule* today in no mood for fooling around, and therefore my sermon today is going to be more serious than it usually is.

And now, after that introduction, let me begin.

I want to ask you a very serious question today.

The question is: What have you learned from this hurricane that nearly swept us away last week? In what ways have you changed?

And in what ways, if any, will you be different from now on, as a result of what you went through?

By the way, do you know what I think was the scariest part of the whole experience?

I don't think that it was the hurricane itself. I think that the scariest part of the whole experience was the week before it arrived, when we sat before the television set hour after hour, day after day, and listened to the predictions of the experts.

What did you learn during those long days and nights when you sat before the television set—and listened to the experts who said that the storm was headed—straight for Boca?

What did you learn as you listened to the governor say that this hurricane was going to be many, many times bigger—and that it was going to do much, much, much more damage—than Hurricane Andrew did?

And what did you learn as you listened to the governor say that this hurricane was going to be wider and longer than the whole state of Florida? And that therefore, no one in this entire state was going to be safe?

And what did you learn when you saw those horrible pictures of the Caribbean in this morning's paper, and you realized that these places—that used to be a tropical paradise—have now become a living Hell?

And what did you learn as you watched those incredible pictures of downtown Houston, where 26 inches of rain fell in 24 hours, and where the only way that you could travel in downtown Houston was by boat?

And what did you learn as you looked at your television screen, and saw those pictures that showed tens of thousands of people from South Florida crowding the highways and heading north … only to discover that they were not running away from the storm, but that they were running directly into it instead?

And what did you learn when the storm that all the weather experts said was going to go up the east coast suddenly swerved at the last moment, and went up the west coast instead?

What did you learn when you found out the next morning that cities like Jacksonville and Gainesville and Naples, that were supposed to be safe from the storm, were hit, and that Boca Raton and the other cities on this coast, which were supposed to be in the greatest danger, escaped with relatively minor damage—at least by comparison?

I hope that you did not learn that the people of Boca are more pious, or that the people of Naples are less pious, because that is not what I believe the hurricane was meant to teach.

I think that we learned the plain and simple fact, that, with all of our scientific knowledge and with all of our sophisticated technology, we simply do not know where, or when, or whether a storm will hit—or not hit. I think that we learned that, with all of our fancy weather-predicting machinery, we simply cannot push a storm out into the sea, and we cannot do anything that will lower it from a category 5 to a 4 or to a 3 or to a 2 or to a 1. And therefore, when a hurricane comes, there are only two things that we can do. We can either try to run away from it—***if*** the roads are not choked with traffic, and ***if*** we know which way to run—or else we can hunker down and hope that we will survive.

And therefore, I ask you: Now that a week has gone by, and now that we are gradually starting to put our lives back in order again, what have you and I learned from this storm, and how long will you and I remember what we have learned?

And how will you and I be different as a result of having gone through this storm?

I think that there is one lesson that we should have learned from what we went through during these last two weeks. We should have learned the inescapable and undeniable fact that my mother, *zichrono livrocho,* was right. My mother used to say: "*Ken bavoorenisht iz bai kainer nisht du.*"

Which means that no one—no one—no one without any exceptions—no one—has control over how long we will live, or over how well we will live.

The plain and simple fact of life is that there are no guarantees. You can diet every day, and you can exercise every day, and a germ that is too small to be seen by the human eye, a germ that is barely big enough to be seen under a microscope, can enter your body, and it can kill you.

You can diet every day, and you can exercise every day, and a car can come hurtling down the street at full speed and hit you. And if it does, all the dieting in the world, and all the exercise in the world will not save you.

You can diet every day, and you can exercise every day, and you can trip over a log that you do not notice on the pavement, and you can be dead before the ambulance arrives.

And so the question that I want to talk to you about today is: How shall we live our lives in view of the fact that how long we will live, and how well we will live, are not in our control?

How shall we live—given the fact that—as many people in Houston and in Florida and in the Caribbean learned this week—our lives are simply not in our control? How shall we live, given the fact that Hurricane Irma or Hurricane Harvey or Hurricane Jose which struck yesterday—or *chas vishalom, chas vishalom, chas vishalom*—Hurricane Marie or Hurricane Lee—can come barreling down upon us … or that they can move away from us at the very last minute—and that there is nothing that we can do about it either way.

What shall we do, and how shall we live, given the fact that we can be here today—and that we can be gone today?

I do not know the answer to this question. I wish I did, but I don't. And therefore, in preparation for this sermon, I turned to all the books in my library and to all the people whose wisdom I respect, and I asked them. And so far, I have found three possible answers to this question. And therefore, what I want to do today is share these three answers that I have found with you in the hope that one of them, or perhaps two of them, or who knows?—perhaps all three of them—will speak to your heart, as they do to mine, and that they will give you some wisdom that will help to guide you in the new year that has now begun.

The first answer comes from my teacher at the Jewish Theological Seminary, Dr. Simon Greenberg, *zichrono livracha*. The second answer comes from a woman named Amy Rosenthal, who lived in Evanston, Illinois. And the third answer comes from Erma Bombeck, whom I hope that many of you still remember.

One of them said that if you want to live well, you have to live gratefully.

One of them said that if you want to live well, you have to be part of something that will live on after you.

And one of them said that if you want to live well, you need to live fully, while you are still alive.

Let me begin with the advice that I heard from Dr. Simon Greenberg, *alav hashalom*, who was my teacher at the seminary. Many years ago, Dr. Greenberg reached the age of 90, and so the Rabbinical Assembly honored him on the occasion of his reaching this milestone. Today, becoming 90 is not such a big deal. Lots of people do it nowadays. I am sure that there are probably some people sitting here right now who have reached this milestone—or who will someday. But a few decades ago, it was rare for someone to reach the age of 90. And so, when Dr. Greenberg reached that age, the Rabbinical Assembly honored him at one of its conventions. A number of rabbis spoke about him—and then he spoke in response. And I can still remember what he said.

He said: "People keep asking me ***how come I have lived so long?*** and the only honest answer that I can give is: I don't know. I really don't. I can only guess that the decision on how long I should live was made by the *Yeshivah shel maalah*—by the Heavenly Tribunal—and I was not there when they voted, and I was not even informed of the decision that they made.

And therefore, I have no explanation to give you as to why I have lived so long.

But ***how*** I have lived my life? ***That*** I think I can tell you.

When I was in college, there were lots of different answers to the question of how you should live that were popular on campus. Some people believed that the kind of life you lived was determined by your genes. Others believed that the kind of life you lived was determined by your economic situation. And others believed that the kind of life you lived was determined by some other factor. But I soon realized that none of these people could prove scientifically that their theory was right, or that someone else's theory was wrong. And so, I decided that I was going to live my life on the premise that there was a God, and that this God created the world, and that this God has blessed the world with many, many good things, and that therefore it was my task to be grateful for all of the good things that I received in my life.

And therefore, whenever anything good has happened to me, I have always said a blessing of gratitude. Whenever I tasted a food that was delicious, or whenever I saw a thing of beauty in nature, or whenever I had some *naches* from my children, or whenever I had a measure of success in one of my ventures, I always said a thank you to God.

And when something bad happened to me? I tried my best not to brood over it, and not to complain about it, and not to wallow in self-pity, but instead, to take the blow as best I could and get on with my life.

And now, when I look back over my life, I believe that it is the fact that I have tried to live my life with a sense of gratitude that has enabled me to live well."

That was Dr. Simon Greenberg's answer to the question of how do you live well even though you know that much of what happens to you is beyond your control. I offer it to you for your consideration today. And I ask you: What do you think of it?

What if we all said, as he did: I choose to live with a sense of gratitude for the goodness of God? What if every time we tasted something good, or every time we saw a thing of beauty, or every time we had *naches* from one of our children, or every time something went well for us in business, we said: thank You, God, for this blessing?

What if, instead of complaining about all the trees that came down on our streets during the storm, we said: thank you, God, that so many people volunteered to help us during this emergency, and that so very few people gouged us when we needed to buy supplies?

What if—instead of complaining about how crowded the roads were between here and Atlanta, we said instead: thank you, God, for the good people of Atlanta who took in, and housed, and fed hundreds of Jews from Boca who needed shelter from the storm!

What if, instead of shaking our fist at heaven and complaining about the hurricane, we thanked God for the hundreds of first responders, who worked day and night to restore our power? And what if, instead of complaining about the water that flooded our streets, we thanked God for the people in Houston who formed human chains, and passed people from one to the other until they got them to dry land? And what if, instead of complaining about the people who took too much at the supermarket, we thanked God for those people who only took as much as they needed, and left the rest for others?

I am no doctor, and I know very little about medicine, but I have a hunch that, if we lived this way, that if we lived with gratitude in our hearts, instead of living as many of us do with complaints about whatever goes wrong in our lives … I have a hunch that if we lived with gratitude instead of with complaining, that we would have less ulcers than many of us have today. And even though I am not a doctor, I believe that ulcers are surely not good for your health.

And so, I offer you Dr. Simon Greenberg's answer to the question of how we should live for your consideration. And I ask you: How would our lives be if we followed his advice and lived with gratitude for all the good things that we receive in this world—instead of complaining? If you like this idea, may I suggest that you try it out in this new year, and see if it makes a difference in your life.

The second answer to this question of how we should live, given that we cannot control our future, comes from a woman named Amy Rosenthal who lived in Evanston, Illinois.

Amy Rosenthal was a very talented writer who lived in Evanston, Illinois, which is a suburb of Chicago. She wrote a number of books for children, and a number of books for adults as well. And then—one day—out of nowhere—just at the time when the youngest of her children was going off to college—just at the time when she and her husband were looking forward to beginning a whole new stage in their lives together—just then—off *tseloches*—she began to feel a constant, rasping cough in her chest that would not go away. And so, she made an appointment to see her doctor. The doctor sent her for an X-ray, and when the report came back, it showed that she did not just have a cough, as she thought. The X-ray showed that she had lung cancer. And the X-ray showed that it was stage four lung cancer—and you know what that means.

At that moment, all the plans that she and her husband had been making for months went out the window. They had been talking about taking a cruise around the world? Forget about it. They had been talking about spending a year in Israel? Forget about it. They had been thinking about taking jobs as teachers together in some far-off country that needed help? Forget about it. Now? After that X-ray, all of those plans simply disappeared into thin air.

As she said: "Now I know why the words 'cancer' and 'cancelled' look alike."

What would you do? What would I do, if, God forbid, something like that happened to us? I don't know what I would do, but let me tell you what Amy Rosenthal did.

Amy Rosenthal did four things. Three of them I think that you or I might possibly do if we were in her situation. The fourth I don't think that I would do … but these are the four things that she did while she was in the hospital.

First, she wrote a note to her husband, telling him where the deed to their graves and where the contract for their funeral services were kept. And she left him the telephone number of the rabbi and of the funeral director as well.

Why did she do that? She did that, because she was the one in the house who kept the family records, and she knew that, left to himself, and especially in a time of confusion and bewilderment, her husband would never be able to find these things by himself.

Would you do that? Would I?

I think that I might … although, to tell you the truth, it is my wife who knows where all the papers are kept in our house. I don't.

The second thing that she did was she wrote out her instructions as to who she wanted to speak at her funeral, and who she wanted to be the pallbearers.

And then, she wrote out instructions for their maid on what food she wanted to be served at the *shivah* house. And she left word for the maid as to where the *milichdik* dishes were and where the *fleishik* dishes were, and where the silverware that was to be used for each of the meals was.

Why did she do that? She did it, because she understood that her maid probably knew these things already, but her maid was very devoted, and she felt like a part of the family, and when you are going through a terrible loss, it is very easy to become confused, and to forget how to make even the simplest arrangements, and so she put them down on paper for her to open up and read when the time came, just in case.

Could you do that?

Could I?

I think so … although I must admit that in our house only my wife knows which dishes are *fleishik* and which are *milichdik*. I don't.

The third thing that she did was she wrote a letter to each of her three children … to be opened up when the time came … in which she told them how much she loved them, and what she wanted for them and from them—after she was gone.

That I could do. In fact, I already have. And I am sure that many of you have done this too. If not, I suggest that you do—and that you do it soon—because you can never know when it will be too late to do it.

But it was the fourth thing that Amy Rosenthal did as she lay on her bed in the hospital that really blew me away.

She did something that I don't think that any of us would do. In fact, she did something that some of us would probably consider ghoulish, or bizarre, or weird.

She wrote her last essay for the Chicago newspaper for which she was a regular columnist. And she wrote it in the form of a want-ad. And she entitled it: "WANTED: A NEW WIFE FOR MY HUSBAND."

And this is what it said:

"If you are looking for a soul mate, may I recommend my husband. He is a good dancer, and he is a great cook. But much more important than that, he is a good husband and a good father. He never forgets my birthday, and he always takes me out on our anniversary. And he always gives me a shoulder to lean on whenever I feel depressed. He is as good a husband as anyone that I have ever known in my whole life. And so, I recommend him to you, if you are looking for a husband."

And then she wrote: "Believe me—I wish that I could have more time to be with him, but that is evidently not going to happen. And I want my husband to have a good life after I am gone, and I know that he is not the kind of person who will be able to live by himself very well. And so, I am writing this want ad, in the hope that somebody who is really nice will read it, and will answer it. For if I can help him find a good wife after I am gone by writing this ad, I feel that I will have done something worthwhile—something that will help my family live on after I am gone."

And then she put down her husband's name, his address and his phone number, and she was just about to sign this want ad and mail it in … when she decided to add a postscript.

She wrote: "Please do not respond to this letter, and please do not contact Jason until after the *shloshim*. I say this because I believe that he will consider that to be gross, and he will not be ready to hear from you or from any other possible *shidduch* until the first 30 days of mourning are over."

And then, after she added that P.S., she wrote: Sincerely yours, and she signed her name, and mailed the letter.

I ask you: Could you write a letter like that?

Could I?

I don't think that I could.

What Amy Rosenthal did may seem strange, and maybe even weird to you, and I am not suggesting that you should necessarily do what she did … but I think that there is a lesson that we can learn from this want ad. The lesson is that even though we may have no control over the future, we can still invest ourselves in some cause—whatever it may be—whether it is the future of our family, or a favorite charity, or a synagogue that we care about, or a school—or whatever it is—we can invest ourselves in something that will live on after us. And if we do, then we will live on too, for as long as that cause lives.

I think that this is one of the reasons why people have children, and I think that this is one of the reasons why people write books, and why they give to charitable causes, and why they belong to synagogues, and why they arrange to have their names put on memorial plaques. They do these things, because they believe that if you belong to something that will live on after you, then you, too, will live on—in this cause, and through this cause, even after your time on earth has ended.

These were the four things that Amy Rosenthal did in her last days. These were Amy Rosenthal's answers to this question of what should you do, given that you cannot control the future. I offer these answers that she gave to you today—for your consideration. You don't have to accept them, but I ask you to think about them, if you will.

And now, let me tell you the third answer to the question we are dealing with today. This one I found in the writings of Erma Bombeck.

Do any of you still remember Erma Bombeck?

Erma Bombeck was a very talented writer, who wrote an essay every week that appeared in many newspapers all around the country. Some of her columns were funny, and some of them were serious. This one—I think is both. It is called *If I Had My Life to Live Over* … and let me read just a small part of it to you today:

> *If I had my life to live over again,*
>
> *I would invite my friends over for dinner whenever I got the impulse to do so, even if it was the maid's day off,*
>
> *And even if the carpet in the dining room was stained, and even if the sofa was faded.*
>
> *If I had my life to live over again,*
>
> *I would burn the beautiful candle that somebody once gave me as a dinner gift,*
>
> *Instead of letting it melt away in the storage room, and never be used, because I was saving it for a special occasion, and I would have realized that*

*every day that someone gives you a gift is—by definition—a special occasion.*

*If I had my life to live over again,*

*I would eat in the good dining room even on ordinary days, and not just on special occasions,*

*And I would not keep the cellophane covers on the good furniture forever.*

(Did any of you grow up in a house where they kept cellophane covers on the good furniture in the living room?

I did.)

*If I had my life to live over again,*

*I would never buy anything just because it was guaranteed to last for a lifetime,*

*Because, if I have no guarantee that I am going to last for a lifetime, why on earth should I buy anything just because it will?*

And she ends her essay with these words:

*Above all, above all, above all,*

*If I had my life to live over again,*

*I would appreciate every single minute of it,*

*And I would live it and love it—as if it were never going to come back again…*

*Because it won't.*

Do you understand what Erma Bombeck was saying in this poem?

She was saying that life is precious, and that life is precarious, and that therefore we should live it, and love it, and enjoy it, and appreciate it, while we still have it …

She was saying that we should not dwell upon the past—for it is gone forever.

And we should not dwell upon the future, for it is not here, and it may never come. She was saying that we should live in the present, for the present is the only reality that we have. And she was saying that there is a reason why it is called the present. The reason we call it the present is because it is a gift.

I think that there are probably a lot of people—in Houston and in Key Largo, and in Miami, and in Broward, and in Jacksonville, and in Orlando, and in a lot of other places around the state today, who understand the truth of what Erma Bombeck wrote in this column. Because yesterday, they lived in nice homes, and they had fine furniture—and today they don't have these things anymore. Yesterday, they had lovely clothing hanging in their closets, waiting to be worn 'one of these days', and today that clothing is in a pile of garbage that is waiting to be picked up outside their homes. I think that these people understand what I tried to say to you in my sermon last year. Do you remember the story of my blue blazer? I told you that I had a fancy and expensive blue blazer, and that every time I was tempted to wear it, I said: "No, this is not a good enough affair to justify wearing this blue blazer. I am going to save it for a special occasion." And when that special occasion finally came, when this synagogue sponsored a dinner on behalf of the seminary, which is a cause that I believe in, and when they chose two people whom I admire enormously as the guests of honor, I decided that this was an occasion that was important enough to justify my blue blazer for. And so I went to my closet and pulled it out, and put it on. And do you know what happened?

I couldn't button it ... which meant one of two things: either that it had shrunk or that I had gained weight. Either way, I had to go out and buy a new blazer, and throw this one away. And so, as I said to you in my sermon last year, the lesson I learned from this experience, and the lesson that I want you to learn is that if you have a blue blazer that you are saving to wear one of these days—or if you have a trip that you are hoping to take one of these days, or if you have an experience that you want to have one of these days—***Do it now!! Do it now … wear it now*** because no one—no one—no one owns tomorrow.

To the best of my knowledge, Erma Bombeck never went to *shule* on Rosh Hashanah. And to the best of my knowledge, those who wrote the High Holy Day Machzor never met Erma Bombeck. And yet, I have a hunch that if they had met, they would have probably found that they had something in common. For how does the Mussaf service of both Rosh Hashana and of Yom Kippur end?

Who remembers?

How did the Mussaf service end yesterday?

Who stayed till the end of the service yesterday, and if you did, how did the Mussaf service end?

Anyone remember?

The Mussaf service of Rosh Hashana and of Yom Kippur both end with the same song. It is a song, whose refrain is *Hayom, hayom, hayom*—which means Today, today, today. It says: *Hayom Ti-amtsenu*—today may you give us strength. *Hayom Tivorcheynu* … today may you bless us. *Hayom Tigadleynu* … Today may you make us feel great. And it goes on and on that way, one letter at a time, all the way through the Hebrew alphabet … until it gets to the very last letter.

Why do we do end the service on *yontif* by asking God to bless us just for today? Why don't we ask God to bless us for a whole year? Or for a whole decade? Or why not for three decades?

I think that the reason why the sages who edited the Machzor ended the Mussaf service with this prayer was because they wanted us to understand that today is all we have. Yesterday is gone—and it will never come back again. Tomorrow is not here yet—and it may never come. Today is all we have. And so this is the last request that we make at the end of the Mussaf service on Rosh Hashana and on Yom Kippur. And this is the lesson that I would have you learn today, after the hurricane. ***If all we have is today, then let us use it wisely, and let us use it well.***

These are the three suggestions that I offer you today on how to live after the hurricane.

Simon Greenberg says that we should try to live our lives with gratitude, and not with complaints. Amy Rosenthal says that we should invest our lives in something that will live on after us. And Erma Bombeck says that we should live our lives in the present, since the present is all we have. I invite you to choose between these three answers. Or perhaps you will consider adapting two of them, or perhaps—who can say?—maybe you will consider adopting all three of them. For if you do, I believe that this new year that now begins will be a blessed one.

I think that it will be a blessed year—for you—for me—and for all those whom we love. And I think that if we choose all three, our days on this earth will be sweet, whether they are many or whether they are few.

And so I offer you these three answers for your consideration.

And I ask you to think about them, if you will. And if you agree, will you join me, and will you say: Amen.

# Jewish Holidays

Year after year, Jewish holidays, festivals, fasts and memorials recall layers of Jewish tradition that extend back through the millennia. The Jewish lunisolar calendar adjusts the shorter, 12-month lunar calendar by adding a leap month in the spring every two or three years. This keeps holidays in sync with the natural cycles of the Earth.

In Judaism, a day begins at sunset. Work is not permitted on Shabbat, nor on the following holidays: Rosh Hashana, Yom Kippur, Sukkot, Shemini Atzeret (the end of Sukkot), Simchat Torah, Passover and Shavuot. During Passover, Jews refrain from work on the first, second, seventh and eighth days.

This guide provides an overview of holidays, starting at the beginning of the Jewish year.

## Rosh Hashana (Jewish New Year)

Rosh Hashana is translated as "Head of the Year," and on 1 Tishrei, as Rosh Hashana begins, the Jewish calendar advances to the next year. Jews regularly adjust their lunisolar calendar to keep the holidays roughly in the same seasons—so this Jewish New Year moves around, but always lands between Sept. 5 and Oct. 5. Friends wish each other a sweet new year and consume honey, popularly as a dip for apples but also in a variety of treats and pastries.

Rosh Hashana also begins the High Holidays, a period of reflection on the past year and hopes for the year ahead. Jews have 10 days, from Rosh Hashana until Yom Kippur, to seek forgiveness and reconciliation with relatives, friends and co-workers.

## Shabbat Shuvah

The Shabbat that falls between Rosh Hashana and Yom Kippur (during the Ten Days of Repentance), Shabbat Shuvah is known as the Sabbath of Return. It is a time of penitence, prayer and charity, and is part of the High Holy Days, or High Holidays. Emphasis is placed on restoration and healing: in particular, on the greatness of the forgiveness of God. Historically, Shabbat Shuvah was one of only two occasions each year when a rabbi would give a sermon to the community.

## Yom Kippur (Day of Atonement)

Often described as the holiest day of the Jewish year, Yom Kippur is the Day of Atonement on 10 Tishrei—a 25-hour period of fasting, intense prayer, liturgies in the synagogue and repentance. There are many historical and spiritual layers to this daylong holiday. Here is one way Yom Kippur often is described: Jews have asked forgiveness and sought reconciliation with others prior to this holy day. Then, they gather in communities on Yom Kippur to seek forgiveness and reconciliation with God.

## Sukkot (Feast of Tabernacles)

For Sukkot, which begins on 15 Tishrei, it is traditional to build a temporary structure, called a sukkah in Hebrew, to "dwell in" during the seven-day festival. These structures, which include a loosely thatched roof that allows families to glimpse the stars, are reminders of temporary shelters used by ancestors. During Sukkot, families have their meals inside the sukkah. Some even try to sleep in it. This is a festive time when friends and relatives visit each other and share stories. Prayers during Sukkot involve symbols reminiscent of ancestors who were more dependent on agriculture.

## Shemini Atzeret

Shemini Atzeret is the eighth day of Sukkot. It is on 22 Tishrei. One ancient practice on this holiday is a prayer for rain.

## Simchat Torah

This holiday on 23 Tishrei marks the end of one annual cycle of Torah readings and the immediate beginning of another. Congregations try to make this an event for the entire family, including a parade with Torah scrolls featuring volunteer scroll-bearers dancing as they move among the congregation.

## Hanukkah (Festival of Lights)

One of the holidays most familiar outside of Judaism, Hanukkah has gained more importance in the United States than it actually holds in the Jewish calendar. The original significance of the eight-day festival, which begins on 25 Kislev, recalls a dire threat to Judaism more than 2,000 years ago. The Temple was desecrated and the future of Judaism was threatened. Then, a group called the Maccabees led a triumphant fight to reclaim and re-dedicate the Temple. As candles are lit today and displayed near windows in Jewish homes, stories are told about a miraculous quantity of sacred oil that seemed too small when the Temple was re-dedicated but burned for eight nights.

## Tu BiShvat (New Year for Trees)

Tu BiShvat is the 15th day of the month of Shvat, which gives the holiday its name. This minor holiday is one of four "new years" and usually occurs in January or February of the secular calendar. In the ancient world, it was important to mark the age of food-producing trees for tithing. Today, Jewish communities celebrate Tu BiShvat with events encouraging environmental awareness.

## Purim

The jubilant, major holiday of Purim, on the Jewish date of 14 Adar, focuses on the story of Queen Esther, who courageously stood up for her people and saved many Jewish lives as a result. In synagogue, the book of Esther is read. In Jewish communities, Purim is celebrated with merriment, noisemakers, sweets and costumes. Children re-enact the story, often in full costume and with robust input from the audience. A Purim meal usually includes plenty of alcohol for the adults, and triangular-shaped, fruit-filled cookies called hamentaschen in Yiddish, or "Haman's pockets."

# Pesach (Passover)

Passover is the most widely observed Jewish holiday. For eight days, starting with 15 Nissan, Passover recalls the ancient Israelites' Exodus from slavery in Egypt. During Passover, Jewish families are reminded of when they were slaves in Egypt. Prior to the start of Passover, it is traditional for observant Jews to clean their homes so that not even a crumb of leavened food, or chametz, is present. Passover usually is experienced as a family reunion, a history lesson, an affirmation of survival and a time of reflecting on ways to help the vulnerable.

Parshat Shemini

The 26th weekly Torah portion is read on Parshat Shemini, when focus is on three things: the consecration of the tabernacle; the deaths of Aaron's two eldest sons, Nadab and Abihu; and the dietary laws of *kashrut*.

# Yom HaShoah (Holocaust Remembrance Day)

Yom HaShoah is a remembrance day, established in Israel in 1953 to remember the 6 million Jews who were killed in the Holocaust, also known as the Shoah. In English, its full title is Holocaust and Heroism Remembrance Day. It is observed on 27 Nissan, the Jewish date of the anniversary of the Warsaw Ghetto uprising in World War II. On the morning of Yom HaShoah, a siren sounds in Israel and all movement stops, including bicycles and cars. While no specific religious customs are mandated, community programs of remembrance often are organized.

# Yom Ha'atzmaut (Israeli Independence Day)

Yom Hazikaron is Israeli Memorial Day on 4 Iyar, established in 1963. In English, the full title of this observance is: Day of Remembrance for the Fallen Soldiers of Israel and Victims of Terrorism. The next day, 5 Iyar, is Yom Ha'atzmaut or Israeli Independence Day. In Israel, these are key events, just as Americans mark Memorial Day and the Fourth of July. The first of the two Israeli holidays is solemn; the second day's expression is jubilant. In the rest of the world, Jewish communities often organize public events.

# Shavuot (Festival of Weeks)

On 6 Sivan, Jews celebrate the major, ancient holiday of Shavuot to celebrate receiving the Torah. Shavuot is usually a time for joyous meals and alternatively is known as the Festival of First Fruits. Thousands of years ago, Shavuot was a time when families harvested first crops and brought them to the Temple. At Shavuot, the book of Ruth is read. Some Jews may follow the custom of trying to stay awake all night in study of the Torah.

# Parshat Mattot

The 42nd weekly Torah portion is read on Parshat Mattot, when the laws of vows, or oaths, is discussed. Readings focus on the destruction of Midianite towns, as well as on the negotiations of the Reuven and Gad tribes, in request to dwell in the land outside of Israel.

# Tisha B'Av (the Ninth of Av)

A major fast day, Tisha B'Av (or, the Ninth of Av) is a time of mourning a number of tragedies that have befallen the Jewish people. According to Jewish teaching, both the First Temple and the Second Temple were destroyed on 9 Av. This is a 25-hour fast and includes prohibitions on bathing, anointing and the wearing of leather shoes. Observant Jews might choose not to work on this day because they are studying and fasting. Jewish congregations place black drapings around the ark, where Torah scrolls are kept.

# Glossary

**Erev**

The day before a Jewish holiday or the Jewish Sabbath. Literally, "eve" or "evening."

**Beth din**

A "house of judgment," a rabbinical court of Judaism. In ancient times, it was an integral part of the legal system in the biblical Land of Israel.

**Rebbe**

A rabbi. Often referring to a religious leader of the Hasidic sect, though this term may also describe to a highly revered rabbi who is respected for his extraordinary ability to understand people and the Jewish religion.

**mitsvah**

A good deed done from religious duty. Also: a commandment, or a precept.

**mentsch**

A good person; someone who respects the needs and wishes of others.

**Al Het**

Literally, "for the sin"; the first words of a formula of confession of sins.

**zichrono livrocho**

An honorific title for someone who is deceased. A way of saying, "May their memory be blessed/for a blessing."

**Simcha**

A Jewish party or celebration. From Hebrew, "rejoice."

**chuppah**

A canopy under which a Jewish couple stands during the wedding ceremony.

**kallah**
A bride. Alternatively, a Jewish communal gathering or conference.

**shule**
A synagogue, or Jewish place of worship. From the Yiddish word for "school."

**kitel**
A white linen robe worn on special occasions, such as the High Holidays, by Ashkenazi Jews. Also, a burial shroud for male Jews.

**daven**
To pray; to recite the prescribed prayers in a Jewish liturgy.

**sedra**
The weekly Torah portion.

**aliyah**
From Hebrew for "elevation," or "going up." Used to describe being called up to the Torah reading at the synagogue and moving to the Land of Israel.

**Rambam**
Rabbi Moses ben Maimon, commonly known as Maimonides. A Jewish philosopher, jurist and physician; the most renowned of Jewish medieval scholars.

**Neilah**
The final service of Yom Kippur.

**sukkah**
A temporary structure constructed for Sukkot.

**yontif**
A Jewish holiday, especially one on which work is prohibited.

**kashrut**
A set of Jewish religious dietary laws. Food that may be consumed are termed "kosher," in English.

**halachah (or halachic)**

The collective body of Jewish religious laws. Also meaning "way," or "path," referring to how a Jew should live his life.

**Yom Tov**

Literally, "a good day." A time of rejoicing. There are six days of the year called Yom Tov: the first day of Passover; the seventh day of Passover; Shavuot; Rosh Hashana; the first day of Sukkot; and Shemini Atzeret and Simchat Torah.

**tallis**

A prayer shawl.

**tefillin**

A set of small black leather boxes, attached to leather straps, that contain scrolls of parchment inscribed with verses from the Torah; worn by some male Jews during weekday morning prayers. The arm tefillin is placed on the upper arm, and the head tefillin is placed above the forehead.

**beit hamidrash**

A Jewish study hall located in a synagogue, yeshiva, kollel or other building; literally, "house of study." Also may be a school where Jews, especially in eastern Europe, study the Bible, the Talmud and later Hebrew literature.

**megillah**

Literally, "scroll" or "volume." Often in reference to the scroll of Esther, but may be a reference to another scroll, as well.

**seudah**

A festive meal.

**zeidi**

A Yiddish term for "grandfather."

**Shoah**

Hebrew for "catastrophe" or "destruction." In current decades, the term has been used in reference to the Holocaust.

**onen**

The halachic (by law) status of an immediate relative of the deceased, from the moment he has learned of the death until the end of the burial.

**minyan**

A minimum of 10 Jewish men, over the age of 13, which constitutes a congregation and is necessary for public worship. Fewer than 10 men (or, in some synagogues, men and women) may not recite certain public prayers.

**bracha**

A recited blessing, or an expression of thanksgiving; recognizing the good that God has given, especially to humanity.

**haftorah**

A passage selected from the Prophets that is read in synagogue services on the Sabbath (Shabbat), following a reading from the Torah. Literally, "concluding portion."

**bimah**

The podium or platform in the center of a synagogue's sanctuary, from which the Torah and Prophets are read and some prayers are led.

**tsedakah**

Charitable giving that is usually seen as a moral obligation. Literally, "justice" or "righteousness."